"Cristina González-Longo has carefully and lucidly analysed one of the most interesting 'architectural metamorphosis' in Rome. The site is studied here for the first time in all its complexities: from Nero's vestibule, and Hadrian's temple of Venus and Rome, to its current configuration of the church of Santa Francesca Romana and the monastery of S. Maria Nova, occupied by the Olivetan Benedictine monks since 1352 and now also partially occupied by the offices of the *Soprintendenza* and the forthcoming Museum of the Roman Forum. With the support of many original illustrations, she has unravelled all the various architectural transformations over more than two millennia, situating them also within their cultural, theoretical and ideological contexts. A fascinating research which challenges existing praxis of architectural conservation."
—Dr Antón Capitel, Emeritus Professor of Architectural Design at the Technical University of Madrid (ETSAM), RIBA International Fellow and author of *Metamorfosis de Monumentos y Teorias de la Restauracion*

"Perhaps only in Rome it is possible to understand that time does not flow, but accumulates. Mankind's creations do not escape this rule. Architecture is made of bricks, stones, mortar, but also and above all of time. A famous and prominent church such as Santa Francesca Romana, very well known to locals and tourists visiting the Roman Forum, is actually the result of an overlapping of constructions, destructions and conservation interventions. Even its beauty is made of time. In the winding of a building on the other, from the great temple of Hadrian, to the solemn medieval church of S. Maria Nova, the sumptuous Baroque church and the intervention in the monastery by the conservation pioneer Giacomo Boni, different generations have followed one another, without ever completely erasing previous architectural layers. Cristina González-Longo has the great ability to unravel the complexity of this site and to explain it to those who are willing to listen. It allows us to understand that architecture is the only art form where past and present manage to dialogue among themselves, giving meaning to our future."
—Dr Claudio Varagnoli, Professor of Preservation of Built Heritage and Conservation at the University of Chieti-Pescara and the Italian Archaeological School of Athens. Member of Italy's Superior Council of Cultural Heritage

"González-Longo provides here a riveting account of the complex evolution of the great Olivetan monastery and basilica, Santa Francesca Romana, leading us for the first time through its integral relationship with the Temple of Venus and Roma, adeptly drawing throughout on primary and contemporary sources, literature and imagery and showing insightful command of the rich instruction they unravel. The author's research revealed phases and aspects of the many engagements with the site unknown until now and which ensure the assessment brings new depth to our understanding of this monumental edifice. Conservation architects and historians, however familiar with the study of destruction, transformation, re-use and regeneration, will also find delight in these well-illustrated chapters in their perceptive discovery of a late seventeenth century emergence of conservation ideology. The monograph traces the development of the conservation discipline following Carlo Lambardi's transformation of the medieval church, through respective ideologies in their application, showing lineage with the later thinking of Ruskin and SPAB, the influential, ground-breaking approach of Giacomo Boni in the early twentieth century and on to stratigraphic architectural conservation or design and the informed conservation we prize today. This is, most satisfyingly, a refreshing and exceptional biography of a building that leaves the reader complete with an intimate appreciation of the subject, its context and its immense significance."

—Dr Deborah Mays, Head of Listing, Historic England

The Temple of Venus and Rome and Santa Francesca Romana at the Roman Forum

This book examines the influence of architectural design in the conservation of monuments by discussing in detail an important building complex in Rome: the Temple of Venus and Rome, the monastery of Santa Maria Nova and the church of Santa Francesca Romana. As the most complete site in the Roman Forum that has reached our times with a rich architectural stratification almost intact, it is a clear product of continuous preservation and transformation and it has not been studied in its complexity until now.

The Temple of Venus and Rome and Santa Francesca Romana at the Roman Forum unravels the original designs and the subsequent interventions, including Giacomo Boni's pioneering conservation of the monastery, carried out while excavating the Roman Forum in the early twentieth century. The projects are discussed in context to show their significance and the relationships between architects and patrons. Through its interdisciplinary focus on architectural design, conservation, archaeology, history and construction, this study is an ideal example for scholars, students and architects of how to carry out research in architectural conservation.

Cristina González-Longo, PhD, RIBA SCA RIAS FHEA FRSA, is the Founder and Director of the MSc in Architectural Design for the Conservation of Built Heritage at the Department of Architecture of the University of Strathclyde, where she has also created and is leading the Architectural Design and Conservation Research Unit (ADCRU). Her research group deals with the challenges of conserving built heritage while allowing changes to adapt historic buildings for contemporary uses, as well as with the design of new buildings to conserve the environment, which requires an interdisciplinary approach. After graduating at the School of Architecture of the Technical University of Madrid (ETSAM), Cristina spent three years in Rome with a scholarship from the Italian Government to study architectural conservation at the prestigious Specialisation School of the Sapienza University of Rome. She is also a practising architect with over twenty years' experience as a Chartered architect both in the UK and

Spain, RIBA Specialist Conservation Architect (SCA) and member of the RIBA Conservation Register Assessment Panel. She has had a central role in taking decisions concerning historic buildings of outstanding national and international importance and wide experience in leading the design, management and procurement of award-winning architectural projects (both conservation and new-build). She was the project architect and resident architect of Queensberry House, a Category A Listed building, part of the new Scottish Parliament complex in Edinburgh (RIBA Stirling Prize 2005). She also designed Bowbridge Primary School in Newark, UK (RICS Sustainability Award 2009), with an innovative lamella glulam structure. She is the President of the ICOMOS (International Council on Monuments and Sites) International Scientific Committee on Education and Training (CIF).

Routledge Research in Architectural Conservation and Historic Preservation
Series Editor: Wen-Shao Chang

The Routledge Research in Architectural Conservation and Historic Preservation series provides the reader with the latest scholarship in the field of building conservation. The series publishes research from across the globe and covers areas as diverse as restoration techniques, preservation theory, technology, digital reconstruction, structures, materials, details, case studies, and much more. By making these studies available to the worldwide academic community, the series aims to promote quality architectural preservation research.

The Temple of Venus and Rome and Santa Francesca Romana at the Roman Forum
Preservation and Transformation
Cristina González-Longo

Architectural Conservation and Restoration in Norway and Russia
Edited by Evgeny Khodakovsky and Siri Skjold Lexau

Reconstructing Historic Landmarks
Fabrication, Negotiation, and the Past
Wayde Brown

Equity in Heritage Conservation
The Case of Ahmedabad, India
Jigna Desai

The Protected Vista
An Intellectual and Cultural History
Tom Brigden

For more information about this series, please visit: www.routledge.com/architecture/series/RRACHP

The Temple of Venus and Rome and Santa Francesca Romana at the Roman Forum
Preservation and Transformation

Cristina González-Longo

NEW YORK AND LONDON

First published 2021
by Routledge
52 Vanderbilt Avenue, New York, NY 10017

and by Routledge
2 Park Square, Milton Park, Abingdon, Oxon, OX14 4RN

Routledge is an imprint of the Taylor & Francis Group, an informa business

© 2021 Taylor & Francis

The right of Cristina González-Longo to be identified as author of this work has been asserted by her in accordance with sections 77 and 78 of the Copyright, Designs and Patents Act 1988.

All rights reserved. No part of this book may be reprinted or reproduced or utilised in any form or by any electronic, mechanical, or other means, now known or hereafter invented, including photocopying and recording, or in any information storage or retrieval system, without permission in writing from the publishers.

Trademark notice: Product or corporate names may be trademarks or registered trademarks, and are used only for identification and explanation without intent to infringe.

Library of Congress Cataloging-in-Publication Data
A catalog record for this book has been requested

ISBN: 978-1-138-89617-8 (hbk)
ISBN: 978-1-315-17924-7 (ebk)

Typeset in Sabon
by Apex CoVantage, LLC

To my parents, Manuel and Clara,
who taught me the importance to conserve and be creative,
in particular to my father, who recently departed,
my husband Dimitris, and our children, Alex and Lucia,
for all their love.

Contents

Foreword xv
BY EMERITUS PROFESSOR GIOVANNI CARBONARA
Preface xx
Acknowledgements xxiv
Introduction xxvii

1 **The First Architecture: From the Velia to the Vestibule of the Golden House of Nero** 1
   1.1 *The Primitive Landscape: The Roman Forum and the Velia hill* 1
   1.2 *The First Settlements in the Roman Forum* 3
   1.3 *The Etruscan Mark* 8
   1.4 *The Velia From Republican to Imperial Rome* 11
   1.5 *Augustus and the Giulio Claudia Dynasty* 15
   1.6 *Nero's Urban Project: From the Domus Transitoria to the Domus Aurea* 19

2 **The Place Transformed: The Temple of Venus and Rome of Hadrian** 23
   2.1 *Flavian Architecture* 23
   2.2 *Hellenism, Mithraism and the Eleusinian Mysteries* 25
   2.3 *Hadrian, Architect of the* Urbs: *Conservation and Innovation of the Classical Temple* 26
   2.4 *The Temple of Venus and Rome* 28
   2.5 *The Fortune of the Temple After Hadrian: The Antonines and Maxentius's Intervention After the Fire of* AD *283* 38

3 Decadence, Destruction and Recovery of the Place: The Churches of Ss. Peter and Paul and S. Maria Nova and Alexander III   41
   3.1 From Pagan to Christian 41
   3.2 The Constantinian Basilicas 45
   3.3 Byzantine Rome, Rome in Ruins 48
   3.4 Honorius I and the Expolio of the Temple of Venus and Rome 49
   3.5 The Church of Ss. Peter and Paul 50
   3.6 Santa Maria Nova From Ninth to Fourteenth Centuries 53
   3.7 The Frangipane Rocca 56
   3.8 Cultural Renaissance: The Work of Alexander III and the 'International Style' 59
   3.9 The Gothic Intervention of Honorius III 62
   3.10 Civitas and Delimitation of Space: The First Monastery 64

4 Architectural Preservation and Transformation, Patronage and Innovation: The Olivetan Benedictine Monks, Carlo Lambardi and Gianlorenzo Bernini   70
   4.1 The Olivetans in Santa Maria Nova and the Regeneration of the Place 70
   4.2 Santa Francesca Romana and S. Maria Nova 72
   4.3 The First Renaissance in Rome and the Tridentine Reforms in Santa Maria Nova 77
   4.4 The Canonization of S. Francesca Romana and the Transformation of the Church (1612–14) 83
   4.5 The New Urban Dimension of the Church: The Facade of S. Francesca Romana (1614–15) 92
   4.6 Bernini's Confessione 97
   4.7 The Monastery and "L'universale ristabilimento" of the Middle of the Eighteenth Century 101

5 The New Conservation Ideology: Giuseppe Valadier and Giuseppe Camporese   104
   5.1 The End of the Seventeenth Century: A New Architectural Awareness 104
   5.2 The Changes at the End of the Roman Settecento: Archaeology, Conservation and the Taste for the Ancient 105

Contents xiii

  5.3 *Napoleonic Rome: Looting, Count of Tournon's Program and the Archaeological Park* 107
  5.4 *Demolition and Reintegration of the Monastery of Santa Maria Nova* 112
  5.5 *The Arch of Titus . . . or the Arch of Pius?* 115
  5.6 *The Love for the Ruins and The Grand Tour* 119
  5.7 *Architectural Conservation in the Second Half of the Nineteenth-Century: Restoration Versus Conservation* 120
  5.8 *The Transformations for* Roma Capitale *and the Monumental Complex at the End of the Nineteenth Century* 122
  5.9 *The First Vienna School, Alois Riegl and the* Kunstwollen *125*

6 **Conservation and Architectural Project: Giacomo Boni as Pioneer of the 'Critical Conservation'**   128
  6.1 *Giacomo Boni: 'The Method', Instruments and Education* 128
  6.2 *Boni, Ruskin, Webb and SPAB* 132
  6.3 *The Innovation in the Conservation of the Cloister of the Monastery of Santa Maria Nova: From 'com'era, dov'era' to Scientific 'Stratigraphic Architectural Conservation Design'* 135
  6.4 *Giovannoni and Mussolini:* Romanità *and Modernity* 140
  6.5 *The* Via dell'Impero *and the Destruction of the Velia* 143
  6.6 *The Restoration of the Temple of Venus and Rome and the Athens and Italian Conservation Charters* 144
  6.7 *Theory of Conservation: Cesare Brandi on Painting, Sculpture and . . . Architecture?* 148
  6.8 *Boni, Cirilli, Scarpa, Brandi and Venturi* 153
  6.9 *The Roman School of Conservation, the 'Critical Conservation'* 155
  6.10 *Rebuilding the Velia: Reflections on Architectural and Urban Conservation in the Second Half of the Twentieth Century* 157
  6.11 *Old and New: The Contemporary Discourse* 161

7 Conclusions: The Architectural Conservation Project: Preservation and Transformation 167
  7.1 The Continuous Architecture 167
  7.2 The Skilful Conservation of the Architectural Idea 168
  7.3 The Conservation Project as Preservation and Transformation of Pre-existences 170
  7.4 Conclusion 172

List of Abbreviations 179
References 180
Index 194

Foreword

From the study of the Temple of Venus and Rome and of the monastic complex of S. Francesca Romana in the area of the Roman Forum and the ancient hill of the Velia, Cristina González-Longo manages in this book to effectively integrate considerations of urban history, history of architecture and theory of conservation, including its historical developments over time, from a distant past to current events.

This makes the book particularly interesting because reflections on historical and cultural values are developed around the buildings studied, including the topography and the occupation of this important site of the city of Rome over centuries. The primitive configuration of the site is presented before analysing the first architectural changes: from the Republican and then imperial age and the substantial transformations that occurred after the death of the emperor Nero, with the construction of the Colosseum, to the destruction of much of the *Domus Aurea*, the displacement and reworking of the Colossus which depicted, as divinized, the emperor himself. The presence of Christians is mentioned as early as the fourth century in this important and above all sacred area, for the presence of the Temple of Venus and Rome, the largest in the city, built by the emperor Hadrian and then restored by Maxentius.

The complexity of the building is evidenced through the events of the church built there and transformed and extended several times in the Middle Ages from the eighth to the fourteenth centuries, and in particular by the Olivetan Benedictine monks who have been occupying the church and adjacent monastery since 1352. The larger intervention was its 'reduction to modern', made with great skill in the early Baroque age by the architect Carlo Lambardi (1612–14). This was carried out on the occasion of the new consecration of the church from S. Maria Nova to S. Francesca Romana (who died in 1440 and was canonized in 1608). Extensive transformations and extensions where also carried out by the Olivetans in the mid-eighteenth century in the monastery. The church was subject to stealing and damage by Napoleonic troops, with the theft and destruction of the precious bronze statue of the saint, part of the *confessio* designed by Gian Lorenzo Bernini.

The book focuses then on the interventions that gave the complex its current configuration. First, during the nineteenth century, with Giuseppe Valadier and Giuseppe Camporese then, at the beginning of the twentieth century, with Giacomo Boni and Guido Cirilli. But the study goes even further, with the *sventramenti* and destruction of the Velia in the fascist era, which have the dramatic effect of making what originally was the back facade of the monastery the main one.

The unravelling of all this history of the place allows the author to advance interesting interpretative hypotheses based on the available material and documentary evidence. For example, about the configuration of the original hill and the Roman temple and its double colonnade, looking at the relationship between the two opposing cellae that distinguish it and their vaulted roofs; they are considered by the author to be Hadrianic based on precise architectural and structural observations. The complex developments of the monastery over time are also analysed in detail.

As all these considerations progress over time and approach modernity, they also take on an explicit connotation of architectural conservation as we understand it today. That is to say of the relationship with the ancient, which is no longer immediate and spontaneous but filtered by an emerging historical consciousness and from values of memory, respect for ancient testimonies and attention to the context. In this sense, significant pioneering work, on which the author very opportunely dwells, is found in the seventeenth-century, by Lambardi. This was an innovative intervention, with a contemporary design but also careful to preserve, in their materiality, medieval testimonies, such as the portico, which is literally incorporated into the modern one, with some difficulties, well resolved with an architectural solution. Also some medieval monuments, pavements and mosaics inside the church are preserved and well incorporated within the new design.

Things matured in the middle of the eighteenth century and, above all, in the nineteenth and early twentieth centuries where the different attitudes of Valadier and Camporese, on the one hand, and of Cirilli and Boni, on the other, are compared. In the first case, Valadier's intervention in the nearby Arch of Titus and also in the monastery, adapted for use as public offices, still occupying it today, are widely discussed. The many novelties of the method operated by Boni are highlighted, recognizable in a truly conservative attitude, attentive to the landscape, to the use of 'flora of the ruins' but also one could say, intelligently 'scientific' and 'critical', intended to "facilitate reading" of the cloister of the monastery, using the words of the Article 4 of the 1972 Italian Conservation Charter, dictated directly by Cesare Brandi. In between, in the mid-nineteenth century, archaeological excavations were carried out in order to join the valley of the Roman Forum to the Colosseum, changing the topography of the place. This operation unnaturally isolated the buildings from the surrounding context and the foundations of the church, and its portico have been as a consequence inappropriately exposed since.

The discussion about Boni includes critically his relationship with English contemporary culture and, in particular, with John Ruskin, William Morris, Philip Webb and SPAB. Very acutely, the author recognizes another line of inspiration, more directly Italian, that she sees in the collaboration with Guido Cirilli in the conservation of the monastery and its partial conversion to a museum. This intervention was clearly an anticipation of some significant operational and theoretical positions of Boni, marked by an open and flexible method. It was also an important experience for Cirilli, who would become later Director of the Fine Arts Office of Venezia Giulia, with interventions, for example, in the Cathedral of Parenzo, the church of S. Eufemia in Grado and the Theatre of Augustus in Pola.

Also interesting is the rightly highlighted link between Cirilli and Carlo Scarpa, who was a pupil, collaborator and from whom he drew inspiration. The rigorous distinction of old and new, the preference for rough surfaces and strong materiality and the 'architectural' use of ivy, are present in Boni and Cirilli's intervention in the cloister of the monastery of S. Maria Nova and, appear many decades later in Scarpa's work, for example in his intervention in Castelvecchio in Verona.

This is why, with good reason, Cristina González-Longo considers this intervention by Boni and Cirilli the beginning of the 'critical' and also 'creative' architectural conservation, which will be later and in different forms theorized. There is on the one hand Cesare Brandi, who gathered ideas from Pietro Toesca for the treatment of *lacune* in painting and by Giacomo Boni for the treatment of architecture and the concept of patina; on the other hand we have Ambrogio Annoni, Roberto Pane, Renato Bonelli and Liliana Grassi.

It is very interesting to read how the author enters in the contemporary debate, with personal, intelligent and stimulating observations, recognizing, for example, an intellectual debt of Robert Venturi—in Rome in the 1950s—towards Brandi and what the Central Institute of Conservation (*Istituto Centrale di Restauro*, ICR) directed by him did at that time. She also traces the Italian comparison between 'pure' preservationists and 'restorers'. The 'pure' preservationists such as Marco Dezzi Bardeschi or Amedeo Bellini, are oriented to absolutize the historical-documentary reasons or, to put it with Brandi, the 'historicity' instance, anticipated at the end of the sixteenth century by the cultured Spanish Dominican Alfonso Chacón, who, regarding the planned intervention in San Giovanni in Laterano, referred to the reasons of *vetustas*. The 'restorers', led by Paolo Marconi, are rather oriented towards the 'recovery of beauty' of the old historic buildings, or, to put it with Brandi, the 'aesthetic' instance or, even earlier, with Chacón, the *venustas*. But the third, more balanced and fruitful way is also illustrated, that of the 'critical conservation', mentioned earlier, promoted by the

Scuola di Specializzazione per lo Studio ed il Restauro dei Monumenti of the "Sapienza" University of Rome, in which both the author and the writer have graduated and which stimulated her first interests, widely developed afterwards, for the site under consideration.

In conclusion, although dealing with an eminently Roman and Italian theme, the study manages to broaden its horizon, not only with reference to the figure of Boni, of sure European relevance, but also with the identification of proto-preservationist and preservationist thought from distant sixteenth-seventeenth century origins, but on even older roots, up to the present.

An interesting parallelism emerges, for example, between Italian anticipations of the concept of stratigraphy and consequent stratigraphic excavation, with Nicolas Steno in the seventeenth century, or of care and cataloguing of cultural heritage with Ulisse Aldrovandi in the late sixteenth century, and John Aubrey, English pioneer of archaeology or Inigo Jones and his excavation and conservation experiences at Stonehenge in the early seventeenth century. Parallelism that continues in the following two centuries with very interesting 'scientific' developments in England and Italy, for example the use of the pendulum in the spire of Chichester Cathedral, to mitigate the effects of the wind, conceived by Christopher Wren, and the same solution, with anti-seismic purpose in this case, adopted in the cathedral of Parma. The two countries arrived at similar conclusions, albeit elaborated independently, around the mid-nineteenth century, with the 'restoration' and 'stylistic' architects on one side and the 'preservationist' front on the other and with the mediation attempted, in England, by George Gilbert Scott and in Italy by Camillo Boito, also with the publication of their respective conservation 'Charters'.

Obviously, this is not just about Italy but about exchanges with the whole of Europe, from Spain to Germany, especially with France. There are, in fact, contacts between Edward Augustus Freeman or the Cambridge Camden Society and Eugène Emmanuel Viollet-le-Duc or, on the opposite front, between Augustus Welby N. Pugin and Adolphe Napoléon Didron. This continues up to the direct contact represented largely by Giacomo Boni and his circle, first Venetian, then Roman.

As we said at the beginning, this book deals with a very specific site but, by deepening the research, it manages to effectively expand the horizons, making the reader retrace pages of history and reflections about the preservation and conservation of cultural heritage, providing also much food for thought.

A final observation, which we also share with the author: near the end of the volume, when she says that there are too many 'Conservation Charters' that today contribute to create more confusion. Above all, because they lack the solid methodological and cultural structure of the first Charters; on the contrary, they are driven by the desire to pursue the 'politically correct' rather than a true historical and intellectual rigour.

Roma, April 2020
Giovanni Carbonara
Professor Emeritus in Architectural Conservation,
Sapienza University of Rome

Preface

The aim of the book is to reflect on the approaches and praxis of architectural design and conservation over centuries. It demonstrates the hypothesis that appropriate and contemporary design in a historic context, adapting buildings to contemporary uses, is a very effective way to conserve and improve architecture. This challenges some existing practices of restoration in which buildings are turned to a fictitious original state or 'former glory', something which is unfortunately still very frequent despite various efforts, including international Conservation Charters providing guidelines of good practice.

The book investigates the historic development, interventions and design processes in the complex site of the ruins of the Temple of Venus and Rome, the monastery of S. Maria Nova and the church of Santa Francesca Romana at the Roman Forum. These processes include new architecture, conservation and transformation of the existing, allowing a reflection on the character, methods and realizations of the architectural project's practice in a temporal arch of over two millennia. It also permits reflecting on the great influence of new design on the conservation of the monument, allowing for alternative conclusions to be drawn, in some instances in conflict with existing orthodoxy on how to intervene in historic buildings or settings.

This is probably one of the best sites in the world to consider issues of continuity and change. It caught my attention from the very first gaze at it during my first visit to Rome, just behind the overwhelming presence of the adjacent Colosseum; this particular view appears at the front of this book. The buildings in the site are rare survivors, having escaped demolition because of their continuous use and occupation by the religious and civil servants looking after the buildings, the Roman Forum and the people of Rome.

It was reassuring to read, many years after starting the research, D. Watkin's (2011) views about the interest of the site, although, in my view, with an unfair criticism of archaeologists: "Santa Francesca Romana is one of the most historic, evocative and attractive buildings in the Roman Forum and its life and wealth make it a unique survivor in a place where archaeologists are contributing to make it unattractive and discouraging." Perhaps he was not aware that Giacomo Boni, the archaeologist who extensively excavated the area, carried also the extensive conservation of the monastery next to the church.

Watkin also considered that the Roman Forum can be "baffling, ugly and frustrating". I said something similar, more concerning the difficulty in understanding the individual buildings of the Forum, to the chair of the panel who interviewed me for the Spanish Academy in Rome scholarship. Unfortunately, he did not like what I told him, saying that he could understand the buildings perfectly! However, another member of the panel, José María Pérez González (Peridis), architect, cartoonist and author, liked the proposal and although I did not get that scholarship at the end, it was a great encouragement to proceed with the research. The *Parco Archeologico del Colosseo* is completing at the moment a similar project to the Museum that I proposed for the scholarship.

As rich as the material remains is also the intangible heritage present in the site; this book has tried to 'capture' it and to encourage integrating it in the presentation of the building. Up until now and due to the complexity in the form and construction of the buildings in the site, research has been partial, as we will explain later. This important architectural and monumental complex has never been studied as such and has not received so far the attention that its rich history and architecture deserve. For this, it is necessary to establish its significance, situating the different interventions in their specific historical, cultural and architectural contexts.

Other buildings at the Roman Forum have, for various reasons, in particular for the search of the ancient remains underneath, been demolished. This site has reached our times with its rich architectural stratification: a product of a continuous process of preservation and transformation. The choice of this particular case study was also based on the existence and possibility of access to unpublished documents that permit dating construction activities that are evident visually, but also those concealed.

The main objective of this research is a coherent analysis of the site and the different interventions in the buildings it contains, including an understanding of the projects' processes, the role of the architect, the patron or client, and the final architectural result. For different circumstances, unlike other buildings in the Roman Forum, this building was always occupied and, as a consequence, adapted for its various uses through the ages. This aspect and the continuous flow of architecture in the building are crucial for this work.

The publication is the result of extensive research in time and space, starting by studying part of the monastery for the specialization thesis at the *Scuola di Specializzazione in Restauro dei Monumenti* of the University of Rome "Sapienza". The fruitfulness of that first investigation, the importance of the site and the fact that it was never studied as a whole, as well as the support and encouragement of the professors in Rome, prompted the desire to further investigate the overall complex (church, monastery and temple), as a doctoral thesis. It was completed at the Technical University of Madrid (ETSAM) (González-Longo, 2015), carried out in parallel with a busy career as chartered architect and academic in Spain and the United Kingdom.

Although I have confronted the study of this complex from the point of view of an architect, I had also taken into account the important archaeology that the site contains, especially considering that the buildings are intertwined and overlapping archaeological remains. The architectural development of a building depends also on the social, economic and cultural circumstances of its owners, architects and occupants, and this has to be better understood while researching and interpreting architecture, as sometimes the focus is more on abstract or fictitious notions of architectural 'styles'. Some of the interventions were largely limited by material, economic or political issues and thereafter each intervention has to be as contextualized as possible.

The research methodology and outcomes are continuously used in my lectures and seminars for the students of the MSc in Architectural Design for the Conservation of Built Heritage, a course that I have created at the University of Strathclyde in Glasgow. I am also very pleased that my research efforts have been useful for the *Parco Archeologico del Colosseo* (formerly, *Soprintendenza Archeologica di Roma*) to inform interventions in the buildings. I am continuing the research as the site is very complex and new elements are being undercovered.

One of the purposes of this book is to further disseminate the research within current and future professionals working in architectural conservation. Hopefully, it will shed more light on the difficult task that architects must undertake every day: to conserve and design on existing buildings, preserving and transforming them to a greater or lesser extent, depending on their significance and condition. There are many publications dealing with the technical aspects of conservation, but the theoretical and design aspects are not, in my view, researched and discussed enough. Understanding these two important aspects—which should be at the base of any architectural project—, the way in which the project is conceived and carried out and the continuous process over a very long period of time, gives another dimension. People come and go but buildings remain for very, very, long time if they are well designed, built and looked after properly.

It is also necessary to clarify the terminology used in architectural conservation, many times inaccurate or confusing. Unfortunately, the terms 'conservation' (*restauro* in Italian) and 'restoration' (*ripristino* in Italian) are frequently used indistinctly. To make things more complicated, in the US—and more recently spreading in other countries—, the term used for conservation is 'preservation' (*conservazione* in Italian). Hopefully, the book will help the reader to reflect about the actual meaning of these terms and inspire more reflective practice and further studies. Ultimately, the intention is to help conserving our built heritage, something very important for our and future generations' well-being, sense of identity and truly sustainable development.

Edinburgh, April 2020
Cristina González-Longo

Acknowledgements

You cannot tackle a topic like this without spending a lot of time in the place, exploring, surveying and investigating the buildings (with four different accesses), consulting a variety of private and public archives, reading all the relevant literature, talking to people and visiting other places to make comparisons. All these activities were made possible and supported by a very large amount of people who I am not able to list in full. Although some access was easier than others, I have been very lucky that places and resources were made fully accessible. This has been fundamental for the research, and I am heartily grateful to the individuals and institutions that made it possible.

This research has been assisted by the constant help and support of the Olivetan Benedictine monks (*Congregazione Benedettina di S. Maria di Monte Oliveto*), who have been occupying and conserving the monastery of S. Maria Nova and the church of Santa Francesca Romana for almost seven centuries, despite the historic difficulties described in this book. It would not have been possible to carry out this research without the help of D. Mauro Dell'Orto (†), who allowed me to visit frequently the church, monastery and archive and brought me to the beautiful Monte Oliveto Maggiore to understand the wider context. His love of art and culture, enthusiasm, encouragement and support was fundamental and also made me to understand the importance of the Olivetan Order not only religiously, but also culturally. He made me also reconsider some aspects about architectural conservation, in particular his 'radical' addition of a lift within the medieval campanile, something that came as a bit of a shock for me as recent architectural conservation graduate. Although, in order to provide the access to the lift, doors had to be opened in the fabric, ultimately this bold intervention made the building habitable for all ages and abilities of occupants. This has definitely helped the conservation of the building more effectively than just the pure preservation of the fabric would have done. I am also most grateful to D. Virgilio Sabatini (†) and D. Vianney Deslandres for providing access to the building and archives and for making me also feel always welcomed, to D. Giovanni Brizzi for providing references and publications and to

Pietrantonio Cavazzeni (†), *Oblato benedettino*, for his help with the *Ministero dell'Interno* archives and interest in the research. I am also very grateful to the Olivetans, in particular to the Abbot Emeritus of Monte Oliveto Maggiore Michelangelo M. Tiribilli, and to Professor Alessandra Bartolomei Romagnoli for inviting me to present my research at a memorable conference at the Capitoline Hill to celebrate in 2009 the fourth centenary of the canonization of S. Francesca Romana.

The staff of the former *Soprintendenza Archeologica di Roma*, located in the southern part of the monastery, were very supportive and incredibly helpful in providing access and archive material. I would like to thank in particular Dr. Irene Iacopi, Arch. Giuseppe Morganti, Dr. Marina Piranomonte and Arch. Claudia del Monti (†) as well as the current staff of the *Parco Archeologico del Colosseo*: Dr. Rosella Rea, Arch, Cristina Collettini, Arch. Stefano Borghini, Arch. Nicola Saraceno and Dr. Sabrina Violante for the most recent information and visit to the building. Dott. Ugo Righini at the *Ministero dell'Interno (Fondo Culto)* has also been very helpful allowing access to their archives, and interested on the research.

A special thanks to Professor Giovanni Carbonara, a key reference for this work. I am immensely grateful to him for his help and guidance, from my beginning in Rome as a student until now, and I am very honoured that he has written the Foreword. I am also very grateful to my other supervisors and professors at the *Scuola di Specializzazione in Restauro dei Monumenti* of the *Universitá di Roma "Sapienza"*: Prof. Giorgio Torraca (†), Prof. Francisca Pallarés, Prof. Piero dell'Amico, Prof. Gaetano Miarelli Mariani (†), Prof. Sandro Benedetti and Prof. Arnaldo Bruschi (†), for their generosity in sharing their knowledge, interest in my work and encouragement.

The supervisor of my PhD thesis at the ETSAM, Professor Antón Capitel and his book '*Metamorfosis de Monumentos y Teorias de la Restauracion*' have been a great inspiration. I am especially indebted for his availability from my first illustrated fax from Rome proposing the topic to the completion of the thesis—with many 'disappearances' in between from my side due to work pressures—, and his time at his studio and house in Madrid and while in his sabbatical at the Bartlett School of Architecture in London.

Thank you also to Professor Claudio Varagnoli, who was the external member of the tribunal of doctorate, for his invaluable comments, suggestions and encouragement to publish and continue the research. Also, to the other members of the tribunal, Prof. Javier García-Gutierrez Mosteiro, Prof. Ignacio González-Varas Ibañez, Prof. Isabel Ordieres Diaz, and Prof. Jose Miguel Merino de Cáceres, for their useful comments and encouragement to publish the research.

I am very grateful for the incredible help from the staff of the *Archivio Centrale dello Stato* (Rome), *Archivio di Stato di Roma*, *Archivio Segreto Vaticano*, *Soprintendenza Arheologica di Roma*, *Archivio del Ministerio dell'Interno- Fondo Culto*, *Archivio della Accademia di S. Luca*, *Comune di Roma*, *Archivio dell'Arma del Genio*, *Archivio dela Soprintendenza Archeologica di Roma*, *Soprintendenza per i Beni Architettonici e Ambientali di Roma*, *Soprintendenza per i Beni Artistici di Roma*, *Archivio Capitolino*, *Biblioteca dell'Istituto di Archeologia e Storia dell'Arte*, *Biblioteca del Dipartimento di Storia, Architettura, Restauro e Conservazione dei Beni Achitettonici "Guglielmo De Angelis D'Ossat" dell' Università degli Studi di Roma "La Sapienza"*, *Biblioteca Nazionale* (Rome), Main Library of the University of Edinburgh, *Biblioteca* of the ETSAM and to the *Archivo del Istituto Lombardo-Accademia di Scienze e Lettere*. These are precious places, truly cultural environments, that facilitate research and make the visits a very enjoyable experience.

These great people and places helped me to continue focused on the research despite the time constraints of a professional career and to publish papers, some of them in collaboration with my husband Dr. Dimitris Theodossopoulos, also a graduate from the architectural conservation school at "Sapienza". I am very grateful to him for patiently going many times to the site to help with the measured and photographic survey of the buildings and, in the early stages of the research, helping to gather the necessary material in archives and libraries. I am also immensely grateful to Dott. Vincenzo Patella for his availability and for making accessible the church and monastery for me, my family and my students and also for his exceptional and very recent photographs, including that of the front cover of the book. A big thanks also to Spartaco Biasini, professional photographer, for his generosity in giving me his excellent photographs of the church, which unfortunately I cannot include all in this book due to space constraints. I am very grateful to Arch. Mari Cruz Gaviria who spent part of her holiday in Rome patiently helping me with the instrumental survey of the façades of the monastery during very hot days, to Dr. Arch. Gaspar Dos Reis Souza Lima, who has always been very generous in sharing his in-depth architectural knowledge and time and has kept me updated on developments and Prof. Eng. Alberto Viskovic for his help in many occasions. A big thanks also to Arch. Carmen Jimenez, Dr. Pat McDonald and Prof. Charles McKean (†) for their continuous interest and encouragement.

Above all, I thank my parents for their continuous love and support and for giving me the freedom to choose and pursue my interests from an early age, and my children, for their love and for making me changing physical and mental perspectives all the time.

Introduction

Preservation and transformation of buildings have been happening in the past as well as today to a bigger extent than is obvious. What has changed over time is the way to carry out architectural design in existing buildings. Until the eighteenth century, architects would perform their projects in the same way, whether they dealt with a new building or an existing one. Since then and alongside the development of archaeology and history as scientific disciplines, architectural design and conservation have acquired a different set of constraints.

Despite common perception, architectural design is not only for buildings ex novo: all architectural projects incorporate some pre-existences in the site, whether tangible or not. Architecture and architectural conservation are complex subjects and truly interdisciplinary ones. Issues such as beauty, functionality, health (we are currently in the middle of the covid-19 pandemic), safety and comfort have to be balanced at the same time, not only for current occupants and citizens but also for future ones.

Rome is a particular site, very useful for the reflection of an architect, for the quality of its buildings and for the long historical periods that they incorporate. It has also been the city of power (religious, artistic, political) for centuries and has a wealth of archival and documentary resources. But the city has also an interesting organised chaos and vitality; Rome is a city built in a cosmopolitan way, but with strong local characteristics.

The desire to deepen the argument has led to the choice of an example as a method of exposure. The monumental complex under investigation is located in the Roman Forum and includes the ruins of the Temple of Venus and Rome, the basilica of S. Francesca Romana and the monastery of S. María Nova (*Abbazia S. Maria Nova de Urbe*). The monastery is currently occupied by the Olivetan monks, offices of the *Parco Archeologico del Colosseo* (formerly *Soprintendenza Archeologica di Roma*) and, until recently, by the *Antiquarium Forense*, now with an undergoing project for the forthcoming Museum of the Roman Forum. The buildings in the site present a great complexity of construction phases, of great architectural interest, representing one of the most significant places in terms of continuity between the pagan, the Christian and the modern city. We can find architectural additions in each period of life of these buildings perfectly visible and in harmonious coexistence with other remains from different periods. Thereafter, it constitutes one of the richest, most varied and interesting examples of architectural stratification that exists in the Roman Forum and the city. We could almost say that knowing the architectural evolution of a building like this is almost knowing the architectural evolution of the entire city, and largely of Europe, in a concentrated way. It constitutes a rare survivor and exceptional example when it comes to reflecting on architectural design and its approach and influence when conserving, preserving, transforming or restoring buildings.

The book is the result of an interdisciplinary research to understand the complexities of the buildings in the site, combining measured surveys and direct observations with archival research and literature review. Exhaustive graphic documentation based on the measured survey of the building was followed by a construction analysis of the buildings and a historical-critical analysis of the monumental site, through analysis also of drawings and another archive material. The theoretical basis of the problem was established through a historical study using national and local archives and a literature review of all publications on the individual buildings that make up the site. This comprehensive study produced new evidence on which to base the reading of the architectural space in the unity of its composition, analysing the successive interventions and resulting configurations. The structure and construction of the buildings are intrinsic to their design, and therefore they have been considered important to provide some light on fundamental issues such as the original configuration of the temple, including its platform and covering, which has many implications for later architecture sitting on the ruins of the temple. In the same way, when studying medieval periods, it has been necessary to undertake the study of the different masonry walls types to understand the complexity of the different phases of the building as a whole. During the Renaissance, an important phase of demolition (and de-construction) began, ending with new façades, for the church in early seventeenth century and for the south part of the monastery in early nineteenth century. These transformations were carried out in very different ways, responding to the skills and education of the architects and patrons, and thereafter are analysed in their historical and architectural context.

This exceptional site had not been studied so far as a whole. There have been, as we will detail in the book, a limited amount of studies about some of its parts, preventing a holistic appreciation of the site and the historical and design processes that produced it. The richness of historical interventions in the same site makes possible a reflection on the character, methods, processes and materialization of architectural design practice within a very long period of time. To understand and identify the different projects over time and their influence on the conservation of the monument challenges the current orthodoxy on how to intervene on monuments.

The transformation that this important site has undergone is studied here in its architectural aspects; therefore, the study has also to address its history, construction and composition, in other words, its significance and the resulting new spatiality, including the role that individual works of art have had in the architectural creation as a whole. The aim is to offer a panorama of the site as a summary of historical events, highlighting those that have had a profound effect on its configuration, identifying the authors and design processes. In particular, the study analyses in more detail the interventions by Hadrian in the second century, the Olivetan Order and Carlo Lambardi at the beginning of seventeenth century and Giacomo Boni in early twentieth century. The analysis of the latter reveals Boni as an innovator and one of the key figures of architectural conservation in Italy, with a clear international impact.

Given the double nature of the temple, there was a curious situation in the Mussolinian era, in which each of the cellae had different ownership and, as a consequence, interventions were executed by two different public bodies. The fragmentation of property and uses is one of the most remarkable characteristics of the complex, which has greatly influenced the current configuration of the site and the conservation of the buildings. Even today, the property is divided between the Ministry of the Interior (Religious Buildings) and the Ministry of Cultural Heritage.

There are some detailed studies of the individual buildings that make up the monumental complex, as a result of archaeological investigations in the temple (Panella, 1985; Panella and Cassatella, 1990; Panella and Del Monti, 1992; Del Monti, 2010), and the church in its early Christian phase (Prandi, 1937; R. Krautheimer, 1937–1977). However, Prandi and Krautheimer reached different interpretations and conclusions about the original configuration of the church. Starting from the original study of the church by Prandi, and the published results of the archaeological excavations, this research has been completed with new surveys and observations of the entire monumental complex, as well as an exhaustive literature survey and archival research.

The first phase of the investigation started from the basis of the extensive survey carried out for the thesis of specialization in Rome. This has been extended to the parts that had not been treated in it, creating the graphic documentation. It has been an arduous task considering the large dimensions of the site and buildings, but necessary for the detailed study of the building fabric and its setting. It has continued with the constructional analysis and study of the materiality of the monumental complex, as well as its state of conservation, in order to get as close as possible to understand in detail the overlapping of its fabrics.

A detailed historical study has been carried out, including an exhaustive investigation in the archives and a review of all the relevant publications as the basis of the historical-critical understanding of the architectural organism. This has sought the 'reading' of the architectural complex and its adjacent areas based on historical analytical knowledge, but at the same time with a formal and structural verification, understanding its internal configuration. Topographic and stratigraphic analysis of some parts of the site have also greatly helped the investigation. The problem can be defined according to different angles: the re-reading of the architectural space in its compositional unit and the analysis of the successive stratifications. Considering the large dimensions of the complex, the detailed study has focused on three of the most important, representative and accessible parts: the platform of the temple, the north facade of the monastery and the church.

It is not the intention of this research to produce a single theory or methodology for architectural conservation, but to demonstrate how each building and site dictate their own intervention, and how research in architecture should be carried out to inform conservation. This has to be conducted always by professionals with sufficient knowledge and skills, able to analyse and make an interpretation of the architecture and the thought processes involved. Architectural conservation is above all an architectural design process and, as in this case, an appropriate transformation project can be an effective method of conservation.

The complex studied is a masterpiece of coexistence between the constructions of different periods, at different topographic levels and that respond to different logics, but equally understandable and with the need to be conserved. It is clear that before undertaking any work, the cultural and architectural significance of the buildings should be established. This should be accredited by historical-critical culture, but without excluding possibilities of innovation when it is indispensable to reveal the formal or historical values of the monument, or facilitate its reading.

Architectural interventions on pre-existences are frequent in the daily work of architects but are increasingly 'harassed' by disciplines complementary to architectural conservation. Sometimes also materials, instruments and misused Charters take an inappropriate role, turning the conservation project into pure repair, a technical and administrative standard process, rather than a creative and cultural one. This reaches the extreme in recent and, considered by some, 'leading' interventions, where the architectural project as such becomes almost non-existent, drowned by a single-focus on the pathology of the stone, non-destructive techniques or sustainability. It is essential that the architect knows these aspects deeply, but the intervention should be based on a comprehensive architectural project. Architectural conservation is not a discipline separate from architecture, although various interests want to present it this way. It is clear, however, that it is a specialism within architecture and, as such, it requires specialist education, ideally well integrated with that of other professionals involved in architectural conservation projects.

The book also attempts to decipher and trace the origins, development and influence of architectural expression and identify how much this is the result of the exercise of artistic freedom, a historical phenomenon of a certain society and culture, or both at the same time. Isolating and describing the specific architectural projects in this complex building, their origin and realization is an important part in this research as it allows to understand in full the significance of the buildings to be preserved and enhanced. Analysing the phases and methods used in the interventions over time on a specific building in a broader architectural, environmental, historical and social context, we can draw extremely useful conclusions. These, although not directly applicable to other cases, can demonstrate the methodologies necessary to understand a building and reflect on successive interventions. Overall, what needs to be researched on and developed in architectural conservation are philosophical principles and rigorous methodologies to follow rather than standard technical solutions.

The patrons, architects, builders and users of the different phases of the transformation of the site have great importance in the analysis of the different interventions and in the narrative. The book identifies the principles and project precedents used in each period, comparing them critically with others of the time. The analysis of the complex has led to the identification of the most significant architectural phases, including those of Nero, Leo IV, Alexander III, the Frangipane family, Bernini and Valadier/Camporese. The most radical transformations of Hadrian in the second century, of the Olivetan order and Carlo Lambardi at the beginning of the seventeenth century and that of Giacomo Boni at the beginning of the twentieth century are analysed in more detail. Following Benedetto Croce's approach, to understand architecture we need to study in detail not only the ideas of these operators but those of their time, tradition and external influences. We also need to understand the practical reasons that have acted on the work of these architects and the decisions of their patrons or clients, trying to contextualize each intervention as much as possible. At the same time, the rich intangible narrative of the buildings evolves and becomes another element of the project.

The book is divided into six chapters and the conclusions. Each of the chapters identifies and analyses the most important projects in the history of the site and buildings studied. In the first chapter there is a critical reconstruction of the primitive landscape and its subsequent transformation by Nero. It attempts to describe what the original configuration and the first architecture of the place would have been, starting with the Velia hill as the original setting and the Etruscan and Republican phases, followed by the construction of Nero's vestibule.

The second chapter deals with the successive transformation of the site by Hadrian into the Temple of Venus and Rome, the largest in the city and one of the largest in ancient times. It analyses to what extent the previous architecture was used, for what purpose and the outcomes. Some contextual information about the previous architecture is also considered and the restoration of the temple by Maxentius after the fire of AD 283 is also explained.

The third chapter covers the process of subsequent decay, destruction and regeneration of the site, due to a combination of natural and human reasons. The transformation of the temple's pagan character into Christian is also discussed, in particular the reoccupation of the place with the small church dedicated to Saints Peter and Paul. The successful recovery of the place as a church and monastery in medieval times is analysed later, identifying the large amount of new architecture added to the site during the intervention of Pope Alexander III and by the Frangipane family, who fortified the site and brought the international and most contemporary architectural trends.

The fourth chapter deals with the greatest transformation experienced by the architecture of the complex since the construction of the temple of Hadrian: the church and the monastery of S. Maria Nova. The work of the Olivetan Order, who took possession of the building in the mid-fourteenth century, is analysed in detail, including how they later transformed the existing medieval forms to those of the Renaissance and Baroque. In particular, the radical architectural transformation of the church at the beginning of the seventeenth century by the architect Carlo Lambardi and the subsequent intervention by Gianlorenzo Bernini are analysed in extensive detail. The subsequent development of the monastery up to the nineteenth century is also discussed.

The fifth chapter discusses the new ideology of architectural conservation during the Napoleonic era and how it affected the whole area, with the intervention in the monastery at the beginning of the nineteenth century by the architects Giuseppe Valadier and Giuseppe Camporese, commissioned by the French government. The context of the intervention and the main theoretical developments in the following period are also discussed in order to provide the required context.

The sixth chapter has as protagonists the architect-archaeologist Giacomo Boni and the architectural design and conservation project that he carried out together with the architect Guido Cirilli. This pioneering intervention at the beginning of the twentieth century to convert part of the monastery into offices and a museum, presenting also the whole site in a didactic way, is analysed in detail, situating it in its theoretical and practical context. This chapter also summarizes the most important theories of architectural conservation, starting with Brandi and continuing with more recent developments, such as the 'critical conservation' and other contemporary discourses on architectural conservation.

The seventh chapter draws the conclusions, beginning with what specifically refers to the monumental complex of the Temple of Venus and Rome-Santa Francesca Romana in the Roman Forum, and then extending the reflection to a more general level.

The term 'monument' is frequently used in the book, as it has been considered a more comprehensive, and international term, also used by ICOMOS (International Council on Monuments and Sites). The Venice Charter (1964) defines it: "The concept of a historic monument embraces not only the single architectural work but also the urban or rural setting in which is found the evidence of a particular civilization, a significant development or a historic event. This applies not only to great works of art but also to more modest works of the past which have acquired cultural significance with the passing of time."

However, the meaning of the term "conservation" used in the book is different to that of the Venice Charter. It is more in line with the definition given in the British Standard 7913: 1998 (a document now superseded): "Action to secure the survival or preservation of buildings, cultural artefacts, natural resources, energy or any other thing of acknowledged value to society."

Throughout the book, there is mention of topics as well as aspects of the buildings and site that require further investigation; this further research is being continued and hopefully more researchers can be involved in the years to come.

1 The First Architecture
From the Velia to the Vestibule of the Golden House of Nero

1.1 The Primitive Landscape: The Roman Forum and the Velia hill

The Roman Forum is the place in which Rome was born and it has been inhabited for at least 3,000 years. Its location in *Latium* (Lazio), to the south of the Tiber River and between a group of hills, was ideal for the primitive settlement: a defensive and strategic position, with good water supply and easy access to the sea. This long human presence has had a profound effect in the area and, despite the destruction that occurred over time, remains of buildings of all the periods are visible.

The territory was covered in the beginning by trees: the primitive kings of Rome were kings of the forests (*reges nemorenses*). This proto-history rotates around forests of beeches and oaks, essential for the naval and commercial life of the population. The bottom of the keel of the warships (*Carinae*), was made of oak and covered with beech. The hills, which are now almost invisible, were then very prominent, with small groups of huts surrounded by earth walls (*oppida*) settled on the top. The valleys in between the hills (*pagi*), crossed by water courses, were partially used as burial places. The Roman Forum developed organically at the foot of the Capitoline Hill (*Campidoglio*), like the Agora of Athens with respect to the Acropolis.

The site of the Temple of Venus and Rome and Santa Francesca Romana is located on the Velia hill, at the east edge of the Roman Forum and next to the Colosseum (Figure 1.1, TVR). The name 'Velia', of pelagic origin, is given to the marsh places: the Roman Forum was in fact a swamp in ancient times. The topographic term 'Velia', was used throughout the Roman era, especially in the first part of it, when it was a '*locus*' of the '*urbs*'. This location is a fundamental reference in the investigation of the different buildings located in it, as we will discuss later.

The summit of the Velia was originally to the north of the area that now occupies the Temple of Venus and Rome, behind the Basilica of Maxentius. From the plan of Reina (*Media pars Urbis*), collected by Castagnoli

2 The First Architecture

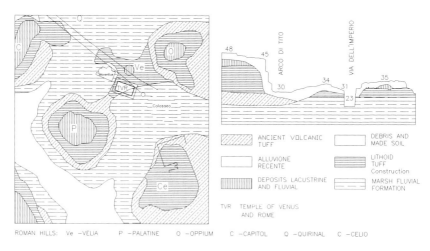

Figure 1.1 Geology of the area (A., traced from De Angelis D'Ossat, 1935) showing the location of the Temple of Venus and Rome (TVR)

(1946), we know that it reached there its highest point: 43 m.a.s.l. (metres above sea level). The Velia was limited by the *Via Sacra* (maximum height of the *summa Sacra Via*: 30 m.a.s.l.), which separated it from the Palatine, to the south, and by the *Via del Colosseo* (24–30 m.a.s.l), which separated it from the Esquiline, to the north. For comparison, the Temple of Venus and Rome is at a height of 34 m.a.s.l. and the *Foro della Pace* at 17.82 m.a.s.l.

During the excavations in 1930s, when Mussolini created the *Via dell'Impero*, the Velia was partially removed in its highest part. As well as ancient buildings in the upper layers, a series of bones belonging to animals of the Middle Quaternary Era (approximately 40,000 years ago) appeared at the bottom, the most striking of all, the skull and fangs of a great elephant. Despite the massive destruction of architectural and archaeological remains, this colossal work gave the opportunity to document the geological constitution of the site (De Angelis D'Ossat, 1935) (Figure 1.1). It chronologically represents the development of natural and human actions in the territory, since prehistoric times. Giacomo Boni, whose extensive contribution will be discussed later, had previously done a detailed report on the geology of the area, which De Angelis could have used (Boni, n.d.a).

The geological study concluded that the Velia, despite having a common origin with the surrounding hills, presents a particularity. The lithoid tuff of construction rests directly on the formation of magma, not appearing the older layers, which indicates a deep hydrological erosion. There is also archaeological evidence of the existence of a stream that, coming from the Velia, and in the direction of the *Forum* Valley, ran alongside huts and tombs (Figure 1.1). This, with the passage of time, would become a sewer, which drained into the *Cloaca Maxima*.

1.2 The First Settlements in the Roman Forum

During the excavation for the opening of the *Via dell'Impero*, the archaeologists found evidence of occupation of the Velia since the eighth century BC (Barosso, 1952). The first inhabited spaces were probably caves formed by the water courses mentioned above. Ancient sources describing the first religious institutions have retained information about this pre-urban period of Rome. One of these sources is the list, mentioned by Pliny the Elder, of thirty '*populi Albenses*' (Plinio III.69) who participated in the celebrations of Mount Albano. The list shows two villages settled in the territory that Rome now occupies: the Querquetulans, inhabitants of the Querquetual (Celio); and the Velienses, inhabitants of the Velia. Mazzarino (1966) indicated that these two settlements would be located in the Velia. Antistius Labeo's description of the religious festival of the *Septimontium*, collected by Festus (348), mentions the league of the seven communities of the seven mountains (although there were actually eight) and the Velia was one of them (Rebert, 1925).

The change in the character of the settlements, the so-called 'urbanization' in archaic times, was a long process. It began with the Iron Age, specifically from early eighth century BC, when the systems of small villages on the top of the high hills started to merge forming larger and more centralized settlements (Walbank, 1989).

The character of some of Rome's original institutions (three tribes, thirty '*curiae*') presupposes the existence of an organizing mind in its first moments of life. Momigliano (1989) follows the views of the Frankfurt school of religious history (Otto and Altheim) about the specifically "numerical" value of many Roman legends. Perhaps this 'mind' was the true founder of Rome, which unfortunately we do not know for sure who he was or at what time he lived. The legend of Romulus is established to the point that his supposed hut is preserved in the Palatine (*Casa Romuli, Parco Archeologico del Colosseo*).

The highest parts of the Roman Forum became cemeteries in archaic times. The *Sepulcreta* (burials), an inseparable component of the primitive habitat, are the oldest vestiges found in the area: we have more data about how cemeteries were than we do of settlements. The study of Roman and Latin cemeteries of this era show the concepts of family and the individual regarding their burial. The families remained gathered around the '*pater familias*' in death as they had been during life. The tomb is in turn a house, and its inhabitant still have social needs.

In the primitive settlement, the administrative organization reflects the model of the family unit. The *pontifex maximus* or king, is the father of the community, as the *pater familias* is of the family unit. The *pontifices* (*pontem facere*: bridge builders) were theologians, guardians and interpreters of tradition and religion, as well as repositories of technical-scientific knowledge, at a time when bridges were a fundamental element for the subsistence of the community. They also had knowledge of astronomy: the first calendar of Rome is attributed to Numa Pompilius, second King of Rome (Romulus being the first) between the end of the eighth century and the first half of the seventh century BC.

Of importance were the cremation tombs (*a pozzo*), a rite of honour, found by Giacomo Boni to the southeast of the Temple of Antoninus and Faustina, dating from the end of the ninth century to the end of the seventh century BC. The most peculiar are the five urns shaped like a house, which represent in clay what would be the aspect of the adobe huts, round or ovoid, with a timber roof structure and straw covering, a kind of 'architectural model', one of the first in history.

The burial tomb *a fossa* (pit) was the most numerous and their location suggests that there were settlements in the Palatine, Velia and Fagutal: this would be the 'centre' of primitive Rome at the time. After the beginning of the eighth century BC—a time in which writing was introduced—the Forum ceased to be a general burial site, limiting it to children who were still buried under the huts, a practice that would last during the eighth to seventh centuries BC. The new cemetery was located in the Esquiline, and would remain there at least until 630 BC.

Initially, there were no buildings for religious rituals, instead, '*Templum*' was for them a celestial or terrestrial space, within which the signs of the divine could be observed. This could even be a lake, like the one on the Via Appia, where its inhabitants, the '*Carmenae*' or '*Camenae*', prophesied through the whisper of fountains. The oldest constructions for religious rituals as such were altars, and a famous altar we know about is that of the Lares on the Velia. Subsequently, small buildings ('*aedicula*' or '*aedes*') were built to preserve objects of worship, for example, the *Sacrum Silex* (siliceous stone), in which Jupiter's lightning force was believed to be enclosed (Quilici, 1979). These were inviolable places, and the material offered to the divinity was also buried in graves. The first priests were the *Auguri*, which were three, a 'magic' number. This type of construction would continue until the end of antiquity, constituting a continuity with the early period and we will see later how this tradition continues even in Christian times.

During this first settlement in the Roman Forum, three main phases of construction can be identified in accordance to the three successive pavements in the area (Gjerstad, 1953). During the first phase, it was not until the middle of the seventh century BC when the change appeared evident, with the construction of monumental tombs by the elite. It is at this time when the first important transformation of the place occurs:

the huts in the *Via Sacra* were demolished, executing a rough paving in their place (Quilici, 1979). This would be the first *Forum*, as a result of the transformation from residential to public area with ceremonial buildings.

The Forum shared with the Palatine the centre of power. The archaeological remains give us a good account of the enrichment of the population, probably as a result of the fact that, since the eighth century BC, the Tiber had become a river of international trade, which in turn implied movement of people, goods and ideas, especially from Greece. There is archaeological evidence of the existence of Greeks living in Rome since at least the end of the seventh century BC.

In the second phase, around 625 BC, the paving of the Forum was renewed and extended to the northwest and the natural depression between the Palatine and the Velia was filled. The route that led from the *Forum* to the place later occupied by the Arch of Titus perhaps did not exist before this time. As soon as these changes occurred in the morphology of the land, large houses occupied the area, giving this district a noble character, which would maintain during the Republican era. From this same time, we have evidence, through material found in the Velia, of houses built of stone and covered with ceramic tiles; similar buildings discovered in the Palatine date from the beginning of the sixth century BC. This new technologies constitute a revolution in construction, not only with regard to the materials used for greater durability, but also in terms of the scale of the buildings. It went from simple individual spaces to more complex bipartite or tripartite buildings.

Earth and straw are no longer used for construction and are replaced with square blocks of stone for the plinths, raw bricks for the walls and terracotta tiles ('Roman tiles') for the roofs, supported on timber structures. All the stones used were volcanic (tuff) and the only locally extracted until fouth century BC was *cappellaccio*, of not much quality. From inscriptions we know that other two types of tuff used were brought from other places farther away: *Grotta Oscura*, a yellowish stone, coming from the area near the Tiber and *peperino*, a grey stone coming from Mount Albano. Subsequently, as Rome's authority extended, the use of *peperino* was increased and *lapis ruber* (red stone) *and Monteverde* (tuff) were also used during the last Republican era.

These advances in urban organization and construction technology, which produced a genuine transformation of the city, were made in a relatively short period, probably a deliberate act, which could be in direct relationship with the foundation of Rome. This period coincides with the traditional date of the coming to power of Tarquinius Priscus (616–578 BC). Although we cannot identify the person directly responsible for such changes, we could say that the true history of Rome begins at this time (Cornell, 1995).

During this second construction phase of the first period of settlement in the Roman Forum, in particular during the last third of the sixth century BC, archaic Rome reaches its cultural climax (Gjerstad, 1953). Two buildings stand out for their importance: the reconstruction of the Regia and the construction of the Jupiter Optimus Maximus temple in the Capitoline hill, comparable with archaic Greek temples such as that of Artemis in Ephesos (Gjerstad, 1953).

The oldest public building in the Roman Forum identified to date is the Regia (625 BC). The current building (c. 500 BC), to the East of the Roman Forum, was identified as the fifth and last of a series of similar buildings constructed in the same place. They all had the same basic elements: two small rooms connected by a vestibule, which opened onto an irregularly shaped courtyard with columns. The design would remain unchanged until the arrival of the Principality, despite successive reconstructions. The new plan symbolized the introduction of a new republican figure, the *rex sacrorum*, a public official, created by the founders of the Republic in order to deal with the originally private cults in the Regia, just as the Vestales were in charge of keeping the fire of the public home in the temple of Vesta (Cornell, 1995). The *rex sacrorum* had his residence (*domus regis sacrorum*) on the Velia. The last monarchs would be tyrants (magistrates for life), reducing the king to a simple ceremonial role. With the arrival of the Republic, the *rex sacrorum* was evicted, and the palace was occupied by the *pontifex maximus*. In the late Republic, the occupant of the Regia was still the *pontifex maximus*, but he did not live there: his official residence was in the nearby *domus publica*. The Regia was fundamentally a public building, consecrated as a temple, seat of the *pontifex maximus*, of the Pontifical school and its archives, and custodian of the famous fetishes of Mars: the spear and the shield, guarantee of the fortune of the city.

Coarelli (1983) has given a new interpretation: he considers that the Regia, the House of the Vestales with the temple of Vesta and the public domus belong to a single complex. It would be a palace containing the residence of the king and associated cults, in particular that of the home (Vesta), that of the pantry (Penates) and those that symbolized the roles of the king as a warrior (Mars) and as provider of wealth (*Ops Consiva*). The primitive Roman religion made an everyday object an object of worship, with a large number of domestic deities that protected the house from the entrance of evil spirits. *Lare* was the spirit of the family and had a funerary character commemorating the ancestors.

Tullus Hostilius, the third King of Rome, lived on the Velia, at the site later occupied by the temple of the Penates; Ancus Marcius lived at the top of the *Via Sacra*, where also later the temple of the Lares was erected;

and Tarquinius Priscus, the fifth King, lived at the top of the *Via Nova*, near the Mugonia Gate and the temple of Jupiter Stator. According to Coarelli's reconstruction of the topography of the upper part of the *Via Sacra*, these places are contiguous and could in fact have been part of a single palatial complex that would cover the entire eastern end of the Forum and the western slope of the Velia.

At the end of the sixth century BC, the monarchy was abolished. The complex was declared public domain and divided into separate units. Its various sacred areas became the centre of public cults: the temples of Vesta, the Lares and the Penates, and the shrines of Mars and *Ops Consiva*, in the new Regia. Only a small residential area of the palace became the residence of the *rex sacrorum*. Other types of public buildings during the second phase of the first settlement in the Roman Forum were the *tabernae*. These were public spaces, preceding the basilicas, whose form was preserved almost invariably during the Republic and the Empire, and the cisterns, such as that of *Scalae Caci* on the Palatine: a circular tank of 6 metres in diameter, built with two leafs of cappellaccio blocks and 0.50 metres thick clay leaf in the middle.

During the third phase of construction of archaic Rome (c. 500–c. 450 BC), the Roman Forum is transformed from an open space to a piazza-like area, enclosed by a series of buildings. It was limited to the southwest by the Temple of Saturn (dedicated in 497 BC), to the northwest by *tabernae* and the temple of Castor, to the northeast by the *Sacellum* in the *Comitium* and *tabernae*, and to the southeast by the *Regia* and the Temple of Vesta (Gjerstad 1953).

We do not know how the city defended itself from attacks during the first period of its existence. According to tradition, Romulus would have carried out the ceremony of the foundation of the city on 21 April of 753. This first city, or "square Rome" (*Roma Quadrata*, as it is frequently represented), would be within a masonry wall of not much height, of which very few traces are left. There is a rest of the wall on the north side of the Palatine, towards the Velia, with a history of continuous reconstruction. Another wall would be built in 675 BC, which would remain in place until 600 BC. None of these walls, due to their characteristics (too low and too light) could have been a defence wall. For this reason, it is thought that they could have constituted a sacred enclosure in the Palatine rather than used as fortification. This is reinforced by the fact that the 50 Roman feet area inside the wall was a building-free zone. During the sixth century BC the outside boundary was maintained with a wall, which would be rebuilt during the same century (Holloway, 1994). We consider that due to its size and position, a series of cyclopean blocks of *cappellaccio* to the northeast base of the Temple of Venus and Rome could be part of Rome's primitive wall and it should be further investigated (Figure 1.2).

8 *The First Architecture*

Figure 1.2 *Cappellaccio* blocks in the northeast corner of the Temple of Venus and Rome (Vincenzo Patella)

1.3 The Etruscan Mark

The Etruscan civilization developed between the ninth and second centuries BC and Etruscan art had its flourishing time in sixth century BC in Rome (Ducati, 1938). It seems that they were a population descending from the Mediterranean culture, a close relative of the Greeks, from whom they took the model of organization.

The Servian wall that surrounds Rome dates from the fourth century BC. It enclosed four administrative regions: Palatina, Suburana, Esquilina and Collina, in addition to the Capitoline Hill. Tradition, however, relates this organization and construction to the sixth king of Rome, and second founder of the city, Servius Tullius (578–534 BC), the Mastarna of Etruscan memories (Ducati, 1938). Tradition also recalls that he set the city limits, gave the city formal definition as an authentic community and that he was Etruscan, although other versions suggest he was Latin. The definition of an exact edge (*pomerium*), the sacred limit drawn by the founder of a city according to an Etruscan rite, was an important moment in the urbanization process. In parallel and based on this distribution, Servius Tullius conducted the first census and also organized the rural areas into districts. The Romans always made a distinction between the sacred limit of the city (*urbs*) and the limit of the territory of Rome (*ager Romanus*).

The primitive city walls were of earth (*agger*), five to six metres high and with a moat, replaced by stone walls (*murus lapideus*) later. In this period the typical construction materials were, in addition to timber and terracotta, the *cappellaccio* or tufa of inferior quality, with puzzolana in the lower strata. After the Gallic invasion of 390 BC, a new wall was built (378–353 BC), and the *Grotta Oscura* tuff replaces the cappellaccio. The Roman foot (29.6 cm) is adopted as a unit of measure and very large square stone blocks of two feet (59.2 cm), or of length of three (88.8 cm) to five feet (1.48 m) are used (Ducati, 1938).

Around 530 BC a hollow beneath the walls north of the Palatine was filled. Atrium houses were built in this new area, in addition to a new road that led to the Forum, also equipped with a sewer, which follows the line of what is normally considered the *Via Sacra*. This route, leading from the Capitoline Hill to the Colosseum valley, was the axis of the Roman Forum, and was also used ceremonially in religious and political celebrations, as well as in the parades celebrating military triumphs. In spite of having changed part of its route, this particular section of the *Via Sacra* was largely conserved in the successive historical epochs. The Caesarean paving of the Roman Forum is still preserved, 7 metres under the current paving of the *Via dei Fori Imperiali* (formerly *Via dell'Impero*). The level of the primitive terrain in the Forum Valley, contemporary of the huts and sepulcretes of the tenth century BC, was 13.5 metres under the current *Via dei Fori Imperiali* (Quilici, 1979).

As it is the case today, the Romans gave great importance to their roads and their durability, and therefore paid much attention to the lower strata. The typical construction technique was the use of a sand layer on which four different strata were placed, with the addition of a simple concrete. The *rural viae glareatae* consisted of a set of gravel conglomerate strata, and in more advanced age, concrete, with thickness ranging from 80 centimetres to one metre. The *urban viae stratae* were composed of four strata: the *statumen* of slabs, the cyclopean concrete *rudus*, the *nucleus* of fine cement and the *summum dorsum* made of slabs. These slabs were thick blocks of basalt hard stone, sometimes up to half a metre high, in polygonal pattern, usually hexagonal (*silices*). Of this last type is the *Via Sacra* and the *Via Appia*, the "*regina viarium*", paved in 293 BC) (Ducati, 1938).

In a world in which the head of each family was also the priest, it is difficult to distinguish between the private and the sacred. Domestic architecture went from simple houses to atrium houses, more functional. The courtyard, which had lost its original agricultural function, became a vestige, with a simple fountain in it. There are no remains of archaic buildings of this period in the Palatine, but two examples have appeared on the *Via Sacra*, and they clearly illustrate how the place was at the end of the sixth century BC: an authentic city. The ground floor contained three adjoining rooms, forming a rectangle, with a wooden porch in one of the major sides, towards the *Via Sacra*. On the opposite side of it, towards the inner courtyard, there was the staircase that led to the upper floor, which probably contained three other rooms. All the dimensions of the lower floor turn out to be round numbers of feet: the thickness of the walls, 2 feet; the central room, 11 × 12 feet; the sides, 13.5 × 12 feet; the distance between the axes of the wooden supports, 8 feet. The height of the floors was calculated based on the extension of the stairs (Gjerstad, 1953).

It is interesting to note the adaptation of Etruscan architecture to the topography of the area and the fact that the Etruscans were experts in hydraulics. The *Cloaca Maxima* (main sewer) is believed to have been built by them and there are still preserved galleries of the time excavated in the volcanic tufa, sometimes more than 15 metres deep, 1.50 metres high and between 0.70 centimetres and 1 metre wide. Some of the existing extensive infrastructure under the Temple of Venus and Rome could be Etruscan, and it should be further investigated.

Servius (I, v.422), states that an Etruscan city was truly considered as such when it had three doors and three temples respectively dedicated to Jupiter, Juno and Minerva. Instead of three different temples, we must imagine only one with three parallel cellae, in the middle the masculine divinity and the feminine to the sides. Every temple dedicated to this Capitoline triad was called *Capitolium*. In Rome the *Capitolium* was built on the hill of the same name: the temple of Jupiter Optimus Maximus. It was the most important temple in ancient Rome and the place where several villages met once a year. Its construction began during the reign of Lucius Tarquinius Priscus (c. 616–c. 578 BC), completed at the time of his son Lucius Tarquinius Superbus (c. 534–c. 509 BC), seventh and last king of Rome, and inaugurated by Marcus Horatius Pulvillus in 509 BC.

The temple had an altar to the north provided with a well: the *mundus*, a way to communicate with the underworld. The tripartite temple is essentially Etruscan and the cult of two different divine triads seems to have its deep roots in the Cretan-Mycenaean religion. The old Capitoline temple was destroyed in the fire of 83 BC. It is likely that the architect Vitruvius Pollio, who wrote his treatise *De Architectura* (The Ten Books) between 25 and 23 BC, would have had this temple as a model when describing the Tuscan-type temple (Vitruvius 7, I). This description has been the subject of debate since the time of Fra Giocondo and Leon Bautista Alberti.

The Tuscan Vitruvian temple was quadrangular in proportion 6:5 in length and width, close to a square shape and thereafter different from the elongated Greek temples in which the length is twice or more than the width, as in the Temple of Venus and Rome. The Etruscan temple had a wooden roof structure and terracotta tiles. The plan of the building was divided into two equal parts: the former (or *pars antica*) or vestibule with a portico and the rear (or *pars postica*) with the three cellae. If the width of the temple is divided into ten parts, the central cella occupies four and the smaller or lateral, three. In the vestibule there are two rows of four columns placed in correspondence with the pilasters of the triple cella. The height of the column is equal to one third of the width of the temple. The lower diameter, which serves as a module, is one seventh of the total height. The base of the column has two equal parts: a cylindrical plinth and a torus; the shaft is not fluted and ends in a capital divided into three equal parts: the abacus, the echinus and the gola. This type of column would be widely used by the Romans. Massive *peperino* blocks of height 56 centimetres can be attributed to the third century BC during the Etruscan rule. Some of those blocks could also have been reused at the platform of the Temple of Venus and Rome.

The measurements of the blocks of the remains of the foundation walls of the temple of Jupiter Optimus Maximus show that the unit of measure used by the architect was the Greco-Roman foot (29.6 cm). Thus, the height of the podium was 12 feet, the width of the central cella 40 feet, the total inter-axial width of the facade was 168 feet, the total width 180 feet (53.28 m wide). Based on Vitruvius and his description of the Tuscan temple, we can deduce that the diameter of the columns was 8 feet, which coincides with the module of the temple, with all its dimensions multiples of 8. Only a few Greek temples could be compared to the grandeur of this temple: the Artemison in Ephesus (55.10 m wide), the Heraion in Samos, the Olympeion (Temple of Olympian Zeus) in Athens (42.90 m wide), the GT temple in Selinus and the Olympeion in Agrigento.

Unfortunately, we do not have enough data to indicate the presence of an archaic temple in the Velia. We have only some minimal evidence: the appearance in the vicinity of a decorated architectural terracotta during the construction of the *Via del Imperio*. This fragment, which was displayed in the Antiquarium Forense (Room VI, no. 3305), by comparison with similar ones, can be ascribed to the sixth century or the beginning of the fifth century BC (Ryberg, 1940).

The first temple built on the Velia of which we know about, is that of the Penates (*Aedes deum Penatium*), from the beginning of the third century BC. According to Rebert (1925), we can consider the origin of the expression *in Velia* as associated to the construction of this temple. Other small sanctuaries in the area were those of Vica Porta and Mutunus Tutunus (Festus 154), which could date from primitive Italic settlements.

1.4 The Velia From Republican to Imperial Rome

At the beginning of the Republic, Rome saw the temples multiply and Greek architects and craftsmen temporarily emigrated to Rome to build them. However, the planimetry of the Forum and the Temple of Jupiter in the Capitoline Hill were preserved. The area that was the highest point of the Velia (that is, behind the Basilica of Maxentius) would be occupied, especially in the late Republic, by those buildings mentioned *in Velia*, such as Domitius Calvinus's house (Festus, 154). Around that time, other buildings mentioned as existing *in Velia* or *sub Veliis* were: the house of Tullus Hostilius, a shrine of the Argei, the *sacellum* of Mutunus Tutunus, the *murus* Mustellinus, two houses of the Valeri (one *in Summa Velia*, the another in *sub Veliis*), and the temple of Vica Pota. However, the Velia is not named in buildings mentioned *in summa sacra Via* such as the house of Tarquinius Priscus and Tarquinius Superbus, the temple of Jupiter Stator, or in those located at *ad portam Mugonis*, as the house of Anco Marzio. The old Attii family would also have their residence here (Colini, 1983).

It is important to mention the existence, in high-Republican times, of the fortified houses of the Valerii on the Velia (Quilici, 1979). It is said that Publius Valerius (Publicola) began to build a house on top of the Velia in the same place that Tullus Hostilius's previously occupied. Due to the misgivings of the people towards such imposing and impregnable construction, Publius Valerius had to change the location, moving it to the bottom of the Velia. Livy (II, 7) and Dyonysius (V, 19) recorded this event and Dionysius (I, 68) also states that the expression '*sub Velia*' refers to a small path that, starting from the Velia, led to the *Carinae*. Two texts by Cicero (Rep. II, 53; Har. Resp. 16) also recorded the event but contradict each other: while the first one presents P. Valerio moving his house to *sub Veliam*, after people's misgivings, in the second he is granted, with public funds, a house in Velia, as a prize for his services to the state. All these contradictions mean that the story cannot be taken as a completely rigorous fact. On the other hand, Valerii graves were found behind the Basilica of Maxentius closely associated with the ancient sacellum of Vica Porta. They confirm, as transmitted by the classical authors, their *sub Velia* situation, indicating a continuity of the family clan with their ancestors. This fact confirms the preservation of the memory and toponymy of the archaic settlements through religious celebrations that still took place around these centres (Rebert, 1925).

The architecture of Rome in the Republican era focused especially on utilitarian works. The period 81–80 BC, corresponding to the mandate of the dictator Lucius Cornelius Sulla (138–78 BC), marks a major building renovation in Rome and its surroundings. It affirms the grand, solemn architecture, evidently inspired by Hellenistic models, although with a clear Roman character. The prevailing form of construction is the *opus incertum*, a robust masonry construction composed by strong lime mortar and small stone cubes. This constitutes the prelude to *opus reticulatum* (small stone pyramids, with the smooth base facing outwards). The use of lime since the second century BC contributed to the development of vaulted constructions, as the lime mortar together with the tuff stone was a tremendously versatile and strong material.

The Forum was at the time the centre of great building activity: Sulla limited the area with ritual wells, rebuilt the *Via Sacra*, connecting it with the *Clivus Capitolinus* through a viaduct with arches, in addition to the construction of the vault of the *Cloaca maxima*. He also consolidated and fortified ancient towers and added buttresses to support the ancient walls. According to Plinio (N.H., XXXVI, 45), Sulla, in the reconstruction of 69 BC of the temple of Jupiter in the Capitoline Hill (as we mentioned before, destroyed by a fire in 83 BC), used Corinthian marble columns extracted from the Temple of Olympian Zeus (Jupiter for the Romans) in Athens, of which we will talk about later. However, the coins of M. Volteius (after 83) and Petillius Capitolinus (43), show a temple with columns more similar to the Doric order. Sulla wanted the temple to be entirely in stone, and this temple is the first example of the use of marble in a sacred public building.

Marcus Porcius Cato, 'the Censor', a Roman politician (234–149 BC) promoted the fight against luxury and corruption of traditional customs. He opposed the influence of Greek civilization, contributed to the expulsion of philosophers from Rome and wrote, among other works, an agricultural treaty in which he said that the owner should sell rather than buy. He wrote the first historiography work in Latin language, *Origines*, in which he narrated the history of the Roman people since its legendary foundation by Aeneas until the second century BC. When Lucio Licinio Crasso (140–92 BC) adorned his residence in the Palatine with six columns of Cipollino marble, he was given the nickname of 'Palatine Venus'. For the austere Republicans, who followed the Catonian traditions, this was an unacceptable sign of luxury and refinement. It would become an open criticism when Licinio Lucullo (c.106–56 BC) introduced the dark (African) marble into Rome, which took the name of Luculleo. In fifty years the use of exotic marbles became common practice in Rome, and an example of the new artistic appreciation (Erder, 1986).

There are existing examples of temples of this era in Rome in Largo Argentina. These temples stand out for their Hellenism, but with the Etruscan-Latin character provided by the height of the podium. Temple B, perhaps identifiable with the temple of Hercules Custodio, was later expanded (probably in the early years of the empire), destroying the wall of the primitive cella, extending it to the colonnade, which was closed with a brick wall, extending also the podium. But, without doubt the most important work of the time of Sulla is the *Tabularium*, on which the Senate Palace of the Capitoline Hill is now erected; this is another interesting case of preservation and transformation, to be researched in more detail.

Pompeo was also a building renovator in Rome, especially in the Campo Marzio. He erected the first stone theatre in the city (55 BC). Although they already existed in other places, in Rome they were prohibited for reasons of public morality, although there were wooden theatres. Pompeo copied, according to Plutarch (42, 3), the theatre of Mytilene, on the island of Lesbos. To extinguish any scruple of a religious nature, he erected a temple to *Venus Vincitrice* at the top of the central part of the cavea, so that the stands looked like the steps of the temple. He thus used the Hellenistic design composition of joining a theatre with a porticoed courtyard, which appears already in Pompeii from 200–80 BC. According to Vitruvius (V, 9, I), this design composition becomes peculiar to Roman architecture.

Caesarian architecture (after 70 BC) marks the affirmation of Hellenism in Roman construction. Marble began to be used more extensively; that of Lumi (currently Carrara) made its appearance at this time in Roman constructions, although it will be Augustus who will use it on a large scale. The peculiar construction technique of this period is the *opus reticulatum*, an opus caementicium wall with an external layer of diamond-shaped blocks of tuff, lined with travertine or marble. This makes a difference between the structure and the cladding that did not exist in Greek architecture.

The great projects of Caesar were the Basilica Giulia and the Forum. The Basilica, inaugurated in 46 BC, measured 101 × 49 metres and was completed by Augustus, who also rebuilt it after a fire. It was rebuilt again by Diocletian after another fire in AD 283, although always retaining the same shape. Caesar also gave the Forum a new paving and built the temples of Fortuna Virile and Vesta (actually Portuno) in the Boario Forum. It seems that he also turned the Tiber Island into a ship, following the Hellenistic trend to play with forms and figures. The dimensions of Rome within the *pomerium* at the end of the Republic was around 285 hectares.

As we have seen, since Republican times the Velia was a very desirable area for the residences of the upper classes, as the remains found during the opening of the *Via dell'Impero* also testified. In the northwest corner of the platform of the Temple of Venus and Rome are still today, at a level of 3.75 metres below the current level (25.30 m.a.s.l.), the remains of a sumptuous Roman house discovered in 1835 by A. Nibby and investigated by Giacomo Boni, and later by Antonio Maria Colini and Maria Barosso in 1931–32, during the works of the opening of the *Via dell'Impero* (Barosso, 1952). The *Governatorato* of Rome commissioned Maria Barosso to reopen the excavation that Boni had done. Barosso surveyed the remains of this structure of semi-underground environments and published a graphic reconstruction (Barosso, 1938).

The building, probably the rest of a *nymphaeum* (Morricone, 1987), consists of an octagonal room 8 metres in diameter, with curvilinear walls and two orthogonal cryptoportici, towards north (Capitoline Hill) and west (Palatine) (González-Longo and Theodossopoulos, 2009). The structure is of small blocks of tufa, and, due to the absence of brick, it was dated between the last years of the Republic and the first years of Augustus. The main interest of this construction lies in a very fine glass paste flooring with beautiful colours: green, ultramarine blue, turquoise, amethyst red and black (Boni, n.d.b.). The design of the pavement includes triangles and rhombuses, similar to the *sectilia pavimenta* described by Vitruvius (VII, I, 4). Based on this pattern of the pavement design, in particular the circle filled with triangles (motif called shield), and on the materials used in it (veined marbles), Maria Luisa Morricone (1987) has dated the building around the last years of the Republic (first century BC).

Curiously, these spaces seem to have remained in use, or at least their structure has been reused, until the time of Hadrian, and incorporated into the temple platform. Unfortunately, the spaces are now not easily accessible and some of the structures recognized by Barosso, such as the stairs, or the walls of opus incertum (through which Barosso also dated the structure in the first century BC), are no longer visible.

1.5 Augustus and the Giulio Claudia Dynasty

The years between the assassination of Caesar, in 44 BC and the triumph of Cesare Ottaviano (not yet Augustus), in 29 BC, were of crisis, although they continued erecting buildings and conserving ancient ones. Roman construction was not like the Greek, fundamentally sacred, but instead extended to all public services: in 33 BC Marcus Vipsanius Agrippa restored the *Cloaca Massima*. Instead of individual artists (although there were some, such as Vitruvius, author of the famous two-storey basilica of Fano), there was a whole series of workshops, craftsmen and artisans divided into different guilds, but united with religious ties, and with the tradition that passed from master to apprentice and from generation to generation, but always improving. The guilds and professional associations were subject to state regulations. This organization, with which *redemptores* (entrepreneurs) were eliminated, would continue even in medieval times.

The section of the *Via Sacra* visible today belongs to the first years of the empire, before the reconstruction after the fire of Nero in AD 64 when it would be built to a higher level. During the extensive excavation of the Roman Forum at the end of the nineteenth century, this Neronian route was demolished, along with some contemporary buildings, confused with medieval constructions. The *Via Sacra* of the Republican era, upon reaching the Velia, turned eastward towards the *Carinae*. In the time of Augustus, this direction changes and goes towards the Palatine. This route is very clear in the vicinity of the Temple of Venus and Rome and the arch of Titus (Coarelli, 1989). A section of the Roman road is also still visible outside and under the nave of the church of Santa Francesca Romana (Figure 1.3), as we will discuss later.

16 *The First Architecture*

Figure 1.3 Remain of the pavement of the *Via Sacra* from the first imperial era adjacent to the church of Santa Francesca Romana façade (A.)

A new construction material, brick, started to appear, which would be used extensively throughout the empire. Vitruvius reports on *opus latericium*, composed by bricks (*lateres*) made of clay pasted with straw and simply dried in the sun or cooked in an oven (*lateres cocti, lateres testacei*) (Vitruvius, II, 3, 5, 6; VII, 2). Lime and mortars were of great importance; Vitruvius distinguished between quarry sand (preferable) and sea or river sand. With the first, the lime:sand ratio in mortars was 1:3, with the second 1:2. Vitruvius also discusses the cohesion between lime-based mortars and stone, based on the combination of the four elements of nature: air, earth, water and fire.

Opus latericium derives from Etruria, although it was also used in Greece and Asia Minor. The Etruscan brick would be, because its dimensions, what Pliny (XXXV, 171) calls *lidio* and which corresponds to the "theoretical" Vitruvian brick "*longum sesquipede, latum pede*" (Vitruvius, II, 5; VII, 2). From this brick, half was obtained by cutting it. Other types of brick prevailed: the *bipedali* (60 cm sq.), which were used not only for arches, but also in the levelling layers of the walls, and the *laterculi bessales* (20 cm sq. and 4 cm of thickness). They were often cut in a triangular shape, that is, of an isosceles triangle, with the base as an external wall and the tip towards the inside, giving the wall a great consistency.

The relationship between the dimensions of the bricks, the thickness of the joints, and the regularity of the execution have been studied extensively, allowing for chronological classifications. However, it is easy to fall into serious errors if exaggeration is reached with these systems. The use of new technologies such as 3D laser scanning can achieve more accuracy and we expect the studies to benefit from it once information can be more rigorously extracted, analysed and interpreted. For now, we can make a general distinction, saying that during the first century of the Empire, the bricks are usually of small thickness (around 3 cm), regular, carefully executed and with joints of less than one centimetre. In the following centuries, the bricks increase in thickness, until they reach about 5 centimetres (third and fourth centuries), with irregular lengths and joints up to 3 centimetres. This way of building contributes to a solidity that we can still admire today.

With Emperor Augustus and the *Pax Romana* or *Pax Augusta*, Rome becomes the centre of Mediterranean or classical art, and from there it spreads to all the places of the empire. Augustus boasted that "he had left marble where he had found brick" (Suetonious, XXVIII, 3). He continued the truncated enterprise- because Caesar's death-, of turning Rome into a splendid metropolis. Later Nero, Domitian, Trajan and Hadrian would continue this idea. Augustus (IV, i; X, 2) himself wrote the history about works he had carried out. The long inscription c. AD 14 on the walls of the temple of Rome and Augustus in Ankara was also an official account of *Res gestae divi Augusti*, composed by Augustus himself. Among other things, he divided Rome into fourteen regions in 7 BC, extended the Philippi porticus and in 28 BC he restored eighty-two temples in Rome. He also built the temples of Augustus and Rome in Pola and in Ancyra (modern Ankara). It is interesting to note that in the Mausoleum of Augustus, which marbles were used for the construction of the *Duomo of Orvieto*, the entrance is to the South, as in the Etruscan temples. Modest families, however, were buried in the so-called *colombarium*, especially from this time, a typology of Egyptian derivation.

Augustus, in his list of buildings constructed or rebuilt under his mandate, mentions the temples of Lares at the top of the *Via Sacra* and the Penates in the Velia: *Aedem Lararum in summa sacra via, Aedem deum Penatium in Velia* (Augustus, IV, 7). The description *in Velia* is used exclusively in this period in connection with this *Aedes deum Penatium*, located at the foot of the hillside towards the Forum, near the present church of Ss. Cosma and Damiano (Van Deman, 1923). In the *Ara Pacis*, which was originally in the place of San Lorenzo in Lucina and was rebuilt in its actual location with the remains found (not all), we find a trace of Hellenism in the relief in which a mountainous terrain appears, with the temple of Penates and the oak tree. It seems that the author of the *Ara Pacis* was inspired by this reconstructed temple of the Penates for the scene of the sacrifice of Enea (Castagnoli, 1946), constituting an anachronism, since the temple was built long after the time of Enea, but very useful from the point of view of communicating the object represented. The small temple of a single cella and which is accessed by steps, appears located on a curled hillside; the images of the Penates were identical to those of the Dioscuros (Castor and Polux, sons of Zeus).

Augustus also built his own Forum, including a temple dedicated to Mars. The Basilian monks built in the ninth century a small church on the temple cella and excavated the podium to make a crypt for the dead. This means that the elevation of the temple no longer existed or was in ruins, and that the columns had been torn down. The building was later occupied by the Knights of Rhodes, in 1230. In 1465 Cardinal Marco Bembo rebuilt the Priory of the Order and built the loggia. Then a convent and houses were built and the only element that emerged from the Forum was the *Arco dei Pantani* and part of the colonnade of the temple. The complex was later unearthed and is how we see it now. Similar developments occurred at the Temple of Venus and Rome, as we will see later.

Among the architectural works of Tiberius (AD 14–37), the temple and library of Augustus at the foot of the Palatine towards the Forum stand out. He also built the Tiberian domus (extended by Caligula AD 37–41), in addition to many other buildings and also carried out restorations. Claudius (AD 41–54), like Tiberius, constructed not only religious buildings, but also public utility works. Claudio's large constructions are characterized by the use of triangular brick, more convenient from a constructive and economic point of view. They derive from the already mentioned *laterculi bessales* (20 cm side and 4 cm thick) and there were two types. The first type was obtained from the diagonal cut, obtaining a base of 30 cm and the second was the result of a double diagonal cut, obtaining four 20 cm base bricks. The cut was made when the *laterculos* were still raw, or when cooked, with the martelina. In the case of the arches of Claudio's constructions, large bricks (*quadrellani*) were used as centring.

A new type of construction, probably from the Claudian era, is the underground building in Porta Maggiore. It is a hypogeum about ten metres below the old level. It consists of a corridor with long inclined plane, an atrium and a vestibule (12 m long and 9 m wide), with three naves, and a semicircular apse at the end. All this gives the appearance of a Christian basilica. The communication between the central nave and the lateral ones, all of them covered with a barrel vault, is through four semicircular arches on quadrangular pilasters. This room was to serve as an initiation to religious mysteries, and was built underground through wells and trenches, in which the concrete was laid, and when it set, allowed the excavation of the space.

An interesting finding of the excavation of the tombs of the Roman Forum, a process passionately followed by local and international observers, was the discovery, on 20 March 1904, of a travertine block belonging to the foundations of an imperial-era statue, which protected a set of amphorae and other pieces dated in the seventh century BC. It seems that these would be offers made to one of the damaged tombs during the erection of the imperial statue, which were subsequently piously arranged and protected there (Holloway, 1994). Although anecdotal, this demonstrates that imperial builders had a certain respect for the pre-existing.

1.6 Nero's Urban Project: From the Domus Transitoria to the Domus Aurea

Nero (54–68) developed a building activity divided into two periods: before and after the fire of July 64. During the first period, he built the *Domus Transitoria* between the Palatine and the Esquiline (Tacito, 39; Suetonius, 31, 1), of which there are very few remains in some spaces under the Flavian Palace in the Palatine (Morricone, 1987). After the fire, Nero built the *Domus Aurea* (Golden House), in addition to other buildings, such as a Porticus on the *Via Sacra,* and rebuilt the house of the Vestales. The *Domus Transitoria* and *Domus Aurea* had sumptuous internal and external spaces including fountains and gardens. The arch of Titus is supported by Neronian foundations, which clearly mark the level of Neronian paving around the area, but, due ti the short time between the two main building phases of the two Neronian residences, there is still some confusion today.

The Julio-Claudio period concludes with a great work of art: the *Domus Aurea* of Nero. After the fire, three of the fourteen Roman regions were totally destroyed, while another seven were seriously damaged. The *Domus Aurea*, which had begun construction four years before the great fire, was largely built when Nero escapes and dies on 8th June, 68. The architects were Severus and Celer, *magistri* e *machinatores* (Tacito, Annales, XV, 42; Suetonius. Nero, 31; Milizia, 1768). The palace was a large rectangle, well- oriented, with the main facade facing south, preceded by a triple Porticus one thousand feet long. In the palace dominated the barrel vault, but the cross vault also appeared. In the place of the current Flavio Amphitheatre (Colosseum), there was a salt water lake.

The square vestibule of the *Domus Aurea* was built on the Velia, in the western part of the area which now occupies the temple of Hadrian (Figure 1.4), next to the lake and with a strategic position, between the Palatine, Oppio and Esquiline hills, and visually very prominent. In the centre, to the west, the 30 m high bronze Colossus, by the Greek Zenodoros, was erected. Interestingly, this height is very similar to that of the current medieval *campanile* and the overlapping of the plans seems to clearly indicate that it was perhaps in this same position (Figure 1.4). Existing Roman structures under the campanile seem to confirm this interpretation and they need to be further investigated in detail. The Colossus represented Nero as the Sun god and the design composition was full of optical illusions, following Eastern Hellenistic design principles.

Also, as part of the great transformation that took place in this area of Rome after the great fire, Nero built on the *Via Sacra* a great

20 *The First Architecture*

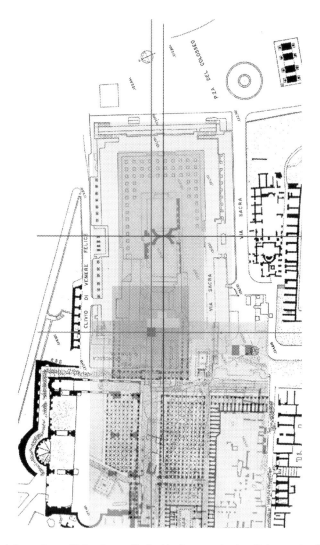

Figure 1.4 Location of Nero's vestibule (darker grey), the Colossus in the center and the Porticus of access, based on Van Deman (1923), in relationship with the temple Venus and Rome and the church of Santa Francesca Romana (A. on Photogrammetry from Rome City Council)

Porticus of access to the *Domus Aurea*. It aligned with the central axis of the Vestibule built on the Velia, creating a total symmetry (Figure 1.4) and providing an effective fire protection strategy for the surrounding buildings. The Porticus was two metres above the

Republican *Via Sacra*, which was widened by twenty metres, creating a monumental access and an impressive visual central perspective towards the Vestibule and the colossal statue (Barosso, 1952). The American archaeologist Esther Van Deman established at the beginning of twentieth century the level of the *Via Sacra* at the time of Nero and identified the remains of the Neronian brick Porticus and its concrete foundations made of siliceous stones (Van Deman, 1923; Van Deman and Clay, 1925). Barosso later also recognized other structures under the Basilica of Maxentius, which had in turn been built on the commercial area of the *Horrea Piperataria* (Barosso, 1952).

In order to create the platform for Nero's vestibule and achieve the desired extension and symmetry, a great engineering work was carried out, modifying substantially the original topography of the area. The slope of the Velia was cut and supported by thick concrete retaining walls made with siliceous stones, which become visible after the opening of the *Via dell'Impero* (Figure 1.5). Nero's successor, Marcus Salvius Otho (15 January–16 April 69) concluded the colossal enterprise.

Figure 1.5 Retaining concrete wall made of siliceous stones, part of Nero's vestibule (A.)

The south front of this retaining wall presents a structure with buttresses, creating quadrangular spaces and a corridor, with similarities to that in the front of the platform of the Temple of Venus and Rome towards the Colosseum, an area then occupied by the lake of Nero. This is a very effective retaining structure used even used in more recent constructions, such as in the Villa Rivaldi and in the Mussolinian retaining walls along the *Via dell'Impero*, and found also outside Rome.

The Neronian transformation changed not only the topography of the area, but also the existing routes, including the *Via Sacra*, which originally went more directly to the east, now deviating to the south, creating also another path to the north. Nero's architects and engineers demolished only what was strictly necessary to reach the necessary levels, which is why precedent structures are partially preserved to a certain level. But the most radical change is that of the character of the area. It is clear that it was occupied in Republican times by rich private residences, with gardens, fountains, porticus and cryptoporticus and became in Nero's time a public and religious space (Colini, 1983).

2 The Place Transformed

The Temple of Venus and Rome of Hadrian

2.1 Flavian Architecture

After Nero's death, the Flavian dynasty restructured the Velia area. Their buildings were of great quality, especially those of Vespasian (69–79) and Domitian (81–96); Titus's empire (79–81) was too short and difficult. During the stormy events in Rome during the brief empire of Vitellio (19 April–21 December 69), a fire destroyed Sulla's temple of Jupiter in the Capitoline Hill, but was quickly rebuilt.

The most important building works of Vespasian were the *Foro della Pace* (71–75) and the amphitheatre (Colosseum), which Titus would inaugurate in the year 80, although it would be completed by Domitian. The building displayed all the experience accumulated until then by the Romans in terms of architecture and construction and was a real wonder for visitors until medieval times. Vespasian, responding to the complaints of the people of Rome, only reserved for his residence a small part of the *Domus Aurea* and the rest was destroyed. The transformation of Nero's Colossus into the Sun god began at the same time as the construction of the Flavian amphitheatre, which took the name Colosseum from the statue.

The *Foro della Pace* was of the Hellenistic type, that is, it had a great quadrangular portico (*temenos*), in whose centre the temple emerged. The name 'Peace' (*Pace*) was because it was inaugurated in the year 71, after the victory over the Jews and the subsequent pacification of the East. In AD 80, there was another great fire in Rome, which destroyed the temple of Capitoline Jupiter, and also left its mark here. It may also have been damaged by a fire in 191, was restored by Settimius Severus and was later affected by the strong earthquake of 408, which lasted seven days. In the sixth century, Procopius (IV, 2) says that the building had been destroyed for some time.

Domitian had an even bigger building activity than his father, Vespasian. The architect-engineer Rabirius designed for him the magnificent Flavian Palace in the Palatine (Milizia, 1978). After the death of his brother Titus, he built the arch in his honour to commemorate the capture and plunder of Jerusalem, in addition to erecting several altars to remember the Neronian fire, and in 96 he built the *Meta Sudans*. The Arch of Titus is in the southwest corner of the temple of Venus and Rome, and, as we have mentioned before, is built on Neronian foundations (Figure 2.1). The surrounding terrain was excavated at the end of the nineteenth to early twentieth century, so the visible levels around it are pre-Neronian. Its position shows a slight rotation with respect to the Neronian axis, probably responding to the urban actions that occurred when the Colosseum was built. We will talk later about the emblematic intervention in the arch of Titus made by G. Valadier in the early nineteenth century.

In 1848 the mausoleum Haterii *gens*, dated early second century AD, was found near the Torre di Centocelle in the ancient via Labicana. Today almost destroyed, it consisted of an almost square space partially excavated in the tuff. The owner was Q. Haterius Tychius, *redemptor* (contractor) of public works in Rome under Domitian. The reliefs of the tomb, now in the Vatican Museum, are a very interesting document of the construction practices in the early second century AD. On the left of the representation of a temple appears, in excellent detail, a construction machine used in its building, a crane—which from its configuration may have been used to erect the columns of the temple—which is operated by a wheel human-powered by slaves walking inside. It probably displays the high technical capabilities of the family business during the Flavian dynasty.

Figure 2.1 Southwest of the area of the Temple of Venus and Rome, showing also the foundations of the Arch of Titus (A.)

2.2 Hellenism, Mithraism and the Eleusinian Mysteries

Rome was the heiress of Hellenism. The Italian-Etruscan precedent had already fed on this, coming from Greece from the first century BC, but already present between the fourth and third centuries BC, when there was a flow of phylo-Hellenism as mentioned before. It was a rich urban culture that produced some of the greatest buildings of antiquity and its cosmopolitan eagerness permeated the culture of the time. The Hellenistic age continued an ancient tradition, enriched by the great discoveries of Hellenistic and Roman historical thought: the historiography of culture and legal historiography, or history in general (Mazzarino, 1966).

The contact of the Roman world with Hellenism is especially intense with Nero, Domitian, but especially with Hadrian, as we will see with the construction of the Temple of Venus and Rome. Between 312 and 286 BC, Capua takes the symbol of the wolf breastfeeding the twins and the expression 'Roman' for their coins. The singular temple or building loses individual importance to become an urban piece, and conditioned by this, the *stoa* becomes an architectural element that indicates the extent of the intervention.

The monumental public buildings served, among other things, as a social centre, banks and markets. Public temples were frequently renovated and rebuilt, and new projects for the emperor's various gods were constantly emerging (Ducati, 1938). In the continuous cultural exchange from the Hellenistic period, new religions appeared and eventually they took a position alongside the classical temples of Rome, often copying their forms. In some cases, however, new forms of worship appeared restricted to the private domain, for which housing was adapted. Thus we find a small tholos on the *Via Sacra*, near the arch of Titus, privately dedicated to the members of the Haterii *gens*.

The second century was a time of apogee of the Roman Empire, and Rome was the capital of the vast empire, the *Urbs*, with about one million inhabitants. There was a fusion of the East and the West, including their gods. During the Hadrian Empire new cults arise and the old ones are reinforced. The city, divinized as *Dea Roma*, was founded as a unit on its own cult, the cult of Rome and Augustus. The cult of Cibeles becomes important and the cult of the Persian god Mithra begins to emerge.

Among the Eastern religions, Mithraism was a unique Roman phenomenon, which had a rapid diffusion especially at the end of the second century. In this case it is possible to speak of an architectural type, and the dominant symbol is the cave. The vaulted ceilings of the *mithraeum* were sometimes decorated with stylized stars. The main room was an elongated hall (the "cave" itself) with the altar or small sanctuary in the background. It had benches running to the sides. Sometimes the entrance was restricted through a vestibule (pronaos) and occasionally through other rooms. It was common to find *mithraea* built inside pre-existing buildings. Mithraism, along with most other forms of paganism did not survive beyond the fourth century.

Hadrian was a frequent visitor of Athens, where he participated in the rites of Eleusis (Lepsina), on the outskirts of the city and accessed through the *Via Sacra*. It is interesting to understand what they consisted of, because they can give us some insights on what Hadrian intended when building his Temple of Venus and Rome. The Eleusinian Mysteries, as they are still called, were secret and performed in the Temple of Demeter, goddess of the earth, which was an important pilgrimage centre throughout antiquity. In March, there was the initiation to the Lesser Mysteries preparatory to the Greater Mysteries which took place at the end of September and lasted ten days. Processions were made from Athens to Eleusis, with stations for prayers in sacred caves, with sacred objects and rites of collective purification, which served as preparation for the great day of 21 September, the sacred union of Zeus and Demeter. The mysteries ended with a libation towards east and west. The strictly secret rituals were performed in the Telesterion, a large rectangular columned hall (54.15 m × 51.80 m on its sides), partially carved in a rock and with eight bleachers that could accommodate 3,000 people. Theodosius ordered to close the sanctuary and it was devastated by the barbarians in 396.

2.3 Hadrian, Architect of the *Urbs*: Conservation and Innovation of the Classical Temple

Roman architecture reached one of its peaks of maximum originality under the Empire of Trajan (98–117), who was called *optimus princeps*. He not only built great buildings and infrastructure in Rome, such as the baths, the Forum and the market, but throughout all the empire, for example, the Alcántara Bridge and Segovia Aqueduct, both in his native Spain. He continued the Flavian program, especially Domitian's and Nero's, to make a general masterplan for the city, but, unlike these other emperors, he was interested in benefiting the community. His architect-artist was an Asian Greek, Apollodorus of Damascus, with a different approach than the Roman architect-engineer Rabirius.

Under Hadrian (117–138), also Spanish and a well-known phylo-Hellenism, architecture continues its development, reaching a decisive point, but at the same time suffering the inevitable reaction of academicism. The Hellenic influence returns to the city, and the building activity of this emperor was very extensive. Unlike Trajan, who built his imperial forum, Hadrian decided to build a temple on the edge of the Roman Forum, perhaps inspired by the Olympeion of Athens restored by him (González-Longo and Theodossopoulos, 2005).

As phylo-Hellenist, Hadrian appreciate and practised geometry, especially valued in the Platonic Academy; tradition says that the sentence

"Let no one ignorant of geometry enter" was engraved in its door. It also seems that Hadrian was akin to the ideas of the Stoics, citizens of the world, especially through his contemporary Hierapolis Epictetus (50–138), on which philosophy the Roman emperors seem to have found the basis of their universal empire.

Hadrian considered himself an architect (Cassius Dio, LXIX, 4). Apollodorus, although he had dedicated his work *Poliorketikà* to him, criticized Hadrian's projects, particularly that of the Temple of Venus and Rome, which led him into exile and perhaps death. Cassius Dio (LXIX, 4) tells how in the presence of Trajan, Apollodorus told Hadrian that he should not design buildings but should draw pumpkins. Perhaps Hadrian had, as executor of his architectural projects Decrianus (arbitrarily transformed sometimes into a Greek Demetriano or Demetrio), who designed the transport, upstanding, of the Colossus of Nero to make room for the Temple of Venus and Rome, as we will see later.

Hadrian's intense building activity consisted not only in the construction of new buildings, but also in a large number of interventions in existing temples that had a particular meaning. He built new temples dedicated to Trajan and Matidia, his mother-in-law, built the Athenaeum and preserved several buildings, with a variety of interventions ranging from conservation with contemporary architecture to restoration. His main buildings were the reconstruction of the Pantheon (after 126), the Temple of Venus and Rome (dedicated in 135), its Mausoleum, the *Mole Adriana* (finished in 139), with the Elio bridge (finished 134), and, of course, his own residence, *Villa Adriana*. All these buildings have been preserved almost entirely, testament to the quality of their construction, and also the architectural design that we could define with modern terms as timeless, and able to adapt to new uses over time.

The primitive Pantheon of Agrippa caught fire in AD 80. Domitian rebuilt it, but it caught fire again in 110 due to lightning, which evidently tells us that the ceiling was made of wood. This fire risk was surely something to consider in future constructions, including that of the Temple of Venus and Rome. The Pantheon was rebuilt by Hadrian between 115 and 127 with totally different forms and other orientation, but, strangely for our modern mind, he credited it to Agrippa in the inscription of the façade. By doing so Hadrian conserved the memory of the place and the original intention, but reconstruction copying the old building was not an option. The construction of its 43-metre diameter concrete dome was made possible thanks to the technical development on the elaboration of concrete, in which the use of puzzolana and structural lightening played a fundamental role. In the circular wall seven niches are opened to the interior, which are alternately circular and rectangular, a feature that will be repeated in the Temple of Venus and Rome.

2.4 The Temple of Venus and Rome

The Velia had important symbolic and urban values for Hadrian. It connected the parts of the old and new city, establishing an axis with the Capitoline Hill in the same way that happened in Athens between the temple of Olympian Zeus—as mentioned before, restored by Hadrian—and the Acropolis. However, the topographic conditions of the two temples were diametrically opposed. The one in Athens was set in a large plain, while the place chosen for the Roman was on a hill full of pre-existences; a closer setting, however, to the Telesterion, the temple of Demeter in Eleusina.

The temple of *Venere Felix* and *Roma Aeterna* (identified at the beginning of the twentieth century with the *Templum Sacrae Urbis*) was the largest in Rome and one of the largest in Antiquity (Figure 2.2). The author of its design seems to have been Hadrian himself, beginning its construction in AD 121, although there was apparently a project since the beginning of his reign in AD 117 (Lorenzzati, 1990). Hadrian consecrated the building upon his return from Judea (AD 136–137) when it was not yet finished, and was completed by his successor Antoninus Pius in AD 140–143 (Lorenzzati, 1990). Manieri Elia (1992) has offered a very insightful discussion about the significance of the temple, highlighting the uniqueness of its layout with two cellae back to back and discussing the concept behind such a design.

For the construction of this temple, dedicated to the goddess Venus, mother of Enea, and to the allegory of the City, Hadrian chose the tramontana land (north wind) of the *Via Sacra*, between the Roman Forum and the Colosseum, with the remains of the Nero's vestibule on it, which were previously converted into a temple dedicated to the Sun. To build the new temple, Hadrian reuses the Neronian platform—with all the spaces it contained-, as is still evident below the area adjacent to the north and the southern transept of the church, as previously discussed. He may have also reused Nero's granite columns. The granite came from the quarry of *Mons Claudianus*, and its use was a characteristic of the monuments of the eras of Trajan and Hadrian, although it is possible that it was already extracted at the time of Nero (Colini, 1983).

The extent of the structures that could be from the Neronian era seems to be larger than previously thought. The ramp to the northeast corner of the temple could have been part of the accesses to the Neronian lake (Nash, 1961) and later used to move the Colossal statue of Nero converted by then into Helios) next to the Colosseum. The Colossus was placed for transport in a mobile armour designed by Decrianus, supported by the back of twenty-four elephants (Spartianus, XIX).

We have found similarities, in the layout and dimensions, between spaces still visible, incorporated within the Hadrianic temple's platform and others of the *Domus Aurea*, such as cryptoporticus 142 (3.55–3.60 m

Figure 2.2 Section at the same of scale of the temples (from top to bottom): Zeus in Olympia, Parthenon in Athens (Coulton, 1977) and Venus and Rome in Rome (A.)

wide). The new templem being more than twice as large as Nero's vestibule, required that the ground was modified by building towards the Colosseum a huge terrace on an artificial platform with underground spaces. By integrating all the archeological and topographic information available we have been able to find out that the amount of this platform

Figure 2.3 Platform of the Temple of Venus and Rome towards the Colosseum (east) (A.)

belonging to Nero's period is more extensive than it was previously thought (González-Longo and Theodossopoulos, 2009) (Figure 2.3). Even further, as we have previously mentioned, the front towards the Colosseum presents also a structure with buttresses, creating quadrangular spaces and a corridor, with similarities to that still visible from Nero's *Domus Aurea* to the north of the temple.

The huge concrete platform of the temple exposes now the voids that previously contained the foundation blocks of the walls (*peperino*) and columns (travertine) of the temple, removed to be used in other buildings, as it can be clearly seen in the north and south sides, and which we will discuss later (Figure 2.4).

The platform is a fundamental element to investigate, because it contains very valuable information on the buildings that have been supported on it. In a detailed study that we have published (González-Longo and Theodossopoulos, 2009), the original configuration of the platform and its development and subsequent occupation were studied, interpreting it through a plan in which the two main phases have been clearly identified (Nero and Hadrian's) (Figure 2.5). This has permitted discover a difference of only three degrees in their alignment, rotating counterclockwise, highlighting Hadrian's design statement and purpose to preserve the place, transforming it at the same time. The slight rotation could be the result of an intention to orienting the building towards the temple of Jupiter in the Capitoline Hill, aligning it also with the entrance of the Colosseum. This extreme construction effort clearly shows the importance that Hadrian gave to the concept and design idea, more than the technical difficulties involved. The design unity, however, does not seem to be a design aspiration for Hadrian, who gives more importance to the symbolic, ideological and even iconic aspects of the project, as he makes clear in its eclectic arch in Athens, near the Olympeion.

Figure 2.4 South section of the platform of the Temple of Venus and Rome, showing the area where a propileo was located (A.)

Considering all the available information about the area, we have also produced a schematic section in which the original configuration of the hill has been deduced and all levels of successive constructions established (Figure 2.6). This has allowed a better understanding of the area and the elements that were preserved and transformed. We will discuss more about this later while looking at subsequent developments in the site. A more recent instrumental survey (Fabiani and Fraioli, 2010) has also identified asymmetries in the plan of temple. Only a detailed 3D scanning of the building and platform could allow further detailed studies of these complex remains.

The temple has dimensions of 113 × 56 metres in plan and was about 30 metres high. Its design is both unique and eclectic, combining Hellenistic proportions, urban presence and appearance, with Roman spaces and construction techniques. But its great originality and uniqueness is the design of the double cellae, presenting an unusual configuration, joining back to back, with a double orientation to east and west, just like the libation during the Eleusinian Mysteries. The cella towards the east was dedicated to Venus and the west (oriented towards the centre of Rome),

32 The Place Transformed

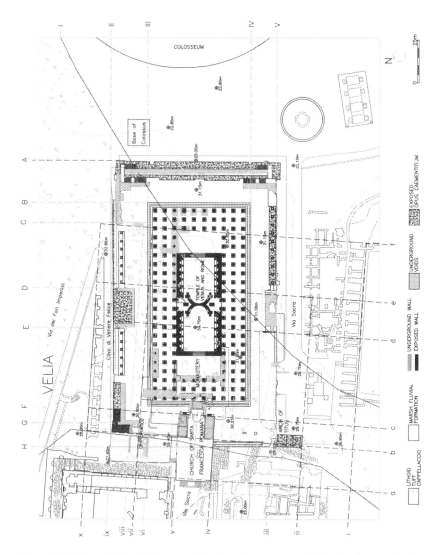

Figure 2.5 Plan of the Velia area showing the extent of the platform and the Temple of Venus and Rome on the Velia Hill with indication of topography (A.)

The Place Transformed 33

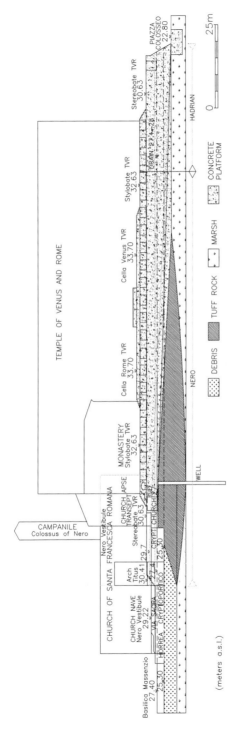

Figure 2.6 Section of the building showing the original hill and levels of the subsequent buildings (A.)

34 *The Place Transformed*

Figure 2.7 Interior of the cella dedicated to Rome (A.)

to Rome. The latter is better preserved because it was later incorporated in the monastery of S. Maria Nova (Figures. 2.7, 2.10).

The temple was built on the central esplanade of the artificial platform described above, which constituted its crepidoma, and did not have the usual podium of Italic-Etruscan origin, although the square plans of the cellae are close to those of the Tuscan temples. The stereobate was 145 metres long by 100 metres wide and was accessed from the Forum through seven large steps and from the east, on the side of the Colosseum, through two narrow side stairs. There is enough evidence to assume the existence of a ramp in the northeast corner, as we have already mentioned above. The was a porticus around the temple and there is evidence of propylea-like structures in the middle of each long side, and perhaps others in the front, towards the Roman Forum.

The peristyle was formed by a double line of Corinthian fluted columns of white marble, ten in the front of the temple and twenty-two in the sides, on the seven-step stylobate. The cellae are elevated with respect to the peristyle by five steps and were accessed through a vaulted vestibule both east and west. Contrary to the publications that hitherto attribute the vaults to the intervention of Maxentius, we believe that the cellae of the time of Hadrian were already covered with a coffered barrel vault, as the fragments that are preserved, and as in the Pantheon (González-Longo and Theodossopoulos, 2005). There are other similarities with the Pantheon, such as the niches along the lateral walls, alternating triangular and semicircular pediments. Apart from the design quality of the spaces, there is also another important architectural and structural reason to build a concrete vault rather than a timber frame structure: the prevention against damage from fire. As we have mentioned, Rome suffered large fire devastation in the previous years and for sure Hadrian would not have liked to expose the building to the damage that the temple of Jupiter at the Capitoline Hill repeatedly suffered in previous generations. Changes in construction regulations after the great fire in Nero's time, the quite recent fire in the Pantheon of Agrippa mentioned before and the high quality and extensive use of vaulting construction at the time, are powerful reasons to conclude that the Temple of Venus and Rome had originally Roman concrete vaults rather than timber roof structures.

According to archaeological excavations (Panella, 1985, Panella and Cassatella, 1990, Panella and Del Monti, 1992) and our own survey and study (González-Longo and Theodossopoulos, 2005), we have been able to draw the plan of the temple as decastile (10 columns in the front and 22 columns on the sides), Corinthian, dipterus (2 rows of columns on all facades), systyle (columns separated by a distance of 2 diameters), and amphiprostyle (isolated columns in the pronaos). The diameter of the columns was, according to our calculations 1.74 metres (about 6 Roman feet), similar to that of the columns of the Olympeion in Athens. Considering the archaeological evidence, there are two possible configurations for the temple plan (Figure 2.8).

It is also possible that the temple followed the *hypæthros* canon, meaning that it was open inside. Vitruvius describes it in his Book III and mentions the case of the Temple of Olympian Zeus in Athens, restored by Emperor Hadrian (González-Longo and Theodossopoulos, 2005), saying also that this typology has inside two stories of columns all round, at some distance from the walls, as it is the case in the temple of Venus and Rome. The opening at the top would be not unusual, if we think about the Pantheon or the Telesterion in Eleusina, where there was also an inner *sanctum* in which the most precious objects were kept (Clinton, 2016).

The two cellae end in apses, which housed the statues of Venus to the east and Rome to the west (Pollak, 1838). The two goddesses were seated, and the criticism of the architect Apollodorus of Damascus on problems of scale in the building is famous: if the goddesses rose, they would not enter the interior of the temple. This would be a strange comment if coming from an Asian Greek architect, since this problem would happen in most Greek temples, which poses questions about his background and design approaches. In Hadrian and Antonine coins, the goddesses appear with a spear in the left hand, small divinities to the right (sometimes Rome carries a globe), with helmet and epithets (Venus *Felix*, Rome *Aeterna*) (Cassius Dio LXIX, Lorenzzati, 1990). The fresco of the

36 *The Place Transformed*

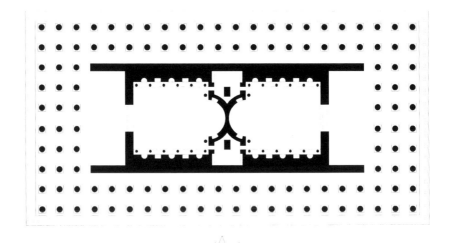

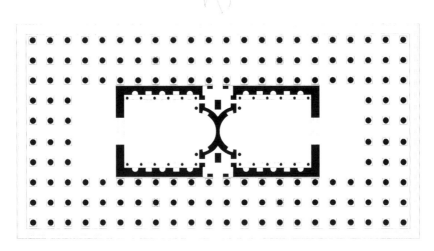

Figure 2.8 Possible architectural plans of the Temple of Venus and Rome, based on archaeological evidence (A.)

first quarter of the fourth century AD, found in the seventeenth century near the baptistery of St. John Lateran, called 'Roma Barberini', may be a representation of the goddess Venus of the temple. It has a winged victory in the right hand, a Psyche in the right shoulder and perhaps Eros in the left; the helmet would have been added during its seventeenth century's transformation, turning it into Rome (Cagiano de Azevedo, 1954). A fragment of the goddess dress could be a fragment of porphyry still visible today in the cella of Rome (Lorenzzati, 1990).

There is also an intriguing structure above the apses of the Temple of Venus and Rome, accessed by staircases between the apses which could also be related to astronomical observation- on which Hadrian was very much interested-, in line with G. De Angelis D'Ossat's ideas, reported by Manieri Elia (1992). Alberti's church of Sant'Andrea in Mantova seems to take inspiration from the Temple of Venus and Rome both for the arrangement of the vaults and the structure above the entrance.

The entire brick construction, now visible, was covered with marble and niches within the walls contained statues of *numi*; exterior columns were made of Proconnesian marble, the interior ones of porphyry and the pavement was geometric and polychrome. The roof was of gilded bronze tiles, removed in 630 by order of Pope Honorius I to place them on the roof of the old basilica of Saint Peter, as we will see later. The pediments of the temple were adorned with sculptural scenes, remains of which exists in a fragment now at the Roman National Museum, representing Romulus and Remus breastfed by the she-wolf. There was also a fragment of the cornice of the temple in the cloister of the monastery of S. Maria Nova (Figure 2.9), which has now been moved as there are ongoing works; hopefully it will return to the site with a more suitable presentation.

As also happens in the reception hall of the Palace of Diomitian in the Palatine, in the Temple of Venus and Rome we have a clear example of the conjunction of a vaulted interior and a lintelled exterior (Figure 2.2), a design that we will find much later in many Christian churches. Although the temple was double, outside it appeared as a single design.

Figure 2.9 Fragment of the cornice of the Temple of Venus and Rome (A.)

We interpret this duality as in line with Hadrian's political intention to give the urban presence of the temple a Hellenistic, cosmopolitan image, while inside he is freer to continue with the innovations of his time, and to achieve spaces of a more human scale, although with a sacred atmosphere.

The temple clearly has a Hellenistic influence, in particular its urban articulation (Manieri Elia, 1992). It is not casual that the main entrance of the Colosseum aligns with it and all indicates that there was a close relationship in the functions, rituals and performance in both buildings since the beginning. Although more investigation is needed to fully understand this relationship, we consider two aspects, one in terms of religious and civic ceremonial performances and another, more practical, concerning hydraulics. It is clear that Hadrian built the temple with the intention to be the most important in the city in terms of public use and events. It is interesting that somehow these public rituals have been reinstated today for the Pope's Via Crucis. Concerning hydraulics, the huge platform of the temple and the presence of ancient water systems described previously may contain the solution for the so far unresolved problem of how it was possible to drain the Colosseum in such a short time after the naumachias, staging naval battles.

There are still many aspects to investigate about the temple, and one is the door communicating the two apses that clearly appears in some historic views, for example Overbeke (c. 1700) and Rossini (1821). It is normally considered to be an opening made later, but considering how it is built and how thin the common wall between the two apses is, we believe the door is original. This fact would give a whole new interpretation of the rituals that took place in the temple, particularly considering the unusual arrangement of the two apses and how this door could have made possible to communicate the Colosseum with the Roman Forum during the rituals. Hadrian wanted to sign with his intervention new times, as well as satisfying his cultural interests, leaving a lasting mark in the city.

2.5 The Fortune of the Temple After Hadrian: The Antonines and Maxentius's Intervention After the Fire of AD 283

The main building activity of the three Antonine emperors focused on Asia Minor and Syria. In Baalbeck (the old *Heliopolis*), in Syria, the smaller temple of Bacco contains a magnificent cella adorned with half Corinthian columns and niches in two orders. These can be compared with those of the Temple of Venus and Rome, with the elevated adyton, an exotic element in a classic-looking building. The situation of Rome copying the East is reversed, with the East copying Rome now.

Antoninus Pius, apart from completing buildings of his predecessor Hadrian, such as his Mausoleum and the Temple of Venus and Rome, restored temples and other buildings, including the house of the Vestales and the Colosseum and built new buildings, for example the temple of the *Divus Hadrianus* (now the building of the Stock Exchange in Rome) and the temple of Faustina in the Roman Forum. Thanks to its continuous use and transformation, the temple of the Divus Hadrianus is preserved and eleven of its original fluted Corinthian columns of marble and a rich entablature are still visible in one of the long sides of the building. The cella and the columns were raised on a high podium adorned with reliefs; those below the column represent allegorical figures of provinces, and in the intercolumni they reproduce trophies of victories. The temple arose in the middle of a rectangular portico, so that the entire construction was comparable to an agora or a Forum, similar to the Temple of Venus and Rome.

Marcus Aurelius (161–180) and Commodus (180–192) continued an intense building activity. Under the Empire of the Antonines appears the type of basilica with the *tribuna* separated from the nave by a colonnade, as seen in the basilica of Otricoli, from the time of Antoninus Pius. In 176 by decree of the Senate, the silver statues of Marcus Aurelius and Faustina were placed in the Temple of Venus and Rome (Cassius Dio LXXII, 31, 1), indicating that the temple was still in use. It was probably damaged in 191, when a great fire destroyed the Vesta temple, the Pace temple, the Capitolian library and the *pipetaria horrea*; in the place of the latter, adjacent to the temple and Venus and Rome, the basilica of Maxentius would be built.

Emperor Maxentius (306–312) exercised great building activity, with which he intended to return to Rome the splendour of other times. He had the title of '*conservator Urbis suae*' which appears in coins and medals. His main work was the so-called *Basilica Nova* in the Forum, adjacent to the Temple of Venus and Rome and finished by Constantine. After the damage suffered during the fire of AD 283, Maxentius restores the Temple of Venus and Rome—which did not appear to be in use then— and reinstates in AD 307 the cult in the temple. The fresco 'Roma Barberini', which we have already discussed may be from this period.

There is a common belief that Maxentius practically rebuilt the temple (Krautheimer, 1983), which we have challenged (González-Longo and Theodossopoulos, 2005, 2009). The reason why the two apses joined behind are considered to be from this period is the existence of numerous bricks with stamps from the time of Maxentius and the similarity of their lacunari in rhombus with those of the Basilica Nova. We think, however, that while Maxentius restored the temple after the fire, this intervention was not as extensive as it is believed: he only rebuilt and repaired the damaged areas and hence the presence of bricks with the seal of Maxentius.

As we will see later, the cellae were restored in the first half of the twentieth century, and curiously on that occasion the walls of the cella of Rome (west) were consolidated with a 'brick sheath', in an operation similar to

40 *The Place Transformed*

Figure 2.10 Interior of the cella of Rome showing the twentieth-century 'brick sheath' (Vincenzo Patella)

what could have occurred at the time of Maxentius (Figure 2.10). Maxentius is also credited with the construction of the cellae vaults, based on the unfounded belief that the thickness of the walls could not withstand the thrust of the vaults, which we have refuted through a simple structural analysis (González-Longo and Theodossopoulos, 2005). The preservation of the Hadrianic structure was part of Maxentius's promise to preserve the whole urbs as *conservator urbis suae* (Dumser, 2005, 2018).

We will see in the following chapter the subsequent destruction of the temple and the reuse of some of its elements. There are also many fragments of the building in various different locations (Ferrajoli, 2016). It would be desirable to reunite them, physically or virtually, for a better understanding of the temple's design, significance, construction and materiality.

3 Decadence, Destruction and Recovery of the Place
The Churches of Ss. Peter and Paul and S. Maria Nova and Alexander III

3.1 From Pagan to Christian

The transition of the Temple of Venus and Rome from a building of pagan cult to Christian worship is not sufficiently documented both literarily and materially. We do not know exactly when the first Christian building was constructed in this place, an important and visible crossroads, as we have already discussed.

It is believed that Pope Saint Sylvester (314–335) had erected a church in front of the vestibule of the *Domus Aurea* (Nibby, 1839; Prandi, 1937), collecting the apostolic memory of the Saints Peter and Paul stay in Rome. Two *selci* (slabs paving of a Roman road)—similar to those usually found in the paving of the *Via Sacra*—, are the only visible memory of the building. Peter and Paul had prayed that Simon Magus fell when he tried to fly in front of Nero and the Roman people. According to tradition, the erosion present in the *selci* would be the footprints of the knees of the Apostles, left during their effective prayers to prevent the flight-duped people, a legend that has been transmitted through the so-called apocryphal gospels.

This first Christian construction in the site was perhaps a simple aedicule with a small oratory, enclosing only partially a paved public area of the *Via Sacra* and including the two *selci*. According to a legend referred by Saint Gregory of Tours in the sixth century, the rainwater collected in the bowls effectively created in the stones by the knees was miraculous, reinstating health to those who drank there (Lugano, 1922, 1924). The hypothesis of the existence of a place of Christian worship in the site since the time of Nero or shortly after is strengthened by the presence still in the church of the two *selci*, inserted in the south wall of the transept and protected by two small bars (Figure 3.1).

There is also the possibility that, before the erection of this small building, the spaces we have already mentioned incorporated in the platform of the Temple of Venus and Rome could have been used as a place of Christian worship. These spaces are of great complexity and have been

42 *Decadence, Destruction and Recovery of the Place*

Figure 3.1 The two *selci* in the south wall of the transept of the church of Santa Francesca Romana (Vincenzo Patella)

used over time as described in other chapters; an extensive archaeological excavation would be necessary to determine the earliest use.

Archaeological discoveries in Rome and in the Middle East during the eighteenth and early nineteenth century shed new light on the period of the first Christian churches, quite unknown until then. In particular, the discoveries of Giovanni Battista de Rossi (1822–1894) were crucial for the further development of the Roman school of early Christian archaeology, exploring the catacombs and underground levels beneath churches and cathedrals. These works constituted a fundamental reference for further research, such as the project undertaken by Richard Krautheimer (1937–1977), analysing the underground levels of the oldest churches in Rome, bringing a global vision.

The early churches were called *tituli*. The best known case is that of the Basilica of San Clemente, which is traditionally believed to have been owned by Clemente and donated by him to become church around the year 95. Krautheimer (1959) suggested the distinction between places of worship and those dedicated to burials. He also identified three areas of historical development affecting architectural decisions: liturgical formalization, organization of clergy and other community functions. These developments were responding to needs of worship, without considering other social factors.

Based on his extensive studies in Rome, Krautheimer (1959) suggested also some architectural periods ranging from the New Testament to the fourth century. For him, until the year 200 there was not authentic Christian architecture (even hitherto Christians were not recognized as a group). Only the state religion built temples in the Greek and Roman architectural tradition. The romantic vision of the use of catacombs to perform services has been replaced in more recent times by the historical and archaeological evidence that initially residential buildings were used for Christian worship. The meeting place begins to develop more specialized needs, and the structural and architectural adaptation of the Roman house as a place of worship occurs. This new type of building is called *domus ecclesiae*.

At the end of the second century and beginning of the third century, the adaptation of the Roman house for Christian worship was a characteristic form of intervention. Between 165 and AD 212, with the *Constitutio Antoniana,* which granted Roman citizenship, the Christian material culture began to emerge, and Christian art, funerary symbolism and construction began to have their own cultural definition. Access to the property through patronage and donation was perhaps the key to the development from the house-church to the *domus ecclesiae*, benefiting from the conversion to Christianity of components of the social elite.

However, the specific form of realizing depended on local styles, conventions and circumstances. In general, no changes occurred outside of the buildings with respect to domestic appearance. Inside, the basic structure of the rooms around the central courtyard remained. Interventions included substantial internal restructuring, with demolition of partitions and cluster environments. The main adaptation was the extension of the dining room (*triclinium*), knocking down the dividing wall to create the great hall (*aula ecclesiae*) for the community meetings. Benches were also built in the courtyard and windows were opened in the walls to connect it with the great hall, becoming then visible. In most *tituli* in Rome at the end of the third century, such as San Clemente and San Martino ai Monti, the construction of the great hall for community meeting was made outside pre-existing buildings. In both cases, they were incorporated during the construction of subsequent basilicas at the beginning of the fifth century.

Adapting homes for religious worship was a process widely accepted by pagans, Jews and Christians. During the third century, buildings of Christian worship were becoming recognizable landmarks, mostly in the context of large cities, despite the fact the buildings had not yet reached a monumental architectural definition. Inside, the rooms were broader, and joint space became more sophisticated, differentiating the area of the clergy and the elevated platform, called the pulpit or tribune. Porfirio—a student of the philosopher Plotinus and contemporary of Paul of Samosata—who was in Rome c. 262–263, considered Christians inconsistent and irrational, from the point of view that were "constructing large buildings imitating the construction of temples".

The Christian historian Eusebius (Books VII and VIII), who wrote during the violent years of the great persecution (between the death of Cipriano at 258 and the first edict of Diocletian in 303) referred to a big "boom" in the second half of the third century. He mentioned the "destruction of churches" which would perhaps have caused further architectural development in building new ones. In his Book VIII he said: "they built up from the ground large churches in each city." The language used is often similar to that we find in inscriptions on buildings. In particular we note that the phrase "built up from the ground" (εκ Θεμελιων ανιστων), which also appears in synagogues and mithraea, normally referred to the reconstruction of an existing building of which some remains exist. However, Eusebius was referring to the renovation of buildings more in terms of growth of the community and social status, rather than architecture.

No cases are known from this time in which the previous house was eliminated by building the new church, but it is possible that there were some, now invisible under existing churches. As the first act of persecution in 303, Diocletian ordered the destruction of a church in Nicomedia, Bithynia (eastern capital at the time), while he watched it from his palace (White, 1990a, 1990b). It seems reasonable to think that the first phase of construction or reconstruction after the persecution continued the lines of *domus ecclesiae* and *aula ecclesiae*. Most of the edicts of tolerance contained some provisions for the restoration of confiscated church property. It seems that most of the Christian buildings were merely confiscated and closed, rather than destroyed.

The change of the meeting around the *triclinium* to the meeting in the *aula ecclesiae* was an important point, which required a more formal arrangement of the congregation during the meeting. We can have some idea of this in the Syrian order of 270, called *Didascalia Apostolorum* (Connoly, 1929). This document determines the separation between clergy and laity; priests sat on the east side of the house, with the bishop in the middle. Behind them would be, first, adult men, sitting east to west, then women, in a separate part, also sitting east to west, and at the bottom mothers with babies and other children, sitting or standing on the sides, on the back of the room. One of the deacons, placed at the entrance of the room, was responsible for putting the people in the right place. These formalities would lead to the creation of a gate and the chair of the bishop even before the creation of the basilica form.

Something also architecturally significant about the continuity of the *aula ecclesiae* is the trend towards the standardization of the rectangular plan for the assembly, with adjoining rooms around it. This layout allowed for future extensions, overcoming the limitations of the previous building design, but always in relation to it. The interiors tended to be articulated to a greater extent, following the development of the liturgy, clerical orders and the seat of the congregation, attending orientations along the longitudinal axis of the floor of the great hall. The focal point of the room was the front, where the altar, the clergy and the bishop were. This type of intervention, characteristic especially of large urban centres and buildings of Christians in prominent places, which some contemporary observers referred to as "haughty temples", will run from the middle of the third century to the end of the fourth century, contemporaneously with the Constantinian basilicas.

The best example of the new dimensions of the *aula ecclesiae* can be seen in San Crisogono in Rome, dating back to the year 310. At the beginning, it was a rectangular room without naves or interior partitions, something more like a warehouse than a house, but with an external porch. Only later, as in other churches in Rome, it was remodelled, becoming a basilica plan, adding an apse and a crypt and dividing the entrance area to form a narthex. As we will see later, the first church in the site under study had a similar configuration.

In the adaptation of the buildings there were two fundamental points: the social extract of Christians and the models taken from their environment for the community organization. These works needed a certain purchasing power, dispelling the myth of the proletarian origins of the Christian movement. Christian groups would be similar to other existing in the urban context, like professional associations or philosophical schools, and the adaptation of domestic buildings to community ones for social or religious functions was not exclusive to them. For the renewal in the third century of the *aula ecclesiae Byzantis titulus* (Ss. John and Paul) in Rome, it was necessary to acquire a complete *insula* housing, which speaks for itself of the economic power of the Christian community. The thirty three percent of residential space in Rome at the time was occupied by the houses of the social elite, which was only the three percent of the population of the city; the rest lived in *insulae* or apartments.

3.2 The Constantinian Basilicas

The term Basilica applied to the great Roman buildings for civilian use rose in the Roman Forum, and later Christians will use it for their early buildings of worship. The typology was just a development of the civil Basilica of Greek character, with the main entrance in one of the short sides and with modifications due to the demands of the new religion. During the rule of Constantine (312–337) the great building of the Basilica Nova, begun by Maxentius next to the Temple of Venus and Rome, is concluded. The ruins that remain from this building still amaze us by their colossal scale, although it would have been less impressive when the Temple of Venus and Rome, the largest in Rome and with its shiny bronze roof tiles, was erected in its entirety, giving it a very different scale and context. The time of Constantine is considered one in which Rome could be viewed in all its glory, but also the turning point of the path that would lead to its decline. This process, from the constructional point of view, starts with the practice of the reuse of architectural elements from other buildings, of which the Arch of Constantine is an example.

The fourth period of the development of Christian worship buildings identified by Krautheimer (1959) begins with this Constantinian revolution. Constantine was the first emperor who recognized as such the Christian faith, which would be reflected directly on buildings. Works and donations from the emperor to the Christian church were recorded by Athanasius Librarian (Duchesne, 1955). After the Edict of Milan, the basilical plan became the prototype of religious buildings. Ward-Perkins (1954) believes that there was no Christian monumental architecture before the 313 to serve as a model and that the first Basilica in the strict sense of the word was the Lateran Basilica (church of San Giovanni in Laterano, of which the date of construction is uncertain, but it seems that was finished in the 319–320, built on an imperial palace donated in 314.

The Constantinian basilica innovation was not as steep as the previous adaptation of buildings. However, it represented a new and radical imposition of scale and style of architecture and aesthetics, although presenting some form of continuity with previous places of worship. The basilica can also be seen as a subsequent adaptation, monumentalization and finally a standardization of various pre-Constantinian models. It also continued the previous practice of patronage and adaptation. But the most important point is that the church as building became physically identifiable from the outside. The Constantinian revolution would provide an architectural metamorphosis that reflects the substantial changes in the status and composition of Christianity.

We know through the Catalogue of the Roman Regions in the fourth century AD that at the time of Constantine there were 1,800 domus and 44,000 *insulae* in the city. Given the difference between the patricians and the plebs, it can be considered that one third of these *insulae* were bourgeois houses, spacious and with certain amenities, while the rest would be small houses for workers, four or five stories tall. Rental houses existed since the time of Hadrian in Ostia, and they multiply in the time of Constantine. These developments had three or four floors, with an internal courtyard, and built with simple, uncovered, brick.

A building of this era that has come down to us is the Basilica of the Nativity in Bethlehem, built before 333, although greatly transformed. The entry was made as required by the ritual, from the west. It was preceded by an atrium surrounded by porticoes. This is an oriental element in various cults, and in the Christian case it seems to have Jewish influence, as seen in its presence in the Temple of Solomon in Jerusalem. In the middle of the atrium, or *paradisus*, there was also a fountain, or *cantharus*, for ablutions. The narthex was the part adjacent to the church atrium where via the door, which in this case introduced into the vestibule (esonarthex or pronao), then via a second door, there was access into the Basilica. The interior consisted of five naves and entablature on columns. The triumphal arch separated the naves of the transept, the same length as the width of the church, and it is topped with two apses at the ends, a clear difference with the Roman Basilica. In the transept there was a quadrangular space flanked by four pilasters forming the choir, and the terminal part of the nave is an apse (*presbyterium*), with the altar in the centre. Instead of the two small rooms and a continuation of the aisles, there appear the *prothesis*, for the preparation of the rite, and the *diaconicum*, where the treasures of the church were kept.

An example in Italy of a building of this period is San Salvatore, in Spoleto (fourth to fifth centuries), which incorporates the cella of a Roman temple. The parts that remain are the facade, the beginning of the nave, chancel and apse. The interior, with three naves, presented a Doric colonnade supporting the entablature. The facade recalls the Palace of Diocletian in Spoleto and the smaller temple of Baalbeck. It was covered with marble slabs and it has three doors and three tall windows on the upper floor, divided and flanked by pilasters.

Constantinian basilicas in Rome were created ex novo or were the result of the adaptation of a profane building but not of pagan worship. The basilica form was based on standardized monumental public architecture in Rome forms, limited to religious buildings before the time of Constantine. It was not a result of existing architecture in place, but a form imposed on it. Roman basilicas had the following characteristics: the facade is oriented to the west, according to the liturgical norms (the Church of Ravenna changed direction from west to east); they have a cruciform plan, as an architectural expression of the symbol; and they had a vestibule and a peristyle, elements taken from the gentile Roman *domus*. However, even primitive forms of *domus ecclesiae* and *aula ecclesiae* continued in some cases. In Rome, some of the oldest titular churches continued functioning without being transformed into the new Lateran or St. Peter's basilica style. San Crisogono was transformed into a basilica plan in the fifth century, like Ss. John and Paul and San Clemente.

From the period that Constantine moved the empire to the East in 330 and during the reign of Constanzo II (337–361), building activity decreases. During the reign of Giuliano the Apostate (361–363), his brief reign being anti-Christian, religious buildings are interrupted. The pagan cult had great roots in Rome and during the late fourth century and early fifth century still had a place there. Honorius was the last Roman emperor who showed a marked building activity. The basilicas of this period continue Constantinian lines, but with a progressive impoverishment in execution and with an inevitable influence of Roman pagan buildings.

3.3 Byzantine Rome, Rome in Ruins

In 410 Alaric, king of the Goths, sacks Rome. The last of the classical Latin poets, Rutilius Namatianus, recited his farewell to Rome in 416. In 455 the Vandals also looted the city. The fall of Rome is commonly situated in 476, when the last Western emperor is deposed by the barbarian Flavius Odoacer.

The ruins begin then to form part of the landscape of the city, and it is in this period in which the emperors are replaced by the pontiffs (Celestine I, Sixtus III), and, strangely, by the Romanized barbarian king Theodoric, king of the Ostrogoths, in the construction of the city. He proclaimed himself king of Italy in 494 and settled in Ravenna. Theodoric showed particular care to the conservation of the city—although he stripped the Domus Pinciana in Rome of its marbles and columns to take them to Ravenna—and described the necessary qualities needed for the conservation architect:

> It is necessary that the repairs of this forest of walls and the group of statues that make Rome are in the hands of an educated man who could make the new buildings harmonize with the old. Let him read the books of the ancients, but he will find in this city more than in the books... The ancients speak of the wonders of the world ... but this City of Rome surpasses all.
>
> (Erder, 1986)

After the death of Theodoric in 526, Justinian reconquests Italy. The eastern Byzantine culture flourishes in Rome, although still with influences of classical Rome. Between the sixth and ninth centuries, there is the presence of Greek and Oriental Popes. Many Byzantine monks and a colony of Greeks and Syrians settled at the foot of the Palatine and Aventine.

The Gothic king Totila in 546 undertook a siege and subsequent devastation of Rome. He also ordered the depopulation of the city. This year marks one of the last falls of Imperial Rome and the beginning of Papal Rome. After the disappearance of the Goths, the population began to return slowly. Thanks to Pope Gregory the Great (590–604), Rome slowly recovered and the fervour to adapt buildings from the classical past or to build new ones for Christian worship using old materials is renewed. During the sixth and seventh centuries the cultural and artistic activity, including the construction, or better, reconstructive activity, was led by priests and monks. This period would last until the seventh century. Pagan buildings, or their parts in better condition, were used mainly for new civil uses. However, thanks to the transformation in 609, due to Boniface IV, of the Pantheon into a church dedicated to S. Maria ad Martyres, we can see this building today almost intact (Ducati, 1938).

In 800 Leo III crowns Charlemagne, king of the Franks, as Roman Emperor. From Charlemagne's will, referred by his biographer Einhard, we know that he owned a silver round table with a map of Rome (sent to the Church of Ravenna) and a square table with Constantinople (sent to St. Peter). A third table, heavier and more beautiful had three circles representing the whole universe. From this time are the first news of pilgrims in Rome, and circular is the map of the oldest preserved guide of Rome, the Itinerary of Einsiedeln, created by a Swiss monk in the eighth century. Circular is also the map of Rome represented in a fresco of Taddeo di Bartolo dated 1413–14 in the chapel of the Palazzo Pubblico of Siena, displaying the appearance of the city. This image is very similar to the Book of Hours of Duc de Berry (1412–16), which may suggest that they are copies of the same original.

3.4 Honorius I and the Expolio of the Temple of Venus and Rome

The deterioration of the Temple of Venus and Rome began as a result of Gratian's decree in 382 confiscating all the properties of pagan worship. But the real damage to the monument starts when Pope Honorius I, with faculty and donation of Emperor Heraclius, removed (between 626 and 629) its gilded bronze tiles, to be used in the old basilica of St. Peter. From thereon the looting and dismantling of the temple begins, and as a consequence, its rapid deterioration process; as we know the roof is a very important element of a building, and once water penetrates from above, buildings deteriorate very quickly.

Rather than religious beliefs, it was the instability of the vaults that did not allow later Christian buildings to occupy its interior. Landslides due to earthquakes (such as the one in AD 476) in combination with the deterioration caused by rainwater penetration after the removal of bronze roof tiles at the beginning of the seventh century turned the site gradually into a quarry for building materials.

The temple had a rich variety of decoration and precious materials used in its structure. Whole or fragments of the building architectural elements (columns of marble, granite and porphyry, blocks and slabs), as we shall see later, will be used not only in buildings in the area, but also in other buildings in the city. It had more than one hundred columns of Proconnesian marble of a height of 18 metres, and the large blocks of travertine and *peperino* in its foundations were also reused in this and other buildings. The Proconnesian marble was used to make lime, and because of this activity, the area was called in medieval times *Calcarium* (Lorenzatti, 1990). Small elements of the temple structure (brick, tuff, marble blocks, metals and fragments of columns) were also reused in the construction of the medieval and later buildings of the church and monastery, as clearly shown in the north facade of the monastery, to be discussed later.

Despite this dismantling of the building, the Temple of Venus and Rome, which had become in Christian times the Temple of Rome, is remembered with its exact name until the eighth century. Some confusion was created by the similarity of the name with the *templum Sacrae Urbis* comprising the nearby church of Ss. Cosma and Damiano and the Temple of Romulus, son of Maxentius. The transformation of these two church buildings was due to Felix IV, Pope from 526 to 530.

3.5 The Church of Ss. Peter and Paul

As we had discussed before, although there is mention of a first church built on the site by Pope Saint Silvester, the first real evidence we have of a church in this site is one that was built by Paul I (757–767) *iuxta templum Rome*, above the two *selci* we have already mentioned. There are some visible remains of a building of this age, as discussed next. The configuration of the platform of the temple and the position of its cellae have clearly influenced the shape and configuration of the buildings that have been built afterwards (González-Longo and Theodossopoulos, 2008, 2013). Although the concrete platform provided excellent foundation for new buildings, the earlier buildings occupied its western part only, never occupying the cellae. In the early days of Christianity, this would be because of their pagan past, but afterwards it should be attributed to structural problems in the vaults of the temple, or as we said before, because the temple was the *hypæthros* canon, being opened inside.

Looking at the plan of the present church and monastery and its relationship with the temple, we see that the apse of the church is built on the stylobate (Figure 3.2). The transept and the eastern half of the nave rest on the stereobate, probably in the void left by a similar propileo that the temple had on the sides (Figure 2.4).

The western part of the church, as A. Prandi was able to report (Prandi, 1937), has a void beneath the nave (Figure 3.3), in which is still visible the basalt pavement of the *Via Sacra*, as mentioned before (Figure 1.3). After studying the levels of pavements (González-Longo and Theodossopoulos, 2009), we have seen that the *horrea* and pre-existing buildings from Nero's time are at 25.30 m.a.s.l., the crypt of the church at 27.40 m.s.l.m (the same level than the remains of the *Via Sacra* under the church), the nave at 29.22 m.s.l.m. (very similar to the lower level of Nero's vestibule) and the transept at 30.63 m.s.l.m. Thereafter, we can conclude that the pavement of the transept of the existing church is the same than the stereobate of the temple, and the level of the nave of the church is at the same level than the lower part of the vestibule of Nero. This means that Hadrian placed the temple directly on Nero's platform, as we have graphically shown (Figures 2.5, 2.6).

Decadence, Destruction and Recovery of the Place 51

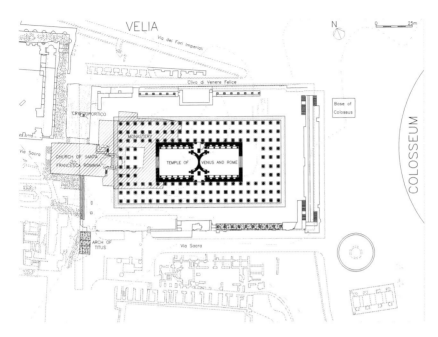

Figure 3.2 Location of church and monastery on the temple (A.)

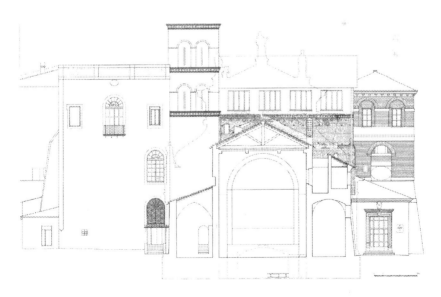

Figure 3.3 Transversal section of the church (A.)

52 Decadence, Destruction and Recovery of the Place

Through a detailed analysis of the masonry of the north wall and the plan of the church, Prandi had identified various pre-existing buildings and the change of direction of the axis of the church that occurs in its central area, in correspondence with the stairs of the stereobate of the temple. We have found that this break in the line of the axis occurs because the western part of the church follows the axis of the Temple of Venus and Rome, while the eastern part follows the alignment of Nero's (now underground) constructions, whose axis is slightly rotated clockwise about the temple (González-Longo and Theodossopoulos, 2009) (Figure 2.5). This clearly indicates that part of the present church was built directly above Nero's structures.

As Prandi claimed, we are of the opinion that the church of Saints Peter and Paul built on the pavement of *Via Sacra* to the West of the Temple of Venus and Rome is the origin of the church of S. Maria Nova (Prandi, 1937). However, we also believe that the western part of the north wall of the church, which Prandi attributed to the ninth century, would be earlier. There is an arch of poor construction, which could be a window of the first building from the eighth century. This window opening was closed in the ninth century, when a door was opened nearby. All this complexity can be represented in a simplified way, proposing that in the eighth century, the church of Ss. Peter and Paul, housing the two *selci*, co-existed with the almost complete but already quickly decaying Temple of Venus and Rome (Figure 3.4).

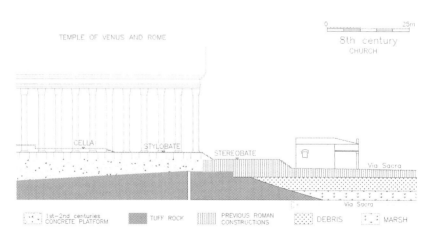

Figure 3.4 North elevation of the first church (eighth century) of the Ss. Peter and Paul and the Temple of Venus and Rome (A.)

3.6 Santa Maria Nova From Ninth to Fourteenth Centuries

The church of S. Maria Antiqua, from late fifth century is the oldest church dedicated to the Virgin Mary discovered in the Roman Forum. It was built in a ceremonial space from the late first century, later transformed into a space for the protection for the adjacent monumental ramp leading to the palaces on the Palatine, where the Roma Emperors and later the Byzantine governor lived. In the church, the different parts of a Christian basilica are identified: atrium, three naves with *diaconicum* and the *prothesis* to the sides of the presbytery, whose apse is partly excavated in an ancient wall. The church, governed by Greek monks, contained the precious icon of the Virgin of the fifth century, the Madonna Glycophilousa, one of the oldest existing (Cellini, 1950; Guarducci, 1989), which is now in the sacristy of the church of Santa Francesca Romana. The church was destroyed in the ninth century as a result of an earthquake, rediscovered in 1702 and excavated by Giacomo Boni in 1900 after the demolition of the early seventeenth century church built above it, which was also built on another of the thirteenth century.

During the Pontificate of Sergius II (844–847), the Saracens desecrated and demolished the church of Ss. Peter and Paul. This was followed by a major earthquake in 847, which may explain the unclear evidence of this construction. This earthquake probably caused the collapse of the vaults of the Temple of Venus and Rome, damaged already by the penetration of rainwater after the removal of the tiles, and thus the building became a ruin and a quarry of materials, its stone and lime providing not only materials for the buildings in the area but also to many other buildings in Rome (Lorenzzati, 1990), as we will see later.

The church of S. Maria Nova was a cardinal title, founded by Leo IV (847–855), when he rebuilt it after the earthquake (Duchesne, 1955) and extends it as a cardinal deaconry. After a fire, Nicholas I reconstructs it in 860 (Duchesne, 1955). According to Ferdinand Gregorovius the first paintings or mosaics in the church were done then (Gregorovius, 1988). The church extended in the ninth century towards the Colosseum, at the East, to the area now occupied by the transept (Figure 3.5).

This first church of S. Maria Nova would have had thereafter two levels: the lower would be the open porch on the basalt pavement then including the *selci* of the apostles, and a large part, to the east, at the same level as the current nave level. The church was probably fortified by Leo IV in the same way as the *Civitas Leonina* in the Vatican. It could also have been built in the same way, by unskilled labourers who were farmers in rural areas from the *Domuscultae* of the Roman countryside administered by the Pope. This would justify the precarious construction of the north wall of the church (Figure 3.6).

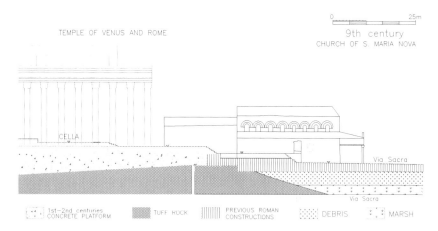

Figure 3.5 The church and temple in the ninth century (A.)

Figure 3.6 North Wall of the church (A.)

Construction materials in this wall are of reuse and the mortars are of low quality. The elements of more quality are the window arches of the nave, despite its irregular geometry, typical examples of Roman construction of the ninth century, but already used since the fourth century, although they were much better built.

There is a construction vacuum in Rome between the ninth and eleventh centuries, although some activity begins in the tenth century, including this building. Sometime between 920 and 982 we know that a church was built in summa sacra via collecting titles and privileges of S. Maria Antiqua, which had been badly damaged during the earthquake, and we assume that this construction was in reality an extension of the leonine church when the transept was added, perhaps when the Greek monks were transferred from S. Maria Antiqua. The precious icon of the Madonna was also transferred from this church.

Between the western cella of the temple of Hadrian (dedicated to the goddess Rome) and the apse of the church of S. Maria Nova, the *diaconicum* was developed for charity functions and to house the clergy. We can deduct that it was built shortly before the pontificate of Benedict VIII (972–982). The oldest Tabularium S. Maria Nova document, dated 7 March 982, describes the church, which had a provost or prior with the respective high and low clergy, and a *Schola*.

There were also homes in the area from the tenth century onwards, from simple brick houses one or two storeys high, with marble stairs in the facade, courtyards and back garden, to stately residential buildings of several floors (*domus solarate*), with fireplaces as evidenced by P. Fedele in his extensive study of the documents in the archives of S. Maria Nova (Fedele, 1900, 1901, 1902, 1903). These documents, which by great fortune have been conserved by the Olivetan monks, and in particular by D. Pietro Maria Rosini and more recently D. Mauro dell'Orto, are a precious source of the medieval history in Rome. They are concerned not only with the monastery but also with the large number of properties belonging to it through donations in Rome and its suburbs.

The area has experienced the transformation that occurred, in line with all Italy, with residential typologies developing between the end of antiquity (fourth and fifth centuries) and the medieval age. In this process, the ancient Roman typologies (*domus, insulae* and villas) disappeared. The city was covered with lighter timber structures and rammed earth, reserving the use of more durable materials for prestigious buildings and without references to ancient traditions (Santangeli Valenzani, 2011).

The church and monastery of S. Maria Nova made thus possible the preservation of the remains of the Roman temple and became a focus of activity for the city centre. This was due on the one hand to material aspects such as the existence of water (wells) and supply of building materials, and on the other hand because of the symbolic memory of a miraculous event held there. As revealed by the documents, the area, called *calcarium*, was occupied by artisans and professionals, from lawyers to bankers.

To reinforce the importance of the church of S. Maria Nova, during its rededication Pope Gregory V (996–999) transported from the Via Latina the bodies of some martyrs: Nemesio and his daughter Lucilla; Olimpio, his wife Esuperia and their son Teodullo; and Sempronio (Landi, 1771).

Thereafter the area under the altar where these martyrs were placed must have been remodelled. This work could have included the construction of the new transept to the east, perhaps using Neronian spaces embedded within the platform of temple. Thus, in the late tenth century, the church occupied the same area as the current one. The study of the building fabric has confirmed that the transept and the east end of the nave are built around the voids left by the removal of a section of the Temple of Hadrian. As we have mentioned before, the level of the nave of the church appears to be the same as the vestibule of Nero (González-Longo and Theodossopoulos, 2009).

3.7 The Frangipane *Rocca*

After the Schism of 1054, the Greek monks from S. Maria Antiqua, then officiating the church, were forced to leave S. Maria Nova, and in 1061 Alexander II installs the Regular Canons of the Congregation of S. Frediano di Lucca, who lived in the attached premises of the diacony (*diaconicum*). The sack of Rome by the Normans in the year 1084, led by Robert Guiscard, destroys the entire area, but not S. Maria Nova, as Cencio Frangipane had agreed protection with Guiscard (Thumser, n.d.). When the Emperor Henry IV (who had just attacked Rome, confining Pope Gregory VII in the leonine city) was forced to retire by the arrival of Guiscard, Cencio Frangipane also helped the Pope and acted as interlocutor with the Normans, perhaps reaching a compromise with them about the devastation of the city (Thumser, n.d.).

It would then start what we might call in this area the Frangipane period, although the name of the family Frangipane appears for the first time in 1014 and again in 1039 on occasion of a donation to the church of S. Maria Nova. Leone appears in documentary sources in 1014 and has two children who are called *Imperato*: Roberto and Giovanni Sardo, the alleged father of Cencio Frangipane.

This powerful family was related to the Normans, and like these, supported the monk Ildebrando (future Pope Gregory VII), who appointed Cencio Frangipane as Roman consul; he was continuously mentioned as a follower of the Gregorian reform of the papacy. His son Giovanni, supported in 1093 Urban II and Ottone, who died in 1120, was made saint. After a long period of support of the papacy, although changing sides, Giovanni begins the filo-imperial policy of the Frangipane, which already started with Cencio the Old, supporter of Henry V, and continued with the notorious attack on Gelasius II, on his election as pope in1118. In January 1145 the Pontefice Lucio II (Gerardo Caccianemico) is assigned to the custody of Circeo and Ottone Frangipane, Cencio's brothers, who was the most powerful support of the Pope during the struggles between Guelphs and Ghibellines. The family survived until the seventeenth century, but their titles and possessions were reduced in favour of the Caetani.

The Frangipane had appropriated the area in 1093 (Gregorovius, 1988), fortifying it and giving important donations to the church of S. Maria Nova. Although today there is no structure to identify with this fortress (*rocca*), there are elements that help us understand how it would be. It seems that the Frangipane *rocca* incorporated a previous one, started around 1000, when the monks of St. Gregory fortified the adjacent *Septizonium*. The first news we have about the existence of the Rocca as such is from 1094, when Urban II (the Pope of the First Crusade), fleeing followers of the antipope Clement III, was welcomed by Giovanni, brother of Cen cio, at his home near the church of S. Maria Nova (Tea, 1921), specifically, in the Chartularia Tower next to the Arch of Titus. He could then reach, with the help of Giovanni Frangipane and Goffredo of S. Maria Nova, his Lateran residence for Easter. The Frangipane, which together with the Pierleoni were the most powerful families in Rome around 1100, built many houses in the Forum, Palatino and Colosseum, and in consequence the area was called the *Campo Torrechiato* (the towered field) (Krautheimer, 1983).

Despite alliances with the Normans, in 1105, there was a fight between Werner II, Lord of Spoleto and Ancona, and Pascual II in the "*templum Romuli ante domum judicis Mattilde*", probably the Temple of Venus and Rome (Tea, 1921). In the thirteenth century, Jacopa of the Normans, friend of St. Francis of Assisi, marries Graziano Frangipane of the Septizonium.

The traditional support that the Frangipane family had given the pope is truncated by the second Cencio Frangipane, brother of Leone. On the occasion of the election of Pope Gelasius II (Giovanni Caetani) in early 1118 in the church of S. Maria in Pallara on the Palatine, Cencio assaults the church during the ceremony, imprisoning the Pope in a house in S. Maria Nova, part of the rocca adjacent Frangipane, although pressure from the nobles and the Roman people forced Cencio to release him. Calixtus II demolished this house in 1119, which from the description of Pandolfo Pisano was a castellated tower that was called 'Torre', and banned rebuilding it, although it was rebuilt twice with the coat of arms of Frangipane (leopard and lamb). The same year, Calixtus II granted custody of the church to the Lateran Regular Canons, and in 1121 demolishes again the towers of the Frangipane in Rome and forbids their reconstruction. The Frangipani lose a fight with the Normans and the church of S. Maria Nova comes under the Norman custody, but Leone reconciled with Calixtus II and continued to own the papal areas.

The real demonstration of the power of the Frangipane happens in December 1124, after the death of Calixtus II. According to the cardinal deacon of S. Maria Nova, Aimerico, Cencio Frangipane, his brother Roberto and Leone Frangipane intervene violently during the papal election, getting their candidate, Lambert (bishop of Ostia), elected with the name of Honorius II. Military control by the Frangipane of the Lateran, where the election unfolded, was crucial, and this strengthened the alliance between the Frangipane family and the papacy (Thumser, n.d.). Honorius II appointed Cencio as Earl of Ceccano, who removed the abbot of Montecassino, Oderisio, in 1125. In the summer of 1128, he went to southern Italy in the company of Aimerico and gave Ruggero II of Sicily the papal document that gave him the duchy of Puglia.

The *rocca* extended from S. Maria Nova to the present church of S. Sebastian and contained the houses of Leone and Cencio Frangipane, sons of Giovanni; his brother Roberto dominated the adjacent *Septizonium*. Leone's house, the "*Domus Franjapanorum de Chartularia*" was in the vicinity of S. Maria Nova, between the Arch of Titus, the Colosseum and Septizonium and became the citadel of St. Peter, protecting imperial incursions and the claims of the resurgent city Commune (Tea, 1921). In 1130, the fort was of such an extent that it could house Pope Innocent II (Gregorio Papareschi) with all his cardinals and family when they fled for his proclamation as Pope in S. Maria Nova, the same day in which the imperial antipope Anacletus II (Pietro Pierleone) was crowned in St. Peter (Tea, 1921). The towers of the fortress, built on Roman ruins (including the mentioned Chartularia, on the Arch of Titus), were then at the centre of Rome struggles in the twelfth century between the town hall, the emperor and the Pope.

The fortress continued to preside over this area of Rome and, in 1139, there was a sale of a manor house near S. Maria Nova made by Gervasio son of Giovanni Pilgi, to Ottone and Cencio Frangipane, illustrious Roman consuls. The Roman municipality (Comune) was created from 1144 by large families (including the Frangipane), which faced the Pope and were made senators. Celestine II died on March 8, 1144 in S. Maria Nova and in 1149 we still have news of the existence of this fortress, which was considered one of the most annoying for the new Roman town hall.

In 1192, Cencius Camerarius made the *Liber Censuum Romanae Ecclesiae*, listing more than forty houses; a group of them, near a public bath, formed the mansion Frangipane, which gave prestige to the area, along with the fact that it was located in the passage of the papal processions. The presence of marsh in the area made necessary that most of the houses were built on higher ground (Krautheimer, 1983). These houses of the twelfth century exposed on their walls Roman remains as a decoration, as we still see today in other buildings in Rome such as the Casa dei Crescenzi. From the mid-twelfth century the owners were forced to cover the house with tiles (Fedele, 1903).

We still have news in 1238 about the Frangipane's domination in the area, near the Mugonia Gate, where Cencio Frangipane had a leopard, symbol of his family. During that period the area of power moves to the Colosseum and the Lateran (Tea, 1921).

3.8 Cultural Renaissance: The Work of Alexander III and the 'International Style'

Twelfth-century Rome experienced a cultural and economic renaissance, establishing an independent Republic in 1143 with the creation of the Roman Senate in the ruins of the Capitol hill. Arnaldo de Brescia, inspired by the love of the old through his master Abelard, was part of this movement. Around 1150 appears the *Mirabilia Urbis Romae*, a guide to the wonders of Rome through walks from St. Peter to the city, as the itinerary Einsiedeln had done previously, and where Christian and pagan monuments appeared. Other guides for pilgrims follow, such as *De Mirabilibus Urbis Romae* of Magister Gregorius and the *Graphia Urbis Romae Aureae* written probably by Petrus Diacunus. In 1162 a document of the Roman Senate establishes the public property of the Column of Trajan and prohibits its damage, an early evidence of protection of built heritage.

Within the long list of benefactors of the church and monastery of Santa Maria Nova, we can highlight Alexander III (Bandinelli, from Siena, 1159 1181), who consecrated the church in 1161 and endowed income. The same year he grants Ugo, Prior and Rector of S. Maria Nova, the church of St. Sebastian in catacomb. The Pope himself was responsible in 1170 for the commissioning of the mosaic of the apse (Figure 3.7), and the campanile (Figure 3.8) and perhaps remodeled the Cosmati pavement.

Figure 3.7 Apse of the church (A.)

Alexander III carries out the work in S. Maria in a time of conflict and complex politics. He was consecrated pope in Ninfa under the protection of the Frangipane, and after a long struggle against the three successive antipopes supported by the emperor. With the help of the Lombard League, Alexander III forced Federico to recognize him as pope, but in 1162 he was forced into exile in France. Back to Italy in 1165 and Rome in 1178, he held the third Lateran Council (1179) and promoted the dissemination of scholasticism. Shortly after the council he was forced again to leave Rome and he will never return.

The campanile, made of brick mansonry, many of reuse, and typical of the Roman twelfth century, is divided into five orders by cornices with sawtooth and mullioned windows with columns of marble on the upper levels and a small aedicule to the west, as protection for an image of the Virgin Mary (Priester, 1993). The tower has majolica bowls and Greek crosses of porphyry inserted into the masonry walls, but the originals, which allegedly were brought from the Crusades by the Frangipane, have unfortunately been replaced during a restoration project.

As the campanile illustrates how the building would be externally in the twelfth century, inside, the apse mosaic indicates the design and decoration of the medieval church (Figure 3.7). Unfortunately, the decoration of the arch of the apse has disappeared, but its design has been preserved in the Royal Library at Windsor through two watercolours depicting it, made between 1620 and 1644 (Osborne and Claridge, 1996; González-Longo, 2013, 2015). The arch contained seven candlesticks, the symbols of the four evangelists and prophets Isaiah and Baruch with two palms on the sides. We can find in Rome mosaics with similar motifs, for example in S. Maria in Trastevere, from the time of Innocent II (1130–1143). The mosaic had already disappeared by 1690, when Giovanni Ciampini recorded the apse in a drawing (Ciampini, 1690), which indicates they would have disappear during the intervention of Giuseppe Arcucci in 1673, which included the reconstruction of the vaults of the transept.

The still-existing mosaic in the apse represents-under a characteristic celestial arch similar to that of S. Maria in Trastevere—, Maria Regina with child, and the apostles: the brothers Peter and Andrew to her left and the also brothers John and James to her right, all inside an arcade with spiral columns and Corinthian capitals of Byzantine influence (Figure 3.7). We do not have precedents in other Roman mosaics of these compositional motifs of arches with figures inside. To find similar iconography we have to refer to Roman sarcophagi and objects of Christian worship and Romanesque architectural decoration that could have been the inspiration (Osborne and Claridge, 1996). One of these objects is the Basel *antependium* at the Museum Cluny in Paris, from the eleventh century Its arches symbolize the celestial *civitas*, in the same way that we believe the mosaic of S. Maria Nova does. The decorative motifs present here (strings, checks, scales) appear throughout Europe, transmitted through the Crusades and pilgrimages in the eleventh and twelve centuries. If we also consider that the church was then, as already discussed, part of the fortress of the powerful family Frangipane, participants in the Crusades, we will understand more clearly the "international Romanesque" influences (Matthiae, 1967; DG AA.BB.AA, 1891–1897, 1908–1924).

The characteristic Cosmati pavements, made with coloured marble (*opus sectile*) of reuse, which originally covered the whole church, are now preserved only in part. They are in the presbytery and a square section in the nave, probably covering the area in which the old *Schola Cantorum* stood (Lugano, 1922); a fragment of the balustrade could be one now at wall in the entrance of the monastery. The geometric pattern of the pavement, with a characteristic square field with other inscriptions and rotated 45 degrees and a quincunx in the centre (Figure 3.8a), is similar to those at the transept of the Duomo di Castellana Civita, the church San Crisogono in Rome (Creti, 2010), and one in the front of the high altar of Westminster Abbey in London (1268). Forcella gives us a reference of an inscription that existed in S. Maria Nova which included the name of Drudus of Trivio (Forcella, 1873), whose professional activity making Cosmati pavements was carried out from the second decade of the thirteenth century (Creti, 2010).

While the presbytery has undergone several transformations, it still shows signs that it is worth noting, such as the presence of several fragments of rectangular sections of Cosmati pavements, many tombs with large slabs of marble in the centre and two fragments of characteristic circular elements, arranged longitudinally in a north-south direction (Figure 3.8b). They do not have the characteristic interlocking circles,

a   b

Figure 3.8 a: Cosmati pavements in the nave (A.); b: transept (Vincenzo Patella)

which may indicate that they have been reconstructed later. We know that the presence of these elements is a clear indication of the design of the church, always marking a central axis of the spaces, and in this case may prove the existence of chapels on the north and south sides of the transept. It also shows that the transept was slightly wider than the current one, before the campanile was built, as the relationship between the fabric of these two elements, clearly visible on the outside, demonstrate. If this interpretation is correct, the pavement of the transept would have been added before the end of the twelfth century. The typology of the various designs present in the pavement also demonstrate their belonging to the twelfth and thirteenth centuries. By comparison with designs of other Cosmatesque pavements (Glass, 1980), some can be attributed to the workshop of master Paulus, a family of marble craftsmen very active in Rome in the middle of the twelfth century. On the other hand, there are clear later reconstructions in the altar area, with more modern designs. The colours of ancient marbles used in this floor are the four characteristic Cosmatesque: white, porphyry (red), antique yellow and serpentine (green). These will mark the colour scheme for the design of the interior of the church that will take place in the next six hundred years.

3.9 The Gothic Intervention of Honorius III

The conflict continues in this part of Rome; between 1202 and 1204, Pietro Annibaldi and his men fought against Giovanni Capocci from the tower between the Colosseum and the church of S. Maria Nova (Torre della Contessa, built on the base of the Colossus of Nero).

The mosaic of the apse was probably damaged during a fire that lasted three days during the pontificate of Honorius III (1216–1227), which destroyed part of the building and from which the icon was miraculously saved. Extensive works were carried out after the fire, including the replacement with masonry vaults of the damaged timber roof structures of the transept and the aisles. Soon after, under Nicholas III (1277–1280), his nephew, Cardinal Latino Orsini Malabranca Frangipane (1278–1294), Bishop of Ostia and Velletri, carried out work in the church: "he built from the foundation the monastery and restored damaged parts of the church" (ASMN, 1793). The now demolished vaults above the transept belong to this time, and these two phases are clearly visible in the church, as we will discuss later.

New windows were also opened to the nave and some remains are still visible in the north wall of the church and in a fresco of 1468 in the monastery of Tor de' Specchi, discussed in the next chapter. Through the study of the fabric of the north wall of the church done by Prandi, we know that the previous eight small windows on each side of the nave of the church, from the ninth century, were closed and replaced with large ogival mullioned windows, which must belong to the interventions of the late thirteenth century (González-Longo, 2015) (Figure 3.9). The conservative design of these windows fits the Italian version of Gothic elements, which often makes little attempt to emulate the structural developments of the type in the rest of Europe.

There are still remains of pointed stone vaults on corbels, probably belonging to this period, in the old space of service to the sacristy (SCVA, 1726), at the base of the bell tower. This medieval vault is supported by a marble architrave, of which Prandi discovered a fragment in the wall between the nave and the left aisle, covered by a baroque wall (Prandi, 1937); the fragment is still visible today (Figure 3.10). These elements confirm the existence of a nave and aisle on each side. The vaults of the transept, which could have been three- resembling those of the transept of S. Maria sopra Minerva-, were reconstructed as a barrel vault with lunettes and decorated with paintings during Arcucci's intervention in 1673. This vault was still visible in 1726 (SCVA, 1726), but it was demolished, probably for structural reasons, in the early twentieth century when it was replaced by a wooden coffered ceiling supported by steel beams (DG AA.BB.AA., 1907). Traces of the springers of this vault imposts are still visible in the space between the new ceiling and the floor slab of the upper level.

The difficulty of understanding in full the transformation of the medieval church is due to all these continuous reconstructions and interventions often as a consequence of the destructions produced by fire and earthquakes, or simply to respond to changes in taste and liturgical needs. To the outside, the facades reflect the taste of the times. As already mentioned, the various fabrics of the north wall of the church—the only exposed masonry wall—clearly show how the windows change over time, with the intention

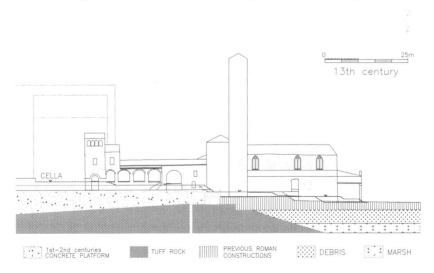

Figure 3.9 The church and monastery in 13th century (A.)

Figure 3.10 Remains of the medieval architrave discovered by A. Prandi (Vincenzo Patella)

of creating an internal spiritual atmosphere in accordance with the times, and taking into account the functional needs of worship and veneration.

3.10 Civitas and Delimitation of Space: The First Monastery

As we have mentioned above, the *diaconicum* developed between the west cella of the temple of Hadrian, dedicated to the goddess Roma, and the apse of S. Maria Nova, in order to provide spaces for charity functions and to house the clerics. The first *diaconicum* was built when the small original church was damaged in the mid-ninth century by wars and earthquakes and rebuilt by Leo IV and Nicholas I. Through archival documents at the monastery, we know that in the year 982, the church had a prior and his clergy, high and low, and a choir (*Schola di mansionari*). As we have mentioned before, it is probable that the monastery was fortified as the *Civitas Leonina* of Leo IV in the Vatican, and it is important to make a more comprehensive consideration of the site conditions at the time.

The successive historic phases of construction of the church affects the monastery, which develops intertwining and overlapping the western part of the Roman Temple of Venus and Rome. As we will see later, the south facade of the monastery was redesigned by G. Valadier during the French occupation, thereafter, the external remains of the medieval monastery are only visible in the northern facade, showing the variety of materials and construction techniques used over the centuries, including the reuse of materials, in a close relationship with local conditions. The data collected through the survey, research in archives and architectural analyses have identified the complex stratification of the north facade, materials and techniques, allowing for an interpretation of the different phases of the building (González-Longo and Theodossopoulos, 2013).

The building experienced activity in tenth century, when the church was restored after the cult was transferred from S. Maria Antiqua, a time in which building activity in the rest of Rome had stopped. The *diaconicum* was extended to accommodate the Greek monks from Santa Maria Antiqua and in the late tenth century the church occupied almost the same space as the current church. As we have also discussed, the construction was also clearly influenced by the fact that the powerful Frangipane family owned and fortified the area.

After the Greek monks left, title Cardinals officiated the church, and to help the diaconate some regular priests or canons were in charge, since the eleventh century, governed by a dean, prior or rector, who lived in the annexes to the church. Alexander III gave the church to the Canons Regular of the Congregation of San Frediano in Lucca. Callistus II changed these to the Lateran Canons, for which Cardinal Latino Orsini Malabranca Frangipane, as we have said, built the monastery "from the foundations".

There are arches in the ground floor of the north facade of the ninth century (Figure 3.11) topped with a later cornice with sawtooth, a typical detail of the twelfth-century, built with reused brick, cut and placed at a 45 degree angle. This is different (probably earlier) than the other cornices of the twelfth century in the building (bell tower, the west wall of the transept and the cloister).

Figure 3.11 Arches to the north of the monastery (A.)

66 *Decadence, Destruction and Recovery of the Place*

As we have seen, during the twelfth and thirteenth centuries the heritage of S. Maria Nova was huge and not only in Rome. It owned a large number of houses and land, including the Temple of Venus and Rome, the remains of the vestibule of the *Domus Aurea* of Nero and vaulted spaces (*cryptae*) at the ground floor of the Colosseum, which was rented for craft workshops and laboratories to *viri honesti* (good citizens) (Fedele, 1903). The Colosseum was owned by the family Frangipane until the middle of the thirteenth century, but was later given a guarantee to Annibaldo Annibaldi. During this period and for nearly a century (from 1270 until the mid-fourteenth century), the monastery went through a period of crisis, which caused the loss of their heritage.

The cloister, built behind the apse of the church, is one of the most interesting elements of the monumental complex. The oldest remains are from the twelfth century, probably contemporary to the apse and campanile, commissioned by Alexander III. After the fire at the time of Honorius III already mentioned, the cloister was probably also rebuilt, and two clear phases are visible. The fabric of the pillars to the southwest of the cloister, made of bricks of reuse, still shows remains of the original reddish stucco, which tried to give more uniformity and perfection to the fabric, a characteristic of the middle of the thirteenth century architecture. These different phases in the cloister were invisible after centuries of transformations, but Giocomo Boni brought them back to light during the conservation of the building he undertook in the early twentieth century, to be discussed later (Figure 3.12).

An important addition to the complex during this period is the Tower House at the northwest of the monastery (Figures. 3.13, 3.14), an

Figure 3.12 Remains of the original cloister as conserved by Giacomo Boni (A.)

Figure 3.13 North elevation of the church and monastery (A.)

excellent example of a fortified construction of the period. It presents a characteristic construction at the bottom, of small blocks (4–9 cm high by 5–20 cm long) of white marble and basalt in horizontal rows, which can be now only seen in few buildings in Rome such as the Caetani (1192) tower on the Tiber Island, the aqueduct Alejandrino (twelfth century) and the nearby Tor 'dei Conti (1198–1216). The top of the wall of the tower-house is built with *tufelli* of *Tufo Lionato* (small blocks of tuff stone), similar to that of the nearby St. Nicholas in Carcere (c. 1280) and Ss. Quattro Coronati (thirteenth century). The cruciform window—the first of its kind in Rome—is a later addition as we shall see later.

The dating of this tower helps us to understand the development of the north facade between the ninth and eighteenth centuries (González-Longo and Theodossopoulos, 2013) (Figure 3.15). The analysis of the types of masonry and architectural elements, as well as their comparison with contemporary buildings in Rome, give evidence of the various stages of the construction of the tower. While the lower part was built in the late twelfth century, the top belongs to the intervention of the thirteenth century intervention, probably by the Cardinal Latino Orsini Malabranca Frangipane. We know he rebuilt the *diaconicum* "from the foundations", and the coat of arms Orsini is still visible, built into the wall of the lower cloister (north side).

Other parts of the monastery were also built in the thirteenth century, such as the south wing, linking the church with the Arch of Titus, forming a courtyard or cloister behind. This wing had characteristic double windows with relieving arches above, as it clearly appears in the drawing of Hieronymus Cock dated 1550, which will be discussed later.

As mentioned before, from 1270 to 1350 the monastery went through a long period of crisis that caused the loss of many of its properties. We know that in 1310 the community of S. Maria Nova was formed by five canons only. It slowly started acquiring some property, and in 1325 we hear about the "Sale all the part of Palazzo Maggiore and Vigna della Contessa

68 *Decadence, Destruction and Recovery of the Place*

Figure 3.14 Tower-house (A.)

Vineyard, made by Andrea Cintio Frangipane in favour of the canons of S. Maria Nova" (ASMN, 1793). Giovanni Frangipane sells also to the canons the other part of the orchards and vineyards belonging to him.

All of Rome was going at the time through a crisis, and the city presented a desolate appearance by the mid-fourteenth century. The papacy

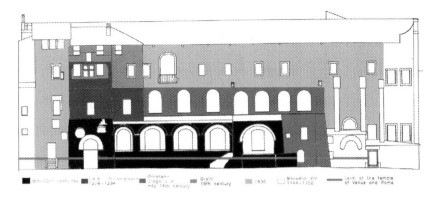

Figure 3.15 Construction phases of the north facade of the monastery (A.)

had moved to Avignon in 1309, where it remained until 1376. Filippo Landi tells us that the most important churches were in ruins having no one else to conserve them (Landi, 1771). The social-economic recession was worsened by the plague and destruction caused by the earthquakes of 1348 and 1349, which led to the ruin of the Basilica of Maxentius, the loss of part of the Colosseum and that surely also affected S. Maria Nova.

The oldest preserved map of Rome is from 1320–1328 and appears in a manuscript on the history of world by Paulinus at the Biblioteca di San Marco in Venice showing a desolate city, 'widowed' and abandoned by the popes and emperors (Scherer, 1955), to whom Dante appealed (Dante, Canto VI, 114). Petrarca also appeals in a similar way to Charles IV in 1350. The *Dittamondo* di Fazio degli Uberti (1350–1367) gives us also a good idea of this aspect of a desolate and abandoned town but still with dignity (González-Longo, 2015).

4 Architectural Preservation and Transformation, Patronage and Innovation

The Olivetan Benedictine Monks, Carlo Lambardi and Gianlorenzo Bernini

4.1 The Olivetans in Santa Maria Nova and the Regeneration of the Place

Pope Clement VI granted the church and the monastery to the Olivetan monks of the Congregation of San Benedict of Monte Oliveto (who still occupy part of the buildings today), with the hope to regenerate the place, which probably was greatly damaged by the great earthquake of 1349. It was at the request of his nephew and titular Cardinal of the church since 1348, Pietro Roger de Beaufort, the future Pope Gregory XI, who would take the popes back to Rome in 1377. With the bull of 25 April 1351, the pontiff placed a prior and twelve Olivetan monks at the service of the church, exempting the existing two canons of S. Agustine (Lugano, 1924). Pietro Tartaris of Rome and Cristoforo Lervini took possession of S. Maria Nova, representing the Olivetan Congregation, on May 29, 1352, four years after the death of its founder, Saint Bernardo Tolomei (Scarpini, 1952).

To understand the importance of Santa Maria Nova at the time, we can mention that Pietro Tartaris, prior of the monastery still in 1372, was later abbot of Monte Cassino and cardinal and grand chancellor of the kingdom (Scarpini, 1952). He died in 1395 and is buried in S. Maria Nova, although we do not know the exact place, like that of many others. A fundamental aspect to consider—and many times forgotten—is the amount of burials that have taken place in the church for almost a thousand years and of which there are only a few visible, but all are still there. The people buried in the church and the position of the tombs, which we have previously discussed (González-Longo, 2013), are important elements because, in addition to the artistic aspect, they mark key points of permanence and change, helping also to understand the history of the place. This should be taken in account when works are undertaking in the building.

Because of their piety and spirituality, the Olivetans quickly obtained the sympathy of the Romans. A quarter of a century after their arrival, the devotion aroused began to manifest itself in a flow of donations, especially buildings. In 1386, Nicolao del Conte donates the remains of the Basilica of Maxentius (named Tempio della Pace at the time) to the monastery (Rosatelli, 1911). Donations reached peak levels during the Holy Year of 1390 and continued at the beginning of the fifteenth century. Most of them were the typical Roman house: a two-storey single-family house (*domus terrinea et solarata*) (Fedele, 1900–1903). In 1391, Iohannes Petri Vecchi, called Giovanni 'the Spanish', donates to the monks a house, "very important", in the enclosure of Santa Maria Nova. However, donations brought with them liabilities rather than wealth, especially in regard to rents, which the Olivetans managed in a personalized way, far from pure speculation. This made economic benefit difficult, as a document of 1408 testifies: the Olivetans could not face the payment of their contribution to the Church of Rome and went to prison (Montenovesi, 1926).

Part of the task to regenerate the place was to contribute to the cessation of superstitions and pagan practices still present in the site. This included regulating the cult around the *selci*, creating a more suitable space for their veneration and cancelling superstitions. Vatican Codex 4265 tells us that the stones were inserted on an altar in 1375 (Lugano, 1922) and, together with the Icon of the Virgin and the burial of Saint Francesca Romana, became the main attractions in the church. This is also recorded by Nicolaus Muffel in 1452 while visiting Rome with Prince Frederick of Nuremberg for his coronation, mentioning also that the stones were placed "in front of the church" (Muffel, 1999).

The current baroque configuration of the church makes it difficult to understand how it was when the Olivetans arrived in the mid-fourteenth century. However, the earlier external and internal elements mentioned previously and still preserved and visible (mosaic, pavements, campanile, north wall), give us clues not only about the previous church but also about the appreciation that the Olivetans gave to the building and all its elements. The vaults can also help us better understand what the church was in the first years of Olivetan presence. Although a large part of them have disappeared or are covered with later decoration, there is evidence that the aisles were covered by pointed vaults after the thirteenth century, and the portico and the central nave by timber structures. The great earthquake of 1349 would have damaged especially the vaults. There is a group of cross vaults, in the western part of the church, that is, in the area that we have previously identified as the one occupied by the preceding church of the Ss. Peter and Paul, on the Roman basalt pavement. This position would make the structure suffer more the effect of the earthquake, and for this reason they have had to be rebuilt, but following the taste of the time, with semicircular arches rather than pointed ones. These vaults, which are similar to those of the adjacent cloister, are still visible in the first and second chapels on the left, but especially in the first chapel on the right and in the vestibule of the south entrance of the church. The vaults of the third chapel on the right and on the left are similar, but they are in the stereobate zone of the temple, and it does not appear that they had been damaged; during the transformations of the seventeenth century, a roundel was added to the key to modernize its architecture. This study of the vaults leads us to clearly distinguish the constructive sequence, consistent with that discussed in the previous chapter and to trace the plan of the church at the time of the arrival of the Olivetans (Figure 4.1).

While the church that the Olivetans found upon their arrival was very similar in size to the current one, there was only a small one-storey fortified building as a home for the canons in this semi-inhabited area in the southwestern area from the city. The monks extended it, drawing inspiration from the old cloister of their motherhouse in Monte Oliveto Maggiore, near Siena. They also carried out infrastructure works shortly after their arrival, as indicated in a 1385 contract in which the prior of the monastery commissioned the construction of a cistern in the cloister, with large stones, most probably from the Roman temple. In 1386, Niccolò di Stefano Conti donates the garden to the monks, between the monastery and the Colosseum; the Conti coat of arms was inside the cloister, towards the Temple of Venus and Rome, and perhaps disappeared in subsequent building transformations.

The *diaconicum* was thus transformed into an important monastery, and a new centre of economic life was developed in a neutral area, between the Vatican and the Lateran, far from the places of power of fourteenth-century Rome but in contact with the *Via Sacra* and the ancient city, in a suggestive combination of pagan and Christian elements. There is a very revealing inscription from the fourteenth century in the cloister, that was originally at the entrance to the monastery from the Roman Forum on the stairway arch. It is the anathema of Pope Gregory XI for those who try to violate the sanctity of the place in any way, to be punished with death:

ANATHEMA—GREGORII
PAPAE—XI—INIVDCIO—NO
RESURGAT—DANATUS
MALE PEREAT CU IVD
INIQVO PARE HABEAT
SI QVIS HVNC—LOCV
QVOVIS MODO SIVE
INGENIO—VIOLARE
PRESUMPSERIT

4.2 Santa Francesca Romana and S. Maria Nova

The life of Francesca Romana, a Roman noblewoman who went to create the Order of the Oblates of Tor de' Specchi, is closely linked to the church of S. Maria Nova. Thanks to this association we have more

Preservation, Transformation, Patronage 73

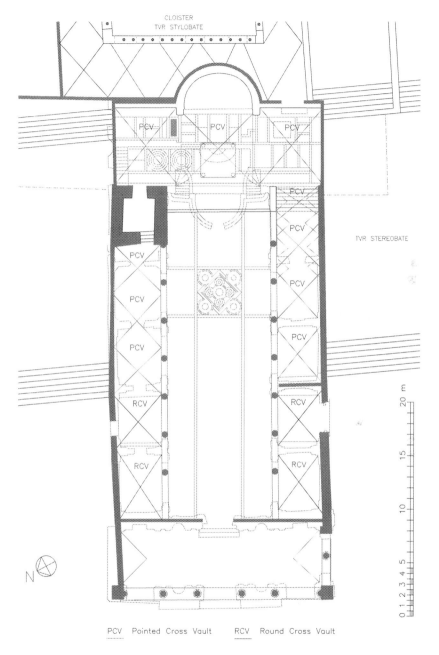

Figure 4.1 Plan of the church of Santa Francesca Romana with the layout of the previous church of S. Maria Nova overlaid in dark line (A.)

information about the medieval configuration of the church. On 15 August 1425, accompanied by nine other women (the future Oblates), pronounced there the solemn Oblation formula and was buried in Santa Maria Nova after her death in 1440. After Francesca's burial, her devotion was still alive and the process for her canonization begins immediately. The church began then to be considered an even more prestigious place of burial, devotion (González-Longo, 2013).

Two frescoes, belonging to a cycle on the life of Santa Francesca in the Oratory of the monastery of Tor de' Specchi, dated around 1468, illustrate these two important events. The first fresco, that of the Oblation, shows us the interior of the church with four Corinthian columns separating the central and lateral nave, which support an architrave that runs along the church, an entrance lateral and four bifora windows pointed in the clerestory of the central nave. In addition to the existence of the side entrance, still in use today, the existence of the bífore is confirmed by the remains of these openings in the north wall of the church (Figures. 3.6, 3.9, 3.13), as already mentioned. However, the material evidence indicates that, contrary to what is depicted in the fresco, the position of the windows was not equidistant. As we have also mentioned before, there is at least one fragment in situ of the medieval marble architrave that separated the naves (Figure 3.10), similar to the one shown in the fresco (Prandi, 1937).

The second fresco represents the funeral of the Saint and gives us an image of what would then be the facade of S. Maria Nova. In this case, the representation cannot be compared with the material evidence because the medieval facade has disappeared, partly demolished and partly covered by the new facade in the seventeenth century. We have, however, other documentary evidence through drawings, incisions and paintings, such as the drawing of the facade of Franzini in 1588 (Felini, P.M. 1969, published also in Gonzalez-Longo, 2013) and the multiple views of the *Campo Vaccino* (Roman Forum), such as that of the Heemskerk from 1532–35 (Prandi, 1937), and Cock's in the mid-sixteenth century (Bartoli, 1911; Augenti, 1996; González-Longo, 2013). The modest medieval facade of the Franzini, with four Ionic columns, probably of reuse, between two pilasters on the sides and a small pediment, is nevertheless represented in the fresco of Tor de' Specchi with a classic portico of seven Corinthian columns, with the aim to relate the interior of the church with the exterior, to be recognizable.

This portico was an important element of the medieval church. If we consider the fortified character of the monastery, as is still evident in Cock's view, this was the only semipublic space in the complex. As a consequence of the historic main access to the site, mentioned before, the portico has always been open towards the front (west, towards the Forum) and towards its right side (south, towards the arch of Titus) and, importantly, the two frescoes of Tor de' Specchi illustrate these two public accesses. An anonymous view of 1551 published by Pietrangeli (1979) evidences the existence of the lateral opening in the portico, with columns similar to those of the front, a configuration that is confirmed and clearer in Dosio's drawing of 1569 (González-Longo, 2013, 2015). The lateral portico would thus have one Ionic column in the middle, and two pilasters on the sides, similar to those shown in the front view of Franzini.

Considering all this evidence, we can conclude that the facade of the church around 1440 had on its front a portico, which would originally have housed the *selci* of Pietro e Paolo. The portico had four ionic columns flanked by two pilasters, and a small pediment on top; the portico would also open to the south, and had an Ionic column in the middle. The gable of the central nave would have windows, which could be two pointed bifora windows, as in the fresco of Tor de' Specchi, or three of a semicircular arch, as in the view of Cock, similar to many other churches in Rome. The south side door of the church is represented in all views, and that is why we do not believe that the side portico extended as much as Prandi (1937) believed, but would be the same size as the current one (Figure 4.2). Inside, on the back wall of the church and adjacent to the main entrance, there was to the left the tomb of Cardinal Alamanno Adimari, with the fresco of Gentile da Fabriano in an arch, and to the right that of Gregory XI. The plan was basilical with three naves: the central nave was similar in size to the current one, and the lateral ones contained tombs and were separated from the central nave by a marble architrave supported by columns. The presbytery was at the same level as the current one, but slightly wider towards the nave than the current one. It had the altar in the centre and the crypt below, and, as Prandi also believed (1937), it was accessible from the nave (Figure 4.1).

Landi (1771) describes the funeral and burial of Santa Francesca after her death on 9 March 1440 (González-Longo, 2013). The Oblates of Santa Francesca Romana promoted the construction of the sepulchre and a chapel, which could also been used by the Oblates as a sepulchre. It was built in the space of the south lateral nave adjacent to the presbytery—currently the fourth and the last chapels to the right of the church—which probably already had a function as a sepulchre of the monks. Its position and relationship with the church and the south cloister (demolished in 1810) are very similar to the *De Profundis* in Monte Oliveto Maggiore. There were several transformations in this space, which now presents three different levels and communicates with the southern transept, at the highest level. It includes the area of the current chapel of Santa Francesca built in the seventeenth century (Cirulli, 2013). The first chapel could have been created at the level of the nave, communicated with the transept through a staircase and separated from it by a large semicircular arch, still visible today, although partially blocked; this staircase would also communicate with the crypt (González-Longo, 2013).

All these spaces are built on underground Roman vaulted structures of the *horrea* type, similar to those below the nearby church of S.

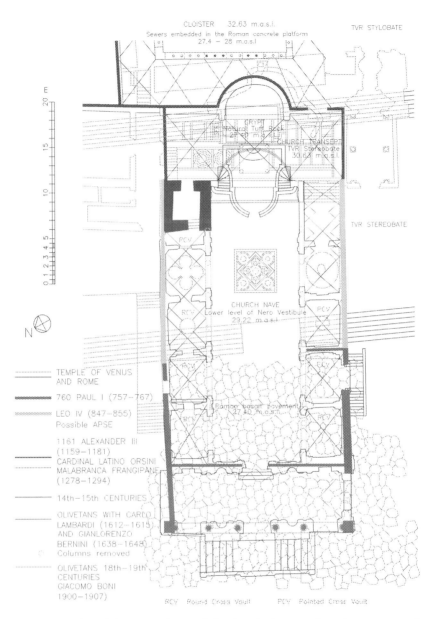

Figure 4.2 Plan of the main phases of the church showing the columns removed by Lambardi (A.)

Clemente (Guidobaldi, 1992). The southern transept now seems remote and dark, but in the fifteenth century it was a very central area of activity and circulation, since it communicated directly with the now disappeared south cloister, and, as we will see later, perhaps also later with the crypt.

4.3 The First Renaissance in Rome and the Tridentine Reforms in Santa Maria Nova

The arrival of the Olivetans brought architectural and constructive innovations to Rome, in particular the cloister, which can be considered one of the first gestures of the Renaissance in Rome (Figure 4.3). They added around 1375 a level to the previous cloister, from the twelfth and thirteenth centuries, taking as reference the motherhouse, the Monte Oliveto Maggiore. The octogonal brick pillars have capitals of simple Florentine Gothic leaves, a motif that was investigated by Arnaldo Bruschi (2008) and bases on reused marble slabs, as some visible Greek marks denote. On the ground floor of the cloister, the arrangement and shape of the variety of pillars reveal structural consolidation operations throughout the ages, with large square brick pillars with chamfer angles and, the oldest, in the angles towards the church, have a 'L' plan. The Olivetans added the slender octagonal brick pillars on the first floor (with those of the angles also in' L ') and small pillars on the second floor, only in the side towards the Temple of Venus and Rome, also octagonal.

Figure 4.3 Cloister at first floor level (A.)

When in 1440 Pope Eugene IV appointed his nephew Pietro Barbo as a Cardinal Deacon, walls were built enclosing the Colosseum together with the Temple of Venus and Rome and the orchard of the monastery, but shortly afterwards the people of Rome demolished the walls. Cardinal Barbo later becomes Pope Paul II (1464–1471) and ordered the removal of the large *peperino* and travertine blocks from the foundations of the Temple of Venus and Rome in order to use them in the construction of Palazzo Venezia. However, the presence of the monastery buildings in the northern part of the temple prevented the plundering in this part. It is interesting to note the similarity of the design of the facade of Palazzo Venezia with that of the tower house at Santa Maria Nova, which probably was the Titular Cardinal's Palace. Both are long facades with a tower in the left side and cruciform windows. We could venture that the monastery building could also serve as an inspiration for the design of the palace; this is reinforced by the fact that the entrance of Palazzo Venezia has a coffered barrel vault similar to the temple's. The cruciform peperine window on the north facade of the monastery, inserted in the upper part of the tower house in the time of Eugene IV (1431–47) (Figure 3.14) is considered the oldest in Rome (Marta, 1995) and also a clear precedent for those at Palazzo Venezia. During the fifteenth century one more floor was added to the north facade of the monastery (Figure 3.15).

Rome commanded the cultural and spiritual world of the middle of the fifteenth century and the popes were great promoters of the arts. This is a period of great construction activity in the city and around the church of Santa Maria Nova. Some of the artists called to work in the city stayed in the monastery, as is the case of Gentile da Fabriano, who lived there his last years and was buried in the church. The interest in the past also developed at the time. Some papal secretaries of the period were interested in antiquities and became historians and 'proto-archaeologists', such as Flavio Biondo (ca. 1450), who compiled a guide to the ruins of Rome, using the old regional catalogues, suggesting how to conserve them. Leon Battista Alberti (1450) surveyed the city for Nicholas V to learn from the ancient Romans. Poggio Bracciolini (1723) recorded Roman ruins, with the intention of studying and valuing them. Varro's Lectures by Pomponio Leto (1484) attempted to interrelate ancient sources with monuments. All this established the principle of modern historical studies.

On the occasion of the Jubilee of 1450 during the papacy of Nicholas V (1447–1455), major construction and restoration works were carried out in Rome and in S. Maria Nova. Andrea Palladio reported that Nicholas V restored the church (Palladio, 1554) and fortified, again, the monastery. Since the thirteenth century there was a presence of the powerful Orsini family in S. Maria Nova, in the person of the aforementioned Cardinal Latino Orsini Malabranca, who restored the church. In 1483,

Preservation, Transformation, Patronage 79

Pope Sixtus IV, who carried out a great "Renovatio Urbis" (Benzi, 1990), appointed Giovanni Battista Orsini as cardinal of S. Maria Nova, but he was dramatically removed from his post in 1493, when Alexander VI (Borgia) granted this deaconcy to his son, Cesare Borgia, who resigned in 1498 when he became Duke of Valentinois. In 1499, S. Maria Nova became a Cardinal Title and Cardinal Raimondo Perauld was appointed as head of the church (Moroni, 1840; González-Longo, 2013).

The north facade of the church reflects again the changes of taste, showing that the large thirteenth-century pointed bifora windows, of which we have spoken before, were closed in the fifteenth century, and other windows were opened, of similar dimensions and location, but with semicircular arcs (Figures. 3.6, 3.13, 4.4). The northern entrance of the church, which existed since the ninth century, was also closed with masonry of large blocks of tuff and marble, probably because the level of the surrounding ground rose or perhaps to prevent passersby from the forum walking through the church (Figure 3.4). The exterior of the church appears on various representations of the area, such as Du Pérac's drawing published, in 1577 (González-Longo, 2015), although normally long time elapsed between drawings and their publication.

Despite events such as the disastrous sacking of the city in 1527, the cult of Santa Francesca Romana lasted in Rome, and Santa Maria Nova retained its importance, as evidenced in a panoramic view of the city by Heemskerk in 1535 (van Heemskerk, 1535), in which it is one of the only three buildings indicated as references. This visibility of the church increased with the opening by Paul III of the boulevard in the middle of the Roman Forum (*Stradone di Campo Vaccino*) for the visit of Emperor

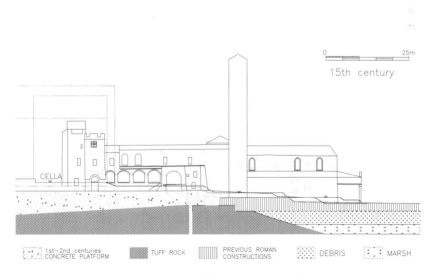

Figure 4.4 Church and monastery in fifteenth century (A.)

Charles V, from Naples, in April 1536. On that occasion many houses and other buildings were demolished to expose the ancient monuments, and thus impress the emperor. As Antón Capitel (1988) has noted, this classic gesture of his triumphal entry into Rome as the last Caesar closed the Middle Ages. The Roman Forum was also levelled and hence the changes in appearance that are seen in the drawings of the time. The Olivetan Congregation had a prominent place in this entrance, not only because of physical proximity. but also because Vincenzo Boccaferri, abbot of the Olivetan monks of San Michele in Bosco and prefect of the Apostolic Palace, prepared the reception of Charles V. A year later Boccaferri died and was buried in Santa Maria Nova, with a great celebration (Moroni, 1840).

During the sixteenth century there was a true artistic explosion in Rome, which attracted artists from all over the world, including some within the Olivetan order, such as Fra Giovanni da Verona (Brizzi, 1989), Olivetan monk, painter, architect, sculptor and carver, who lived in Rome in 1511–1512 while working for Julius II. The Olivetan Congregation was also in relationship and commissioned works from other important artists such as Giorgio Vasari, Luca Signorelli and Sodoma. The monastery also attracted intellectuals and artists: Torquato Tasso was a guest of the monastery between 1589 and 1590.

While the rest of Rome flourished with the great works of the *Cinquecento*, the excavations (*cave d'antichità*) and the pillage of ancient remains continued around the church and monastery. Since the fifteenth century there was the plundering of archaeological remains, and the Forum area and other areas of Rome were intensely excavated. Eugene IV (1431–47) started measures to prevent destruction, and Leo X appointed Raphael in 1514 as commissioner of Roman antiquities. These preservation actions will be completed in 1580 with the edict of Gregory XIII. Despite these actions, excavation permits were still granted. At the same time that the monastery developed, excavations continued in its orchards in order to search for antiquities; there are references to a series of campaigns between 1522 and 1556. There is a record in 1545 of the sale to the ongoing works at St. Peter's in the Vatican of a column that was in the garden of the monks (ASMN, 1793), one of the many of the temple that were transported between 1545 and 1547, a time in which Michelangelo directed the construction works (Lorenzzati, 1990). Some columns were also used in the construction of San Giovanni in Laterano. Flaminio Vacca (Boni, n.d.c) reported how the very fine marble slabs from the temple were also disassembled and cut to make new pavements. The architects of the Rome of the Renaissance, who admired the temple so much, did not hesitate to strip it of its materials to construct new buildings, a clear example of the purely instrumental value they gave to the past. The monks received payments for these excavations, which certainly helped to sustain and extend the monastery: in 1564 the campanile is consolidated with iron braces and a new bell is put on, which unfortunately the Napoleonic troops plundered later (ASMN, 1793).

The second half of the sixteenth century, marked by the Council of Trent, was a period of valorization of the thoughts of the fathers of the Church, and of improving the relationship with the faithful. The opening of the Council on 15 March 1545 (Scarpini, 1952) was chaired by Cardinal Del Monte (the future Pope Julius III), protector of the Olivetan Order. This work of reform lasted almost twenty years. San Carlo Borromeo, after an intense activity of building and adapting churches, publishes in 1577 the *Istruzioni* (Borromeo, 1577), a kind of guide to interventions according to the new rules of worship and liturgy. The intention was that the artistic works had a didactic value for the faithful and that the patrons exercised an effective supervision of the artists. In order to achieve these objectives, it was necessary that employers and designers were adequately prepared: before creating works of art and focal points, harmonious and welcoming environments had to be designed. Although Borromeo gave precise indications in order to harmonize the design, furniture and decoration of the churches, he also clearly indicated the importance to respect the authority and criteria of the architect in matters relating to design. Christian archaeology was also born in this period, promoted by architects such as Andrea Palladio and Pirro Ligorio.

San Filippo Neri, who was also a confessor of the Oblates in Tor de' Specchi, becomes a central figure in the rediscovery of the martyrs in Rome. In the case of S. Maria Nova, although the exact location of the burial was unknown, the memory of the martyrs brought in the tenth century by Gregory V had not been lost (Palladio, 1554). In 1580 their remains were found and placed under the main altar. Although we have no clear indication of its configuration at the time, it would be logical to think that the entire area of the main altar would be reformed, to free it from medieval constructions and make it more visible, as recommended by Borromeo. The only evidence of this intervention is the existence of a balustrade of separation between the presbytery and the nave and the visible alterations in the marble floor in front of the apse, difficult to interpret. The fragment of marbled atomic-medieval plutus at the entrance of the sacristy could be part of this balustrade or, as we have mentioned, of the Schola cantorum (Lugano, 1922).

Shortly after, and in the same Tridentine spirit of recovery of Christian memories and the didactic objective, a new monument to Gregory XI was built in 1584 by Pietro Paolo Olivieri to the right of the transept (González-Longo, 2013). It represents the moment of transition from the medieval church of Santa Maria Nova to that baroque of Santa Francesca Romana, and as such, it is eclectic, with a bas-relief with images of primitive character, within a modern architectural composition, creating a contemporary architecture of the late sixteenth century. Despite the great architectural quality of the monument, it seems that it was erected without the intervention of an architect, as evidenced by the precariousness with which the back wall was left, and the probable destruction of a medieval fresco (González-Longo, 2013).

With respect to the exterior of the church at this time, Cock's view of around 1550 (González-Longo, 2015) shows three windows similar to those of the fifteenth century on the side wall. These windows, wider than the previous ones, would give greater illumination to the main nave. There are also windows on the apse and on the transept, now completely covered by later fabrics. A description and drawing by Ugonio from 1580, published by Krautheimer (1959), shows the existence of a mosaic on the main facade of the church, which represented the Virgin with a cross in her hand, flanked by angels. This is surely the same mosaic that appears in Franzini's drawing of 1588, in simplified form (González-Longo, 2015). This would indicate, contrary to what Krautheimer (1959) thought, that the three fifteenth-century windows that we mentioned earlier, would have been closed sometime between 1550, when Cock draws them (González-Longo, 2015), and 1580 when Ugonio describes the mosaic. This transformation of the church's gable, which would aim to create an internal atmosphere more linked to the mystery, as recommended by Borromeo (1577), undoubtedly also intended to commemorate and make more visible to the public the new work done in the church. The *selci* of Ss. Peter and Paul would have taken a more secondary role, perhaps then placed in their current position in the southern transept (Lancellotti, 1623), although surely on an altar and with a better accessibility than at the moment, altered with the construction in the nineteenth century of the stairs to the crypt.

The number of monks in the monastery ranged from twenty-five to thirty during this period. According to the Rule of St. Benedict, the monks had to sleep in separate beds and with their clothes on, placed in large bedrooms that remain lit all night. The Olivetans did so from the beginning; however, to achieve greater comfort to rest and pray, separate cellae for one or two monks were later preferred. At the beginning of the sixteenth century, separate cells for each monk were built in Monte Oliveto Maggiore, reusing the bedrooms for Chapter meetings. Unfortunately the Book of the Fabric that archival documents at S. Maria Nova say existed already in 1578 has now disappeared (ASMN, 1793). As we have already mentioned, there are several drawings from this period representing the area, but the one that best shows the configuration of the monastery is that of Du Pérac from 1577 (Du Pérac, 1577; González-Longo, 2015). It clearly shows that the two-storey cloister behind the apse of the church, which we have already discussed, was only covering the other three sides. There are another four cloisters or courtyards shown, two to the north, with buildings on one floor, and two two-storey ones to the south, joining the monastery with the arch of Titus. Some the latter were granaries built between 1540 and 1543 by the Abbot Sevagli; they were demolished at the beginning of the nineteenth century, as we will see later.

In 1586 the barn on the gate of the Monastery overlooking Campo Vaccino and joining the arch of Titus was repaired and appears on the A. Tempesta plan of 1593 (González-Longo, 2015). All the complex was enclosed by a wall, probably that built by the Prior F. Celso di Corigio in 1532, and included the Temple of Venus and Rome and the orchards; no standing column from the temple was left by then. However, we cannot consider Du Pérac's drawing a completely rigorous representation since the bell tower appears to the south of the church, rather than to the north.

4.4 The Canonization of S. Francesca Romana and the Transformation of the Church (1612–14)

The most radical transformations of the architectural organism of the church took place on the occasion of the canonization of Saint Francesca Romana, proclaimed by Paul V (Borghese) on May 1608. The grandeur and level of participation in the procession is reflected in a rare Tempesta incision, which features a series of detailed vignettes. It was a true civic celebration, during which Santa Maria Nova was transformed into the sanctuary of Santa Francesca Romana.

Lancellotti (1623) reports that in 1611 the abbot Stefano D'Aversa, is "repair[ing] everything", and at his death, in 1613, the new abbot, D. Clemente Cattaneo (Cattanei di Bologna) continues the work, which will be completed in 1615. Around that time Lancelloti is granted permission to investigate in all the archives and write the history of the Olivetan Order. It seems that while the works were finished and a new image was given to his church in Rome, the sense of identity of the Olivetan Order was also being renewed.

At the general chapter of Monte Oliveto in 1614 "1000 shields for the reconstruction of the church of S. Francesca Romana" are given. In the chapter of the following year, in which the works would be finished, another quota of "2000 shields, of 10 paoli each one" is added. To give an idea of what these sums would mean then, it is enough to say that 300 shields had been paid in 1612 to carpenters Francesco Nicolini da Firenze and Alessandro Castaldi of Bologna for roof construction materials, including scaffolding, and another 925 shields to make the structure, not including paint and gold (Scarpini, 1952).

The church then experienced a major intervention and transformation that the Olivetan monks commissioned to the architect Carlo Lambardi, or Lombardi, also called Lambardo da Arezzo (Arezzo 1545–Rome 1619). Of possible Tuscan formation, he lived in Rome since 1583 (Parlato, 2004) and was seventy years old when the construction of Santa Francesca Romana finished, his most important assignment and last great work before he died. Unfortunately, the figure and work of this architect

84 *Preservation, Transformation, Patronage*

are not very well known, and the critical evaluations of his work and ability are very varied, as we will see later.

In addition to executing the new facade, including the portico and the choir above, he transformed the interior of the church, creating the chapels (Baglione, 1642). The medieval facade described previously becomes a modern travertine composition, with a giant Corinthian order (Figure 4.5). Inside, the level of the western area of the nave rises approximately 1.5 metres. The wall rises between 0.6 and 1 metres in the central nave and on the sides, correcting the irregularities and subsidence of the preceding buildings, creating a series of buttresses and consolidating the structure to support the thrusts created by the new wooden coffered ceiling (Figure 4.6), which is undergoing conservation works at the moment and that we have described before (González-Longo, 2013). To more effectively illuminate the church, four square windows are opened in the nave's claristory and other square and semicircular windows in the new side chapels (Figure 3.6, 3.13, 4.6). The medieval campanile was maintained, but its lower level space (Figure 4.7) was covered by a new baroque decoration.

With the creation of the lateral chapels, the church is transformed from a three-nave basilical configuration, as the 1551 Bufalini plan shows, into a Latin-cross plan, as recommended by Borromeo (1577) (González-Longo, 2015). This Latin cross was already the preferred plan by many architects such as Palladio and had been used before in

Figure 4.5 Facade of the church (A.)

Figure 4.6 Interior of the Church (Spartaco Biasini)

important masterpieces such as S. Andrea di Mantova by Leon Battista Alberti, which Lambardi knew very well for having worked there in 1588 (Parlato, 2004). Maderno was also at the time transforming, for Paul V (1605–1621), Saint Peter's, extending the Greek cross of Bramante and Michelangelo to form a Latin cross plan, following Raphael's original idea.

In the case of Santa Maria Nova, the operation of transforming the plan, in addition to following Borromeo's recommendations, helped the structural consolidation of the church as a whole. This was undoubtedly the most complicated operation executed in the church. In this way, Lambardi masterfully transformed an irregular medieval interior, full of tombs, with naves separated by columns, into a more uniform interior, with a nave and four chapels on each side, accessible from the nave through arches and with pairs of pilasters between the arches, articulating the main space of the church (Figures 4.1, 4.2, 4.6).

Lambardi designs something that we could call a 'structural sheath' of the existing building, partly replacing, partly covering and partly consolidating it, in an addition and subtraction process that minimizes the amount of material needed for construction. This complex design and construction required skills and knowledge of the structural behaviour of the building and great skills in the execution, as well as an excellent organization of the work. It provides a system of new pillars

86 *Preservation, Transformation, Patronage*

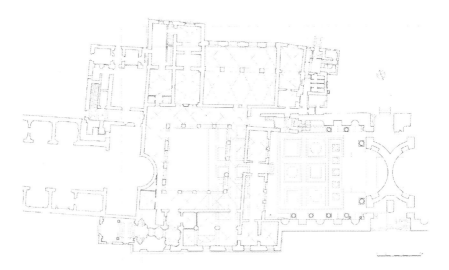

Figure 4.7 Ground floor plan of the church transept, monastery and cella of Rome (A.)

that support the access arches to the new chapels, connected to transverse walls behind, dividing them. The transformation of a lintelled system into one with arches had already been experienced by Lambardi in the interior of S. Prisca, with similar intentions of structural consolidation and visual unity, but with a scale and difficulty smaller than those faced in Santa Maria Nova more than ten years later. As Prandi (1937) already noted, the interior design, with a discontinuous central axis, is a masterful exercise of unification of an existing irregular plant, with a pavement tilted to the west. Prandi illustrates with a longitudinal section of the church the relationship between the old columns and the new pillars. This configuration was also demonstrated by its finding of the architrave fragment that we have already mentioned (Figure 3.10), which is at the level of the imposts of the access arches to the side chapels.

This geometric relationship between the architrave and the new arches aimed to facilitate the construction process. In this way, the pillars and transverse walls that form the chapels would be built first, followed by the construction of the arches, demolishing part of the walls of the clerestory, a critical and delicate phase in the construction in which the stability of the entire building was at risk, as also reflected in the works contract (Bilancia, 2006). Once the new load-bearing structure was put into use, the old columns were removed, and the remaining sections of the architrave was disassembled or cut. Despite the attempt to reuse the precious marble of the columns, structural or operational reasons in the

Preservation, Transformation, Patronage 87

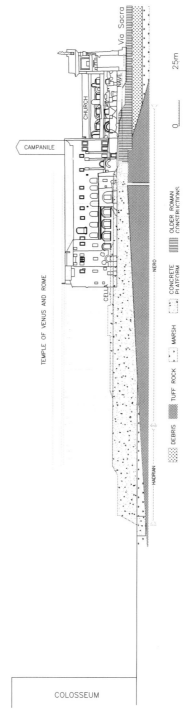

Figure 4.8 North elevation of the church and monastery and graphic reconstruction of the temple (A.)

construction sequence could have caused damage or prevented them from being completely removed (González-Longo, 2013).

If we consider that the total number of the columns was eighteen, it turns out that once the five are removed from the portico (as we have analysed before, four in front and one on the south side) thirteen columns would remain inside: seven to the left of the nave and six to the right (Figures.4.1, 4.2). This number of columns and their position would create thirteen possible intercolumni to place the thirteen candles, which the passage of the Liber Pontificalis of the life of Benedict III (855–858), tells us that this pope had donated to the church (Prandi, 1937). The operation of removing the columns was also necessary due to the fact that the level of the pavement of some parts of the nave was raised.

Despite eliminating the columns, and thanks of the existence of the large architrave (Fig. 3.10), the masonry vaults above them were mostly preserved. As we have already said, the lateral nave and the transept were already vaulted before the intervention of Lambardi; he only repaired and transformed the existing vaults. This material fact is also confirmed by a document dated November 1615, relating to the construction of the new chapel of Santa Francesca, which talks about the vault "half old and half modern" and the intention to modernize the old, which indicates not only that the work in the interior still continued then (Cirulli, 2009), but also that it was a transformation of the structure rather than a completely a new construction.

Also, the contract of works in the nave of the church confirms that Lambardi preserved—surely also for economic reasons—, and transformed the vaults, to the new spatiality and dominant taste at the time. In fact, the contract specifies that the new stone walls that form the new chapels were finished up to the height of the old vaults (Bilancia, 2006). The only completely new vault was the cloister vault at the portico, replacing an earlier wooden structure. It is interesting to note that the most transformed vaults at that time are those above the stereobate of the Temple of Venus and Rome, between the west part of the church and the transept. That is also the area where the change of direction of the axis of the church and other structural irregularities occur. This has surely affected the stability of the vaults, thus requiring major repairs and changes. We must also note the clear principle of economy that guides the project, intervening only in those structurally damaged parts, merely giving the rest a slight surface treatment. This operation is in line with our contemporary conservation principle of minimum intervention.

Lambardi uses in his design previous experiences, but above all he looks at the building and the works of art and devotion that it contains. The most important medieval and renaissance pre-existing elements were preserved, including those at the presbytery (tomb of Santa Francesca, mosaic and monument to Gregory XI), and the southern vestibule (monuments of Cardinal Vulcani and Antonio Rido). The external portal of this preserved vestibule seems to be from the second half of sixteenth century, perhaps from around 1586, when, as mentioned before, the adjacent barn was repaired. The portal and the two monuments inside require further study and the access to and from the church to the Roman Foum needs to also be studied in detail and resolved, as there is at the moment an inadequate relationship between the two. Hopefully with the ongoing works of the Museum of the Roman Forum these relationships and access will improve.

Unfortunately, other valuable works, such as the painting by Gentile da Fabriano on the tomb of Cardinal Adimari at the entrance wall of the church, were sacrificed for the needs of the consolidation of the church and the construction of a new choir and ceiling. Lambardi, however, retained the existing elements mentioned, and was inspired by them when creating the new design. Thus the 'michelangelesque' capital in the monument to Gregory XI is very similar to the Ionic capital with garlands that he uses in the new pilasters, but he adds the faces of the cherubs. The cosmatesque floor would also be an inspiration for the marble finishing of the walls and pilasters, and the colours and gold of the mosaic for the new wooden ceiling (González-Longo, 2015).

It is also interesting how the modulation of the medieval church leaves a clear mark on the new design. The new couples of pilasters of the interior hold an entablature that in turn holds the upper wall of the clerestory, where horizontal rectangular windows were opened, a scheme that repeats that of the medieval church, but inserting a new arch system and giving new proportions, architectural language and articulation of space. As Prandi (1937) had already observed, the projections of the pairs of pilasters vary in depth in order to accommodate the irregular geometry of the pre-existing structure, which was partly preserved. The previous vertical semicircular windows were replaced with rectangular horizontal windows, in order to better illuminate the new polychrome roof (Figure 4.8). These transformations are clearly seen in the north wall, but they are not visible in the south wall because it is covered by a wing built on the south side nave, connecting the Choir over the southern area of the presbytery with the new Choir over the portico (Figures 2.1, 4.9).

We do not know exactly how the church was temporarily decorated for the canonization of S. Francesca, but we know that it was extensive, as indicated by the great expenses (Pelissier, 1893). The permanent decoration of the interior and exterior of the church seems to perpetuate this festive and celebratory spirit, through colours, gold, garlands, angels, shields, sculptures and inscriptions. The architecture of the church thus became a vehicle for the perpetuation of celebrations. We also see that in the church there is a proliferation of angels: on the facade, the cherubs of the abacus of the capitals inside, the two angels of the apse, at the holy water basin in the chapel of Santa Francesca, many in the sepulchral monuments, and in the tabernacle. Their presence in the church can be clearly placed in relation to the importance of the role of the guardian angel in Francesca's life, but it is also a characteristic of the religiosity of the time. Paul V approved the celebration of the cult of guardian angels and Francesco Albertini published in 1612- the year in which, as we shall see, the transformation of the church began-, a treatise on the guardian angel.

Lambardi also designed the new wooden ceiling of the nave, with carved gilded coffers, and with polychrome decoration, as confirmed by the inscription on the ceiling. However, it seems that his role in the construction of this element was not as central as in the rest of the works, as the Olivetans, following Borromeo's recommendations, had great control (González-Longo, 2013). This type of roof was a frequent type of construction then in Rome (Conforti, 2018). In this case, the contracts, which are very detailed, show the special control and the detailed knowledge that Olivetans and Lambardi had. Considering also that these works were carried out at the same time that those of the masons and stonecutters working inside the nave, it required a great organization and coordination, as well as a secure access system that allowed, as stipulated in the contract, that the decorator could begin his work when the carpenter had finished a quarter of the structure. The execution of the structure and decoration was developed during 1612 and the gilding was finished in January 1613 (Bilancia, 2006).

The medieval configuration of the interior of the church, with strong iconographies and focal points, was thus transformed into a more modern idea of the space of devotion, appreciated more as an environment in its material and spiritual aspects, as requested by the Tridentine reform. The transept preserves the mosaic, the raised pavement with respect to the nave and the vaults, which are perfectly in accordance with the suggestions of Borromeo (1577), and which are integrated thanks to the harmonious articulation of the new design and the selection of materials, of coloured marbles and gilding. The *selci* of Ss. Peter and Paul went to the background, following in part Borromeo's guide to avoid representing anything apocryphal. The legend of Simon Magus falls into this category, but the historic memory and its importance in the origin of the church was too great to be ignored, and this ensured their presence in the new one.

The Olivetans have preferred the transformation of the existing church and its facade, and not its demolition and construction of a completely new building, as Paul V had done in 1606 in St. Peter's. Cardinal Baronio had opposed this demolition because of the cost involved (Benedetti, 1999), but also because he considered that the material of the old church is sanctified as a testimony to the life of the Church: "*illi lateres, illae columne, illa marmora tot sanctorum vestigiis calcata*" (Hill, 2001). Surely these were also the main reasons for the Olivetans' choice to preserve the old building, but contrary to what Baronio did in his intervention in the church of the ss. Nereo and Achilleo, they decided to carry out the transformation with all its design implications, thus producing a contemporary architecture that incorporates elements of its medieval past (González-Longo, 2015).

We do not know with certainty the reasons why the Olivetans monks commissioned this important work to Lambardi, but the fact that in one of the last contracts of the work of the façade they refer to him as "*magnificent d. Carolo Lambardo architecto Romanam Curiam*" is a testament to his status (Bilancia, 2006). It is also clear that in addition to his recognized ability to control works, the architect had great capacity as a designer, contrary to what Della Porta had told Monsignor Cosimo Giustini, as he recorded in the documentation relating to the Giustini-Piombino palazzo in the piazza Colonna in Rome: "*Carlo Lambardo è misuratore, et non Architetto, et che non li piace*" [Carlo Lambardo is a surveyor, not an architect and he does not like him] (Hibbard, 1967). This comment, or rather gossip, has damaged the image of Lambardi and needs to be placed in context: it was made in April 1593, in the same month that Lambardi was appointed by Clement VIII general estimator of public buildings (Parlato, 2004), meaning that the comment was made many years before he did the work of S. Francesca Romana. On the other hand, curiously, Lambardi replaced Della Porta after his death in 1602, not only at the church of the Madonna dei Monti, but also in other prestigious works such as, ironically, the Giustini-Piombino palazzo (Parlato, 2004).

There is no doubt that Lambardi's work was much appreciated in his time. Guglielmo Facciotti (1616) reported shortly after the church completion that "This church has been conserved by the monks of Monte Oliveto who live there with a beautiful architecture inside and out." (Orbaan, 1920). This admiration for the work continues fifty years later, as evidenced by its inclusion in the selection of the best architectural works in Rome made by Mola (1663), who mentions the "beautiful travertine facade with that spacious Portico". Titi (1674) is quite neutral in his criticism, although he acknowledges that Lambardi had a "buon nome" [good name]. Milizia (1768) is however more severe despite the conclusion: "we cannot condemn it at all." This critical assessment was based on Lambardi's use of the orders: Tuscan portico outside, interrupted by Corinthian pilasters on high pedestals, and composite order inside the portico; surely too eclectic for the classic taste of critics like Milizia. Reading his comments or those of De Brosses, as observed by Blunt (1982), there is a clear change in taste. We cannot forget that, as discussed, since the "age of vitruvianism" (Forssman, 1989), the architectural critique was largely based on the use of architectural orders in the design.

This negative evaluation of Lambardi's work would not change substantially until the twentieth century, when his figure and his intervention in Santa Francesca Romana was finally appreciated by Adolfo Venturi (1939) and more recently by Gaetano Miarelli Mariani, who considered that "presents an original front and perhaps the one that best responds, from the typological point of view, to the demands of its time" (Miarelli Mariani, 1989). Miarelli Mariani, however, questioned its architectural quality, which, despite everything, was considered of great interest. From our point of view, the fundamental value of this intervention and its architectural result is not in its individual elements, but in the design and construction solution of this complex architectural problem. It was executed harmoniously with the pre-existing and contemporary in its attitude, within great economic and temporal limitations, producing a high quality result from the philosophical, compositional and technological point of view. Lambardi had the opportunity here to realize many of his ideas, to demonstrate his professional capacity and not to limit himself to the restrictions imposed by the sometimes closed Roman architectural environment.

The role of the Olivetan Order was central and fundamental in the process of commissioning, monitoring and approval of the works, as evidenced in chapter 16 of the contract of the works inside the church with magister Thomas: "do this work . . . to the satisfaction of the very reverend father abbot and architect" (Bilancia, 2006). We have no doubt that the Olivetans were not only interested in Lambardi's project capabilities, but also in his demonstrated financial management and control capabilities that were very important in this project which lasted only three years. A document in the monastery says the "since 1663 there was a custom for the house architect to appraise the lists of the mason" which indicates that there was an architect continuously employed for the works of the church and the monastery. We know that in 1673 the architect Giuseppe Arcucci worked in the church, remaking the gallery and the ceiling, and could have been one of these "house" architects (González-Longo, 2015).

4.5 The New Urban Dimension of the Church: The Facade of S. Francesca Romana (1614–15)

The transformation of the church becomes even more visible with the construction of the new facade, which includes an inscription noting the Pope, the patrons, the Olivetan Congregation and the date of construction, 1615: "*Paulo V Burghesio Romano P.M. Sedente-Olivetana Congregatio suis—et Monasterii sumptibus—Templum hoc in hanc forman—construxit et ornavit—anno Domini MDCXV*". After the construction of the new facade, artist's views incorporate it, and Falda dedicates it an incision in 1669. In 1684, De Rossi publishes this new facade and the name of the architect: Carolus Lombardus Architectus f. (De Rossi, 1684; González-Longo, 2015).

As seen in the works contract between D. Timoteo di Perugia, cellerario and procurator of the monastery of Santa Maria Nova, and Giulio Buratto (through an agent), the construction work of the facade did not begin until May 1614, when the purchase and transport of Tivoli travertine is contracted. The contract stipulates that the architect, Lambardi, or the master quarryman Francesco Bettania should be satisfied and insists on the need to proceed with a robust quality control of the material to be used (Bilancia, 2006).

The facade develops the theme of the giant order of two couples of Corinthian pilasters on high pedestals, which support a triangular frontispiece containing the pope's shield, in correspondence with the central nave, which gives the composition a strong centrality, reinforced by the window balcony of the new choir over the main entrance. To this, a minor order is added Tuscan without pedestals in relation to the lateral naves and crowned by a section of tympanum. These two overlapping but perfectly differentiated elements, are connected by a scroll on each side. The design is completed with a portico, three statues on the frontispiece and two on the sides, which followed the guide of Borromeo (1577), that is, they had the Virgin with the Child in the centre and that of Santa Francesca on their right (González-Longo, 2015).

Unlike all other Roman churches of the time, S. Francesca Romana has a giant order and a portico. The basic scheme of a giant order of a pair of pilasters and scrolls had been experienced by Lambardi in other projects, such as the facade of S. Prisca in 1600, although of much smaller scale. His reference could be an architectural language belonging more to civil architecture, which gave a more civic appearance to the facade and established the relationship with the Capitoline Hill. But we also have to consider as precedent the giant order of pilasters and the use of orders made by Michelangelo on the exterior elevation of the southern apse of the basilica of St, Peter's as well as Maderno's giant order of Corinthian pilasters on the sides of the facade, whose final section was built between 1612 and 1617, at the same time as the facade of Santa Francesca Romana. The contract of 1614 between the abbot, d. Evangelist Tornolius perisinus, and the magistri Felix e Clemens de Garzolis for the stone decoration of the façade of Santa Francesca, stipulates that the capitals of the pilasters must be similar to the Corinthian capitals of the Gesù, not only in their appearance but also in their quality and durability (Bilancia, 2006).

However, the facade of S. Francesca Romana has a very clear Palladian influence (González-Longo, 2013, 2015). Palladio superimposed on the facades a giant scale of Corinthian semi-columns, just as Michelangelo and Della Porta had done in the Palazzo dei Conservatori in the Capitoline Hill (1563–1568), with the giant order of Corinthian pilasters. Palladio studied Roman monuments, including the Temple of Venus and Rome (which was called then *Del Sole e la Luna*), which he had drawn in his Fourth Book (Palladio, 1570), and that has certainly inspired his own designs. He resolved on the facade of S. Giorgio Maggiore in Venice (design started in 1566) the problem of how to compose a central volume with tympanum and two lower sides with two sections of tympanum, also giving an urban and pictorial dimension to the facade. The construction of

S. Giorgio Maggiore occurred between 1607 and 1611, after the death of Palladio and shortly before the construction of the facade of S. Francesca Romana, for which it would be a clear precedent. S. Giorgio was for Palladio his first complete reconstruction project of a religious building. He had already experienced similar problems, such as the construction of the facade of S. Francesco della Vigna, also in Venice, in which he had developed the Albertian façade model composed as a Roman arch with scrolls, with a giant order of semi-columns on high pedestals. The case of S. Francesco is interesting because of its resemblance to Santa Francesca Romana's project, although in that case the interior and exterior have been made by two different architects: Jacopo Sansovino (1534–1554) and Andrea Palladio (1564–1566). The final project is from 1535, after having been modified with the proportions suggested by the patron, Fr. Francesco Zorzi (Burns and Beltramini, 2008), a clear precedent also in regards to the design control by the client.

Lambardi considers all these precedents and composes the facade using Corinthian order and double tympanum as if it was a temple and most certainly having present the adjacent Temple of Venus and Rome and the Basilica of Maxentius. Lambardi assimilates Palladian ideas to the Roman environment and converts semi-columns into pilasters, but continues with Palladio's idea of coordinating the interior and exterior of the church, matching the giant order with the central nave. Lambardi designs a façade that successfully solves all the problems that this complex project poses, including the needs of worship, visibility and symbology of the church. The façade has an eclectic and scholarly character, and the architect demonstrates great talent and skills by inscribing the new façade on the medieval building, retaining it almost entirely. The front is covered by a new travertine fabric, and, as Lambardi had already done internally, uses contemporary language, although leaving some evidence of medieval construction, as required by the new image and significance of the project.

Lambardi, following the recommendation of Borromeo (1577) on the provision of an atrium or portico, transforms the old one, following , again, the criteria with which he had already intervened inside the church. In this way, and taking into account the existing structure, the two accesses (front and side) of the portico are maintained with a higher arch in the centre and two lower ones on the sides, with the south arch of the same height as the central one. The Tuscan order, symbol of romanity, is also used on the lower level. Inside the portico, again pairs of composite pilasters mark five bays, as if the architect wanted to leave the mark of the position of the older columns. The wall of the portico towards the church contains alternating circular niches and squares like those of the cellae walls of the Temple of Venus and Rome still visible today. This was a innovative and contemporary design, in which the memory of the preceding building is preserved.

The fact that the portico has been maintained in all the medieval and baroque transformations suffered by the church is mainly due to functional reasons and to the fact that it is at a crossroads. As Prandi (1937) reminds us, the Pope used this portico and the bed that was accommodated there as a resting place during the Assumption procession (Moroni, 1840). The portico is a space of transition, of control of the flow of the faithful to the church and of protection from the inclement weather. Unfortunately, the modern enclosures of the Roman Forum and the archaeological excavations around the church have almost completely removed its urban dimension and direct contact with the surrounding area.

The ground around the entrance of the church was excavated approximately two metres during the archaeological works of the late nineteenth and early twentieth centuries. As an incision by Falda clearly shows (González-Longo, 2015), Lambardi's portico was built on a platform of only three steps, while now the access to the church is through a staircase, which already appears in a drawing of D'Espouy of 1889 (Cassanelli et al., 1998; González-Longo, 2015). The current enclosure of the church, with access only from the North, was created at the beginning of the twentieth century, when the imperial pavement of the *Via Sacra* was excavated in front of it. This operation not only altered the relationship of the building with the surrounding area, but the design of the facade was deformed, since it was necessary to create a base underneath, with the consequent change of its original proportions and the alteration of the minor order side, which originally arose directly from the pavement and now features a modern pedestal of almost two metres, an unfortunate deformation of the original design.

In this new configuration, the foundations of the portico were exposed. These foundations were surely rebuilt by Lambardi, since the previous medieval portico would have been a much lighter structure, with marble columns and architraves and wooden deck structure, easy to disassemble to build the new portico with the choir on top. The volume of the new portico is projecting slightly with respect to the church, and Prandi (1937) found Paleo-Christian remains on this junction wall of the portico and the lateral nave to the north. Er can thereafter conclude that Lambardi reused the existing medieval pillars and pilasters, at the corners of the portico, in the new construction, covering them with new travertine blocks, reinforcing and extending the foundations.

It is also necessary to further consider the urban aspect of the church, which represents so effectively the image of Francesca Romana as saint of the city and the church as the centre of a very visible civic cult. It is important to remember that the current public access to the church, from the north, exists only since the early twentieth century, as a result of the excavations of the Forum and the opening of the *Via dell'Impero* by Mussolini in 1932. The main access to the church had been until then the Roman Forum (*Campo Vaccino*). This justifies how the church is designed: while the west and south elevations contain the entrances, the north elevation has no entrance (Figure 4.9).

Figure 4.9 View from the Palatine (SW) (A.)

Its position at an important crossroads, but especially its presence as the end of the visual axis of the Roman Forum from the Capitoline Hill, makes it even more prominent. The design of the church was intended to reinforce its urban image. With the permanence of the medieval campanile, the antiquity of the building is remembered, and the new facade, with its modern, unitary and recognizable design, reaffirms its identity and gives it a contemporary presence among the classical ruins of the pagan monuments of the Forum, inviting faithful and visitors. With this intervention, the church and monastery, previously fortified and closed to the city, open to it and acquire the true urban dimension of modern Rome.

The plan of the Roman Forum of 1656 published by R. Krautheimer (1985) shows the church and tree-lined elm trees planted by Alexander VII, marking a large avenue between the arch of Septimius Severus and that of Titus, with the new Facade of Santa Francesca Romana as a focal point. Both the Olivetans and Lambardi were aware that the new facade would be present in the numerous views of the Roman Forum from the Capitoline Hill and that these would be carried by travellers throughout Europe. Perhaps it is this point that has also influenced the choice of the Palladian architectural language, more recognizable beyond the strictly Roman environment (González-Longo, 2015).

4.6 Bernini's *Confessione*

Although the Oblates wanted to exhume the body of the Saint during the works of Lambardi, Paul V had not given the necessary permission, perhaps because of the fear that the body would not be found. Upon finishing Lambardi's work in 1615, the Olivetans presented a proposal to the city for the construction of a new chapel in honour of Saint Francesca Romana. The 'Conservators' of Rome then issued a decree for the collection of funds and created a commission for this purpose (Lavin, 1980).

Urban VIII (Barberini) was elected Pope in 1623, at a time when the church of S. Francesca continued to attract the faithful and the monastery is enlarged. In 1629, D. Vittorio de' Greci Paleologi of Naples was abbot general and a residence was established there for the best students of all the provinces of the Order (Scarpini, 1952). In 1634, and following the suggestion of the Olivetans, the Pope made Pietro Maria Borghesi of Siena Cardinal-Protector (Scarpini, 1952). Rome was hit again by the plague and the living conditions were bad. Despite these hardships, and perhaps to raise the morale of people, the Pope approved in 1638 the excavation to find the body of the Saint (Lugano, 1933) and Landi (1771) reports in detail the search (González-Longo, 2013, 2015). The excavation began from the sacristy and the body was found under the main altar (then in the middle of the transept), that is, the space of the current crypt. A chirograph of the Pope on 24 August 1638 assigned to the President of Tor de' Specchi, Suor Maria Madalena Anguillara, 5,000 shields for the *Confessione*, whose design had already begun (Lugano, 1908).

The *Confessione* was executed according to the design of Gianlorenzo Bernini. The design was carried out between 1638 and 1641, the construction of the a edicule between 1641 and 1644 and the sculptural group between 1644 and 1648, as confirmed by the inscription on the urn. The marble work was done in part by Giovanni Maria Fracchi between 1644 and 1649. The project included a funerary structure that was built in the crypt at the level of the nave and in front of the main altar, as it was common practice in the early church (Lavin, 1980). The *Confessione* was inaugurated on March 9, 1649 with the presence of Bernini, who was very involved at the time with the plays he wrote and prepared.

The design consisted of a statue of S. Francesca in gilded bronze, inside a marble aedicule within an area enclosed by a marble balustrade with curved stairs on each side (Figure 4.10). Unfortunately we don't have the original drawings, only two illustrations from the end of the seventeenth century (González-Longo, 2015). In 1641, when D. Carlo di Roma was abbot, permission was obtained to move the altar to the apse and thus leave more space for the confession. The original position of the altar probably was where the aedicule is now and aligned with the rounded cosmatesque pavement.

98 *Preservation, Transformation, Patronage*

Figure 4.10 Confessione by Bernini and Gregory XI monument at Santa Francesca Romana (Spartaco Biasini)

Bernini's aedicule is embedded in the presbytery, with continuous curved entablature supported by two pilasters on the wall and two marble columns of red jasper with golden capitals, forming a polychromy of rich and rare coloured marbles, which gave prominence to the monochrome of the golden sculpture of the Saint. The aedicule is opened at the top, thus creating a zenithal illumination of the sculpture. The *Confessione* was of "such beauty, grandeur and majesty that, with reason, it is admired as something strange and singular" (Landi, 1771). The main references for Bernini's design are Roman: ancient and modern circular temples. We can see many other precedents but we do not know to what extent all these influences- perhaps some pointed out directly by the Olivetans-, were actually considered by Bernini (González-Longo, 2013).

The theme of the aedicule-tabernacle and the zenithal light are central elements for the composition of the *Confessione*. Bernini's design is also based on spatial compositional strategies of concavity and convexity. The marble balustrade is convex, creating a bell-shaped enclosure that goes up to the transept, with an iron gate towards the nave. As he would do shortly after in S. Andrea al Quirinale, Bernini created a convex aedicule that contained the sculptural group. As it had already happened in

Lambardi's intervention, the architectural forms present here have Christian and pagan references: the tabernacle at S. Maria in Trastevere, centre of a scene represented in one of the frescoes of 1468 in Tor de' Specchi, and the pagan circular temples that contained statues of gods. The design of the aedicule could also have been inspired by the niches of Pantheon, held by two columns and with zenithal light.

The balustrade is divided into four zones on each side by pedestals. It has heavily moulded jasper Tuscan balusters, a step as a plinth and a wide ridge as handrail all around, which protects the entire area of the *Confessione*. The well-designed curvature and height of the balustrade increases the visibility line of devotees and visitors. The shield of the Bussa de' Leoni family, to which Francesca belonged, in the very elaborate polychrome marble floor, completes the decoration. The two curved stairs that flank the *Confessione* lead to the presbytery and the new altar, in the apse. The solid balustrade is not only an element of enclosure, but it articulates the space around and creates an illusion perspective, uniting, with a game of concaves and convexes, the nave and the presbytery, and framing the apse that contains the medieval mosaic. As he would do later in St. Peter's Square, Bernini plays with dimensions, scales and spaces, which compresses and expands at pleasure. The two marble statues of angels flanking the apse rest on high pedestals, so that, when seen from the nave, they seem to rest on the balustrade at the level of the transept. This scenery was topped with a large number of silver lamps that, supported by the balustrade around the *Confessione*, burned continuously; in Landi's time (1771) there were thirty.

We do not know with certainty Bernini's design for the crypt since it was completely transformed between 1867 and 1869 by Andrea Busiri-Vici. However, elements of the Berninian project were preserved, such as an Ercole Ferrata medallion, with a bas-relief of Santa Francesca Romana and the angel, inserted in the east wall of the crypt, suggesting that this wall was part of the space created by Bernini and perhaps the same space of the underground altar to which a description of the church of 1727 refers (De Rossi, 1727). All this suggests that Bernini reused the space in which the Saint was originally buried to create the underground altar. The space was transformed in the second half of the nineteenth century, when the space was made publicly accessible and the body of the Saint located where it is today, in the wall towards the nave of the church. All this seems to indicate that Bernini's design did not provide public access to the crypt, only a partial view of the burial space through the two metal lattice windows on the sides of the aedicule. The access to the underground altar was through the mentioned staircase behind the south transept arch, which we have already mentioned, and it was probably limited to the monks and the Oblates.

Urban VIII died in 1644 and Innocent X becomes Pope; considering his criticism about his predecessor, one could doubt that he wanted to continue his work, especially if we take into account that he did not appreciate Bernini's work as much as Urban VIII did. The continuity of the project was assured, without any doubt, because of the commitment shown by the successive presidents of the Oblates and the help of the Olivetans. The long period of realization of the *Confessione* of more than ten years (1638–1649), being a relatively modest-in- scale project, makes us think that, apart from the typical budget problems and the interruption by the death of Urban VIII, there would also be some disagreement about the design.

After the completion of the aedicule in 1644, Innocent X granted his sister, the Oblate donna Agata dei Principi Pamphili, the permission for the commission of the sculptural group, which consisted of a statue in gilded bronze of the Saint in the company of the angel. The golden urn below contained the silver ark with the body closed in another lead box, flanked by two angels. Unfortunately, the *Confessione* was vandalized during the Napoleonic invasion of Rome in 1798, and the bronze sculptural group disappeared when the church was desecrated and reduced to a warehouse. The body of S. Francesca Romana was transferred to Tor de' Specchi, and the monastery of S. Maria Nova was suppressed. Bernini's bronze group and other ornaments of the *Confessione*, as well as the bell, disappeared, probably melted down to make cannons. The current marble sculpture is a work of Giosuè Meli made between 1866 and 1869.

The richness of polychrome and golden marbles and the strategy of the zenithal light create a theatrical stage, while the effect given by the convexity of the *Confessione* and the concavity of the apse convert a compressed space, difficult to transition between the nave and the presbytery, to a fluid passage, giving at the same time a sense of depth greater than the real one. As it is already known, Bernini experienced in S. Francesca Romana for the first time strategies that he would develop immediately after not only at S. Andrea, but also in the well-known Ecstasy of Saint Teresa of Avila (1645–52) in the Cornaro Chapel of S. Maria della Vittoria. Here, Bernini repeats, although in a much more elaborated way, the same global scheme of the design of the *Confessione* de S. Francesca: a curved aedicule on columns and illuminated from above, containing the sculpture of the saint that recreates an episode of her lifetime. The curved aedicule of S. Francesca Romana is also at least ten years prior to that of the façade of S. Maria della Pace (1656–57) of Pietro da Cortona, also a curved aedicule embedded in the facade, which resolves a position of crossing three streets in a small space.

The *Confessione* has its formal unity, but at the same time it merges harmoniously with the rest of the church, with a clear pictorial quality, something that we could compare, in modern language, to a three-dimensional painting. The Berninian design of the monument creates a unitary system, a smooth transition between the nave and the presbytery, effortlessly saving the difference in height and with an effective treatment of architecture, sculpture and natural light around the relics of the Saint. Bernini is considered an artist who integrates all visual arts into his works and this *Confessione* is a clear example of his ability. Even further, at S. Francesca Romana, despite the modest scale, he has visually realized an effective integration of the interior of the church, solving the circulation problem and giving, through the form and continuity of the balustrade, a masterly game of concave and convex that surround the visitor, making a richer spatial experience of moving through the church. In addition to the "*bel composto*" [beautiful whole]—as Bernini's biographers described his works (Lavin, 1980)—of the work itself, with this intervention the whole interior of the church becomes a "*bel composto*".

The *Confessione* masterfully synthesizes the architectural place in which it sits, in the Christian church but also on the pagan temple. We could speculate on Bernini's possible awareness of the location, facing the stairs of the temple stylobate, a place where perhaps there is a singular element such as a propileo, similar to those that existed on the sides of the temple (Figure 2.4). Bernini also used materials, such as coloured marbles and bronze, very similar to those used in the Roman temple and the medieval church. Beyond a clear narrative about the place and the meaning of the Saint, Bernini exercises here his usual practice of "*i contrapposti*" [the opposites] (Lavin, 1980), consisting of the insertion of different elements and the consideration of the rest of the elements, designing and placing them as a composition of colour, form and light, creating interaction with the rest of the elements of the church. He is very aware of the insertion to be executed, which has been carefully dimensioned, so that he manages to give unity to the whole church, following his declared design approach:

> The architect's chief merit lay not in making beautiful or commodious buildings but in knowing how to invent ways of using the small, the bad and the things that are badly adapted to the needs, to do beautiful things, so that it is useful what it was a defect and if it did not exist it would have to be made.
>
> (in Lavin, 1980)

4.7 The Monastery and "L'universale ristabilimento" of the Middle of the Eighteenth Century

After the radical transformation of the church at the beginning of the seventeenth century, the monastery, previously fortified and enclosed, is also modernized, opening it to the city. In 1634 the monks sold "an ancient wall near the garden of the orange trees" and initiate the "fabric of the Novitiate" (ASMN, 1793) extending the monastery to accommodate a greater number of monks. Permission to dig the garden in search of Antichità is given again in 1642. There are also references to payments between 1659 and 1673 in the archive to fix the kitchen and for a new fountain, most likely the one that appears in Bonaventura van Overbeke's drawings from c. 1706 (Overbeke, 1763; González-Longo, 2015). In this collection, we see the transformation of the cella of Rome of the temple into the monastery garden, with the fountain in the centre. The fact that almost seventy years elapsed between the drawings and their publication means that the temple is correctly named as Venus and Rome, while in earlier publications, such as Pieter Schenck's *Eternal Rome*, it is still identified as the Temple of Isis. The cella of Venus was also a garden of the monastery. The eastern part and the facade of the monastery towards the Roman Forum also appear in Schenk's drawings of 1705 (González-Longo, 2015). We also know from the archive that in 1663 the Cardinal-Protector had two carriages, horses and mules in the stables of the monastery. This was housed in the mentioned wing that incorporated the Arch of Titus, and, as we will see, it will be demolished at the beginning of the nineteenth century (González-Longo, 2015).

Three exceptional drawings by L. Cruyl illustrate the part of the monastery towards the Colosseum at this time, although one shows the reverse image and the other does not show the loggia (González-Longo, 2015). There are also some views from the Colosseum, such as that of Jacob De Heusch from 1694 and Warwick Smith from 1776–81, which illustrate the appearance of the monastery at this time (González-Longo, 2015). Thus, as Cruyl's drawings reveal, we know that there was a lodge with three arches, probably with octagonal columns, similar to those of the cloister. This lodge would be covered during the expansion of the monastery in the eighteenth century. The conservation of this facade has recently been carried out by the architect of the Soprintendenza, Claudia del Monti, but no evidence of the loggia has been found.

Giovanni Battista Busiri's painting of 1720 illustrates very well the exterior appearance of the monumental complex at the beginning of the eighteenth century (González-Longo, 2015). In 1696 the monastery was "pretty good"; between 1704 and 1706 more excavations of antichità were carried out in the garden, without many findings. The community was composed in 1705 of 22 monks. Two archival documents give us a detailed report of the contents of the church, the monastery and other properties in 1726: the report of the Sacra Congregazione della Apostolic Visit and the manuscript of B.M. Rosatelli (Rosatelli, 1911). In 1729 the Chapel of Santa Francesca was rebuilt, and between 1730 and 1735 the new sacristy was built (the old one had moisture problems) at the initiative of Pope Clement XII, who promoted architecture greatly and whose bust is in front of the entrance of the new sacristy, dated 1735; there were 24 monks at the time.

A drawing by Canaletto (c 1742) constitutes an exceptional document illustrating the appearance of the monastery just before being transformed

(González-Longo, 2015). In 1744 the monastery was in a terrible state: "falling from a thousand parts" and thanks to the Nolli plan we know its configuration around two cloisters (González-Longo, 2015). Between 1744 and 1750, under Benedict XIV, the Cardinal-Protector and Abbot D. Luca Bertusati of Milan, declared "The universal re-establishment of this monastery has begun". Two new sections were built to the northeast and northwest, giving the monastery two new facades crowned by a painted balustrade, indicating the limited budget available. In 1770 the community was composed of 27 monks.

A drawing of Claude-Joseph Vernet, who spent the years 1734–1752 in Rome, shows the monastery just finished, from a position that also shows the topography of the Velia, heavily excavated later by Mussolini, as well as the fabric of the monastery to the north, demolished by Giacomo Boni, as we will see later (González-Longo, 2015). At the end of the eighteenth century the northern part of the building was very similar to what we see today (González-Longo, 2015).

5 The New Conservation Ideology
Giuseppe Valadier and Giuseppe Camporese

5.1 The End of the Seventeenth Century: A New Architectural Awareness

It is normally considered that the culture of conservation was born in the second half of the eighteenth century (Racheli, 2007). However, before that, there is already a preservationist and conservative consciousness in practice, as we have seen in the case of Santa Francesca Romana, and theoretically; Vasari discusses questions of loss and compensation (Matero, 2007; Rossi Pinelli, 1996). The development of the culture of conservation happens, as we will see next, through the greater appreciation of historic material and classical architecture.

France was the first to officially recognize the importance of ancient Roman architecture. Jean-Baptiste Colbert (1619–1683), the minister of economy of Louis XIV, in his effort to revive the economy of France, promoted public works and architecture. He was also very interested in art and took Bernini to Paris. Colbert also commissioned him to follow the training of young French artists at the Academy of France in Rome, created by him in 1666, which would open the way to the creation of other national academies. This was a time of scientific discoveries, in which science and art were closely linked. It seems that Colbert studied at a Jesuit college, and it may be that there was a connection to the activities of Jesuits like Athanasius Kircher. Scientific and methodological thinking was also applied to architecture, in a collaborative way. Until then it had been sustained by the talents, efforts and observations of individual architects such as Alberti, Vignola or Palladio.

Colbert sent Antoine Desgodetz, who had studied with François Blondel (1618–1686) at the Academy of Architecture in Paris, to Rome (1672–1674). The Academy was created in 1671 to study ancient monuments and use these studies in the promotion of a new French architecture that will influence the rest of the world. Desgodetz published his studies and detailed surveys in a book (Desgodets, 1682), in which he tried to get a more precise description of the monuments, updating old treatises. Although Desgodetz had studied the Temple of Venus and

Rome (then called Isis and Serapis), during his trip in the years 1676–77, as it appears in his manuscript (González-Longo, 2015), it is not included in the final published volume. The reason is that his drawings were not an original survey, but mainly taken from the *Quattro Libri* of Palladio. Desgodets's constitutes the main reference since then for the study of the ancient monuments of Rome, as it explicitly corrects the errors of previous authors. Other architects have since reviewed it: L. T. Piroli (1794), G. Valadier (1822) and L. Canina (1863). The latter includes the Temple of Venus and Rome, establishing that the columns of the entrance were of Cipollino marble and that the foundations of walls and columns were of blocks of Albanian stone *peperino* and Tiburtina (Travertine).

5.2 The Changes at the End of the Roman Settecento: Archaeology, Conservation and the Taste for the Ancient

As we have seen in the case of the monastery of S. Francesca Romana, the additions were made in a contemporary way and without any explicit concern for the existing building, apart from taking full advantage of its functionality. This is also the case in the new facades of San Giovanni in Laterano (1736) and Santa Maria Maggiore (1741–43) in Rome, transforming its architecture. These projects, however, clearly have contributed to the active conservation of these buildings. The architectural conservation mentality appears only in those cases in which it is about finishing a work in the same style as the existing one, as is the case of the façade of the Duomo of Milan or, as in the interventions of James Essex in the cathedrals of Ely, Winchester and Lincoln, about using a philological method of conservation (Racheli, 2007). As an act of active conservation, it would also be possible to mention the case of Sir John Vanbrugh in England regarding his intention to preserve the Woodstock Manor in Blenheim and the Holbein Gate in Whitehall in 1719.

Despite the edicts of the cardinals Albani (1726) and Valenti (1733), in 1740 art auctions began to be held in London, a practice that will spread throughout Europe, with the consequent plundering of Roman art, since the objects came from excavations such as those mentioned in the case of Santa Francesca Romana. After the architectural and scientific innovations of the seventeenth century, the tendency is to a conservatism, which together with the political instability, made to forget the contemporary in favour of the Antiquity, which becomes the artistic and cultural ideal. The image of Rome becomes an object of desire and artists proliferate producing it and dealers speculating with it. There were not enough Roman painters, such as Giovanni Battista Lusieri (1755–1821), and foreigners, to produce paintings for their numerous foreign clients, especially British. Antonio Canaletto spent several years painting in Rome and he made a painting and several drawings of the church of Santa Francesca Romana and the Basilica of Maxentius (González-Longo, 2015).

Roman ruins were not only the object of artistic inspiration (Eco, 2004), but also a means of study and propaganda, as in the case of the Scottish architect Robert Adam's book (1764). Adam used the book on his return from the Grand Tour as his public introduction to his new stellar career in Britain, with major changes to what had been his previous professional practice with his family of architects.

The discovery of Herculaneum in 1738 and Pompeii in 1748 opened up interest in the sophisticated ancient world and constituted the creation of archaeology as a science. Johann Joachim Winckelmann (1717–68), who is considered the founder of art history as a discipline after his publication of his History of Ancient Art (*Geschichte der Kunst*, 1764), becomes a catalyst for antiquarianism and the science of archaeology. He was the librarian of Cardinal Alessandro Albani (1692–1779), a great patron of arts and collector. However, the first large-scale archaeological excavation in the modern sense was carried out in 1788 by the Swedish ambassador in the Basilica Julia of the Roman Forum.

Winckelmann expressed the impossibility of conserving without damaging the beauty of the work of art (Racheli, 2007 cf. Haskell and Penny, 1984), although fe contradicted himself by appreciating the conserved statue of the Laocoön (Winckelmann, 1755–67). In the second half of the eighteenth century, there was in Rome extensive activity of conservation of ancient statues in particular those belonging to the Cardinal Albani collection, which were placed in suitable contexts for a more effective presentation of the 'ancient'. The act of copying statues was intimately linked to conserving them. Winckelmann commissioned many of the conservation work to Bartolomeo Cavaceppi (1716–1799), who is considered the pioneer of the Roman school of conservation (Racheli, 2007). Although this type of activity had begun much earlier— since the fifteenth century ancient Greek statues had been restored—Cavaceppi states in 1768 what we can consider a theory and method, clearly distinguishing conservation from restoration. He set four main principles: researching the work of art to conserve, consulting experts, but keeping always the own judgment; employing artists who are skilful in the use of materials and techniques; integrating the new work with the old; and keeping the irregularity of the old in all the elements used to consolidate or fix it (Cavaceppi, 1768).

The culture of the ancient filled the social *Salotti*, authentic centres of exchange and cultural debate. The *Accademia di San Luca* and the *Accademia dell'Arcadia* were made up of writers who promoted, with the support of the Roman curia, the classicist restoration. The old is admired and used to criticize the present. Art theorist Francesco Milizia openly criticizes the closest past; architecture and urbanism are for him the instrument of good governance, and the *Cloaca Massima* represented the best example of architecture at the service of citizens. For the scholars of the time, the ancient city represented the ideal of a society open to individual talent and at the same time a way of standing out in a city still controlled by religious powers (Donato, 1992).

The taste for the ancient flooded Europe; Rome was the main reference and the trip to Rome an aspiration. The engravings of Giuseppe Vasi continued the tradition of those of Falda of the seventeenth century, with an ease of production and diffusion. This made travellers carry images of the city all over the world, whose main views were easily recognizable, as Goethe himself pointed out. This reached its peak with the views of Giovanni Battista Piranesi and his frantic production between 1740 and 1778. His mixture of antiquarianism and imagination cultivated locals and foreigners. Despite some scale games, his drawings are extremely accurate, as we see in his drawing of the ruin of the Temple of Venus and Rome (González-Longo, 2015). Goethe transmitted from his trip through Italy shortly after (1786–87), the message of a fabulous world.

From 1778 the pensioners of the French Academy (*"pensionnaires du Roi"*) had to work hard studying Roman architectural masterpieces and present the envois in public exhibitions. The Temple of Venus and Rome was one of the monuments drawn and imagined as it would be in its original form, the result of the interpretation of the results of some contemporary excavation campaigns (González-Longo, 2015).

It is in this context and in this same spirit of interest for the ancient and conservation that Abbot Pietro Maria Rosini (1728–1807) organized and preserved the important archive of S. Maria Nova in 1793, where he remained until 1798, after the temporary closure of the monastery occurred in 1797 as a result of the Napoleonic invasion, leaving only the Procure there. In addition to that of S. Maria Nova, he organized and preserved the archives of Monte Oliveto de Naples and Monte Oliveto Maggiore, where he also created a museum of natural sciences (Fedele, 1900). He created inventories and a document synthesizing the history of S. Maria Nova. The work of Abbot Rosini is considered a pioneer in the field of archiving, and thanks to him important documents of the history of the monastery and Rome in general have been preserved.

5.3 Napoleonic Rome: Looting, Count of Tournon's Program and the Archaeological Park

In 1797–98 Napoleon invades the Papal States, bringing to Paris a hundred works of art from museums and buildings in Rome, the so-called '*le bouquet*'. The Architect Camerale of the Papal States, appointed by the French Commissioner for Works of Art, was in charge of safeguarding these objects. Others were destroyed, such as the mentioned gilded bronze sculpture of Santa Francesca Romana, by Bernini. In 1798 the citizens of Rome proclaimed the Republic, celebrating freedom festivals in the Roman

Forum, with triumphant columns and arches of wood and canvas, but Neapolitan forces invaded Rome in 1799. As always, the architecture also served as a means of propaganda for the French revolutionaries in their promotion of the republic, although ironically the buildings that inspired them most were those imperial (Scherer, 1955).

In 1800 Pope Pius VII, after being elected in Venice, made his triumphal entry into Rome and the city looked pitiful. The Pope issued in 1802 an Edict for the protection of monuments called 'Pamphili Edict', protecting the monuments and works of art of Rome: for its historical and pedagogical value, as a model for contemporary artists and to form popular taste (Linstrum, 1982). With this objective, the responsibility for the protection of monuments and works of art was granted to two officials: the Commissioner for Antiquities and the Inspector of Fine Arts. The Pamphili Edict of 1802 would serve as a model for the French legislature on historic monuments, which would begin to germinate in 1810.

The lawyer and antiquarian Carlo Fea (1753–1836), appointed Commissioner of Roman Antiquities in 1799 by the Neapolitan army, excavated in the Roman Forum between 1801 and 1817. In 1803 Pope Pius VII appointed him director of the Forum, with the objective of digging and repairing the monuments. Fea, who had helped establish legislation to protect archaeological excavations and finds, wrote several books and translated Winckelmann's History of Ancient Art. Antonio Canova was appointed the same year Inspector of Fine Arts of the States of the Church and Commissioner of the Vatican and Capitoline Museums. He commissioned a series of paintings in the lunettes of the Chiaramonti Gallery in the Vatican, illustrating the patronage of Pius VII to artists and archaeologists and his Protection Laws. (González-Longo, 2015).

With all this taste for the ancient, the travellers and pensioners contributed to create an ideal image of Rome, evoking a feeling of greatness, splendour and glory. General Berthier refers to the "monuments and their glory" (Linstrum, 1982). This has been until recently the guide of many restorations, and even today in Great Britain, often people refers to the operation of returning a building "to its former glory".

In 1808 the French forces invade Rome, kidnapping and deporting the Pope, and a Commission is appointed for the conservation of monuments. On 10 June 1809, Rome became the second city of the Napoleonic Empire, and, for the first time (after the parenthesis of Sixtus V), it was sought to restore the city to its Imperial Roman past. Napoleon employs all the architects, archaeologists and curators of the Pope: R. Stern, G. Valadier, G. Camporese, C. Fea, A. Canova and F. A. Visconti. Valadier was an early and prolific architect, born in the Roman artistic environment, although of French descent. As *Architetto Camerale*, he was in charge of designing and constructing new buildings in the Papal States, as well as conserving the old ones. Napoleon made him *Chevalier* of the *Légion d'Honneur*.

The architects Valadier and Camporese executed the demolition plan of the Forum designed by the archaeologist Visconti to make the ancient monuments more visible (González-Longo, 2015). Fea established two priority sites: the Colosseum and the temples of Vesta and Fortuna Virile in the Boario Forum. The *Accademia di San Luca* was appointed as a fund manager of 300,000 francs plus 75,000 francs annually and a papal contribution of 10,000 piastres. New architectural projects were also carried out, such as the project of the architect Scipione Perosini, who proposed in 1811 an imperial palace that would extend from Piazza Colonna to the Colosseum, a kind of new *Domus Aurea*, in which the Roman Forum would be an inner courtyard.

Despite being the second city of the empire, Napoleon did not appoint a Governor for Rome, but made Count Camille De Tournon (1778–1833) Prefect of the Department of Rome, and, as such, directed the Public Works that would take place from 1809 to 1814. The aim was to prepare a splendid visit of Napoleon to Rome, which never occurred; in June 1811 the monuments of the Forum were illuminated to celebrate the birth in March of Napoleon's son, the King of Rome.

From an urban point of view, the conditions of the city at the beginning of the nineteenth century were disastrous, and it was urgent to prepare an intervention strategy. De Tournon makes a vast exposition of the problems that Rome presents and the actions envisaged in a letter addressed to the Count of Montaliver, Minister of the Interior, during his stay in Paris in July 1811 (Patrizi and Giovannoni, 1927). As we have already said, De Tournon had the architects already operating in Rome before the French occupation (G. Valadier, G. Camporese, R. Stern), although always under French supervision (LM Berthault, G. de Gisors), in an interesting cultural exchange.

In this program, De Tournon divided the type of interventions into two categories: the conservation of ancient monuments and the sanitation and beautification of the city (*"abbellimenti di Roma"*). De Tournon clearly says in his letter that returning the Forum to its original level was impossible. The first category of works included all the excavation works that would uncover the buildings and monuments of the Forum, their conservation and subsequent connection through an "archaeological tour" (Capitoline Hill-Colosseo, Piazza del Popolo), for which the demolition of existing houses and barns in the area was necessary.

The sanitation and beautification of the city focused on the opening of squares (Colonna Traiana, Portico di Ottavia), the widening of streets (Spina dei Borghi, connection of the road from Naples to Corso), the cleaning and channelling of the Tevere and the construction of bridges (or rehabilitation of some already existing), slaughterhouses, markets and cemeteries. On the other hand, state buildings were requested, especially the convents and monasteries expropriated by Napoleon as a result of the suppression of religious orders, to be used as schools, academies or hospitals. The monastery of Santa Francesca Romana had become one of these.

All these proposals were accompanied by their corresponding budget and calendar, detailing the number of workers and the time provided for each of the works. It is important to highlight their social dimension, providing work for a large number of people (approximately 2,000 workers were hired to remove the rubble around the monuments), especially those who until then lived from the charity offered by the suppressed monasteries. The work was organized in such a way that the non-specialized workers were in charge of the excavations of the monuments, while the craftsmen were engaged in 'beautification' work.

The works also had their detractors, such as Hillard (1853) who described a scene of "desolation that is not beautiful; a ruin that is not picturesque". Because of the fact that the studies did not advance as they should have, there was much confusion about the true identity of the monuments. He also refered to the drawing that an English architect, Charles Robert Cockerell (1788–1863), made of the conserved buildings of the Forum (González-Longo, 2015), whose idealization did not correspond to the reality in situ.

With the project in 1811, by Camporese and Valadier, *Le jardin du Capitol* (Capitoline Garden), Napoleon wanted to link the monuments of the Roman Forum and Palatine through gardens and public tree-lined boulevards, creating a monumental entrance to Rome from Naples, as the one created for Charles V discussed before, and following the lines of trees planted in the Roman Forum in the seventeenth century (González-Longo, 2015). The boulevard of the Via S. Gregorio is reminiscent of this design intention. The same idea, substantially Roman, would prevail after the reunification of 1870 and at the time of Mussolini.

In February 1813, two French architects-inspectors were sent to Rome. The official motive was, in the case of landscape architect Louis-Martin Berthault- who had published in 1788 prints of English gardens and designed the Malmaison gardens in 1805-, to contribute to the project related to the *Jardin du Grand Caesar*, in the Pincio-Piazza del Popolo area. The architect Guy de Gisors (called *Le Jeune*), who was also in charge of conservation works, was commissioned with the inspection of the *Piazza del Pantheon*, the *Piazza della Colonna Traiana* and the *Piazza della Fontana di Trevi*, including the buildings that were to be demolished, and carrying out the new projects. It seems that in Paris they were not happy with the projects by the Roman architects. They believed that a more uniform approach was needed, established according to a rigid geometric scheme inspired by classical models. Thus the real reason for the visit of Berthault and Gisors, who would remain in Rome for a year and were appointed honorary members of the *Accademia di San Luca*, was the realization of projects for the city according to the criteria of the French *Conseil des Batiments*, in addition to controlling all excavation and conservation work that was being carried out. The main objective was to give the Capital of the ancient Roman Empire a dignified aspect as the second city of the New Napoleonic Empire. On March 25, 1813, Berthault presented the project to the *Commission des Embellissements* (Beautification) of Rome, emphasizing on the landscape and accessibility aspects and the project was approved by the commission on May 13 (Boyer, 1943; González-Longo, 2015).

Gisors also reported that some buildings which were consolidated thanks to the enormous stimulus of Pius VII (Colosseum, Temple of Peace, lateral support of the Arch of Titus), were at risk of collapsing. He explained his conservation criteria, proposing to rebuild the masses of the unstable parts in their forms and proportions, for example, in the Arch of Titus, without damaging the lower voussoirs when replacing the upper voussoirs in their original position, after having reestablished, either in stone or brick, the volumes (Boyer, 1943).

Much later, De Tournon will write a book of great interest (De Tournon, 1831), explaining the precedents, forecasts and actions taken. He understood Rome, in its character as a historic city and monumental centre, and valued it as a unique city, while integrating the needs of everyday life. He laments the confiscations of the first invasion of Rome and recalls his classification of the monuments of Rome and province into: Ancient Ruined Monuments, Ancient Preserved Monuments and Modern Buildings of Sacred or Profane Use. He established one of the priorities of the work: to find the old level of the Forum and expose the bases of the columns. He mentions the origin of this idea, which was in fact Raphael, expressed in a letter to Pope Leo X, where he proposed this intervention. As we will see later G. Boni will resume this ambitious idea.

The method followed is also exposed: they bought a large number of houses, and excavated, arranging the soil and debris in a way that did not prevent other excavations, repaired the monuments at risk of collapse and carried out drainage for rainwater in depressed areas. All this at a time when the science and techniques of archaeological excavation and conservation began to be delineated and applied to the most important monuments of Rome. Unfortunately, as Tournon himself reports, to reach the 'old' level, all the ground around the monuments, which we now know contains very important evidence about the buildings, was reused in other works at the Forum or transported to distant places (De Tournon, 1831). In this way, an invaluable source of information on the medieval and later phases of the Forum was lost. Giacomo Boni would later take part of the blame for the damage caused by this excavation.

Thus, in less than five years, a plan was realized that would be the germ of a whole series of future initiatives, starting with Pius VII, who returned to Rome and continued the works begun but without the French financing. It is not entirely clear what are the specific ideas and proposals that can be attributed to French and Italian architects. It is clear that the contribution of the latter was substantial, including practical aspects such as drainage of the area. These works will continue after Napoleon abdication and the fall of the French government in May 1814 when the administration is again Pontifical after a Neapolitan provisional government. The project by Camporese, approved by Monsignor Agostino Rivarola (the equivalent of De Tournon in the commission of the *abbellimenti*), in which he proposed to join the Roman Forum to the walk around the Colosseum, is preserved. Although the events did not allow this *Giardino del Campidoglio* (Capitol Garden) project to complete, the Forum underwent a profound transformation, and its picturesque appearance, with grazing cows, changed to become a desolate place of archaeological excavation and entertainment for the aristocracy (González-Longo, 2015).

5.4 Demolition and Reintegration of the Monastery of Santa Maria Nova

As we have already mentioned, the Napoleonic invasion of Italy in 1797 had produced the temporary closure of the monastery, leaving only the Procure there. With the subsequent proclamation of the Republic in 1798, the monastery of S. Maria Nova is suppressed and the church is desecrated and reduced to storage. Bernini's bronze group disappears along with another decoration of the *Confessione* and the bell (as we have said, probably melted down to make cannons) and the body of S. Francesca Romana was transferred to Tor de' Specchi for protection.

In 1801 the monastery was reinstated and the Saint was returned. With the arrival in 1809 of the French Administration and the so-called "*abbellimenti di Roma*" the monks were forced to leave again the monastery in 1810, going back to their respective nations, in Parke order to demolish it. In the plan that Valadier prepares for the earthworks, levelling and demolition of houses, we clearly see the area of the monastery that was to be demolished (González-Longo, 2015).

In 1810 the demolitions of houses and barns in the Roman Forum were decided, including a part of the monastery of Santa Francesca Romana. It was also intended to excavate the Forum to its former level. The main Bureau of the *Commissione degli Abbellimenti* was located in the building of the monastery of Santa Francesca Romana, and the work around it began on 15 October. Between 1811 and 1812 the demolition of the part of the monastery between the church and the Arch of Titus took place for the creation of the Capitoline Garden. Henry Parke's painting from around 1810, which was commissioned by his teacher, Sir John Soane, shows the facade of the section of the demolished monastery; watercolours by Joseph Mallord William Turner of 1819 shows the new facade (González-Longo, 2015). Undoubtedly, the demolition was traumatic for the area, which had served as a background for so many drawings and paintings, including the portraits of the Duke of Hamilton during his trip to Rome (González-Longo, 2015).

The architects Camporese and Valadier directed the works. This action was one of the direct consequences of the fundamental idea behind the Archaeological Park: to isolate the ancient monuments, in this case the Temple of Venus and Rome and the Arch of Titus. Although, as seen in the project plans, the demolition of the monastery was intended to be total (González-Longo, 2015), only the southeast area of the monastery was demolished, from the southern bays of the main cloister to the Arch of Titus. The project supported the charitable work being carried out at S. Francesca Romana, where stoves, water pipes and a refectory were built to feed the workers. It was also intended to demolish part of the church, turning it into a cruciform form, to better expose the Roman remains (González-Longo, 2015). At the already mentioned session of 25 March 1813, in the presence of Berthault, the Commission for the Beautification of Rome decides to keep the church (both for architectural and religious reasons) but reducing it in its dimensions (De Tournon, 1831; La Padula, 1969). The demolition also had the scope to undercover the remains of the Temple of Venus and Rome, Nero's vestibule and other unknown monuments. De Tournon describes also works carried out to uncover the view of Santa Francesca (which he considered a beautiful church) and the Arch of Titus from the Roman Forum and the precarious state of the Arch and the area. The intention was to join the valleys of the Roman Forum and the Colosseum (De Tournon, 1831)

Apart from the first-hand historical report, De Tournon's text is a manifesto of values. The veneration that the Romans felt for the church was reason enough to save it, and this value prevailed over the aesthetic of making classical monuments more visible, not forgetting the nationalist component, since Pope Gregory XI, who as we have seen is buried in the church, was French. De Tournon's comment on the conservation of the Arch of Titus, which we have already mention and that we will discuss later, also indicates that the intervention had a more Roman origin than French.

When in 1815 d. Placido Ciucci becomes the abbot of the monastery, he found it in terrible circumstances. Between 1815 and 1820 works are carried out in the building under the direction of the master mason Giovanni Conca. In 1816 Valadier and Camporese were still involved in the works concerning the isolation of the Arch of Titus and part of the Temple of Venus and Rome. It included the design of the new south façade of the monastery, which was left with the scars of the demolition. However, it seems that they disagreed about the new design (Gonzàlez-Longo, 2015) and, according to vews of around that time, the facade built was the one proposed by Camporese. He wanted to expose a smaller section of the monastery in front of the south wall of the cella of Rome, while Valadier wanted to incorporate it into a longer, nine-bay, façade. Unfortunately the drawing showing the existing façade and Valadier's proposed one, which was once at the archive of the monastery, has now disappeared. The smaller section of the fabric was also subsequently demolished and the façade is now a uniform, seven-bay, elevation (Figure 5.1) (González-Longo, 2015).

The resulting facade shows the architects' talent in encompassing in a new 'structural sheath' the fabric resulting from the demolition of the monastery wing, which left the façade with irregular openings and at different heights. Their ability is also apparent in the plan, resolving the connection between the old and new fabric through flared window reveals in several directions (Figures. 4.7, 5.1). This way of intervening, conserving the existing fabric and simply covering it with a new 'structural sheath', similar to what Lambardi did in the church before, is very different from what some authors like Ciampi consider: that Valadier made the Santa Francesca monastery almost new (Ciampi, 1887). Valadier himself remembers the work through a sketch in his third notebook, written in 1832, giving 1810 as the date of the proposal (Debenedetti, 1985). With the work of this new facade, it is demonstrated that, as Giulio Carlo Argan has said, more than through an act of faith in the unsurpassed perfection of the ancients, neoclassicism was reached through a critical process of reduction (with Milizia as a guide) (Argan, 1979), and we will add, an intention of simplicity, like many other artists of the time.

Although the works continued under the control of Monsignor Rivarola, who retains Camporese and Valadier as architect, working also in the Temple of Venus and Rome, the Olivetans has also a role to play. In 1814, after four years of exile, and thanks to the Pope, about thirty Olivetanos monks had returned to the monastery and wrote a series of requests to Monsignor

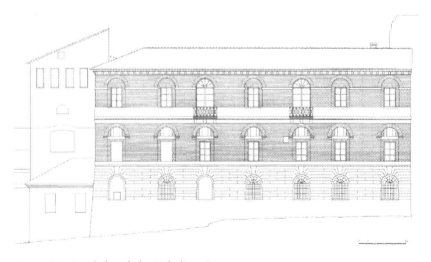

Figure 5.1 South facade by Valadier (A.)

Rivarola to have their land returned. In their report of 27 November 1814, they requested the construction of a modest boundary wall, as advised by the architect Camporese. He supervised the excavations of the Forum in the years 1810–13 and in the Forum of Trajan in 1812–13. He also took care of the conservation of the Temple of Vespasian and Titus, where he inscribed in the new elements of the Vespasian temple 'RESTITUERUNT' (Boyer, 1943), a pioneering example of identifying the new elements. His work seems to be largely in the shadow of Valadier and probably deserves more credit than has been given to his role in the project. Valadier is considered to have designed the southern façade of the monastery, but the controversy with Camporese seems to indicate a prominent role of the latter in the project.

5.5 The Arch of Titus . . . or the Arch of Pius?

The Arch of Titus is a recurring example when talking about the modern concept of conservation and an important case to reflect on architectural conservation at this time. This marble arch went from being an isolated triumphal arch to a mere gate of a fortification and again an isolated arch, as we have explained. The arch, which presents the oldest example of the Roman Composite Order, was probably built in the years AD 81–82 at the top of the Velia in honour of Titus, Vespasian's son, after his death. As Coarelli (1989) already considered, its partial conservation is due to the fact that it was inserted in the fortifications of the Frangipane, discussed before, but it was also more damaged for this reason, since an element was added on top to improve its defensive ability. The arch has been a source of inspiration for artists and architects (González-Longo, 2015). Peruzzi drew the elevation with measurements and Palladio reconstructed graphically the monument. Serlio gave its dimensions in detail and noted that the ornamentation of most of the arches in Rome does not coincide with the writings of Vitrubio. He believed that it was because the arches were built with remains of other buildings and because perhaps the architects did not respect the rules when building the commemorative arches in rush (Hart and Hicks, 1996).

Piranesi's drawings show the state of the arch at the end of the eighteenth century (González-Longo, 2015). As we have mentioned, the arch was attached to the monastery, and Auguste-Jean-Marie Guénepin (1780–1842, Grand Prix 1805), who made a hypothetical reconstruction of the arch of Titus in 1809–1810, documents in his drawing the exact condition of the arch before the restoration (González-Longo, 2015). Desgodets drew the monument in 1676–1677 and there were later discrepancies in the various graphical reconstructions: Giovanni Antonio Dosio (Borsi, 1976), Bellori (1690) and Giacomo Lauro (1699).

Giuseppe Valadier finally reinstated the arch in 1822, after dismantling it and rebuilding the missing parts with travertine. This could have been directly influenced by the report that Gisors had written in 1813 to Paris, in the same lines of intervention, as we have already mentioned. This report was written four months after Canova had received instruction from three Roman architects nominated by the Accademia di S. Luca (Pasquale Belli, Virginio Bracci and Andrea Vivi) to repair the arch by strengthening the brick buttress towards the Palatine, covering the holes of the brick structure left after the demolition of part of the Monastery of S. Francesca Romana (Linstrum, 1982).

Valadier (1822) read and published the details of the intervention at the Roman Academy of Archaeology, starting by noting the value of the monument: the arch was built in honour of the victories of Titus against the Jews, including the sacking of Jerusalem and the destruction of its temple, and it was the first built with the Composite Order. He also pointed out that it is located at the highest point of the *Via Sacra* (*summa sacra via*), the destruction suffered by the arch and the description of the evidence of its design comparing it with the arches of Ancona and Benevento, dedicated to Trajan. Valadier explained the structural condition of the monument, how the Olivetan granary had been built to the east and a buttress to the west and that the monument still had structural problems. It also explains how, by their position, the original elements were identified. Valadier proceeded to the disassembly of the monument, verifying that, although the blocks were designed to have metal connection elements, they were not put in place, which also explains the structural problems. He further comments on this fraudulent and unfortunately usual practice of stealing during the execution of buildings.

Valadier also clarifies that the demolitions suffered in the Roman Forum, although they did not allow the return of its former splendour, they served at least to rediscover the old roads and to restore monuments such as the Arch of Titus, which reinstatement—Valadier calls it 'reparation' (*risarcimento*)—had been commissioned to Stern in 1817. He started it in 1819 with Valadier's help, but died the following year. The intervention of the Arch of Titus was actually devised by Stern, although later conducted differently. Valadier's explanation seems to indicate that Stern's preference would be to consolidate rather than rebuilt. In the drawing by G. Taylor and E. Cresy (1821) we see the wooden structure placed to support the arch, and in the legend it is said that Stern wanted to hold the arch while removing the modern additives, with the intention of leaving only the original elements and achieving structural stability through the use of new travertine blocks, marking the difference with the original ones, of marble (Linstrum, 1982; González-Longo, 2015). Perhaps Stern would have undertaken the work in a very different way if we consider the case of the Colosseum. His intervention there, adding a brick buttress to support the arches, "freezing" the collapse, was rated as "unacceptable" by Gisors. The influence of Gisors could then have led to a change of approach in Valadier's intervention in the Colosseum in 1823–29, copying the original forms but building a brick buttress painted to resemble the original material. In those years, among many other monuments, he worked on the Temple of Venus and Rome (Linstrum, 1982).

Instead of holding the arch as Stern would have wanted, Valadier (perhaps with the help of Camporese), dismantled it and rebuilt it with the appropriate support, covering the fabric with travertine and copying the elements of the old decoration. Stern had commissioned his student Pietro Bosio the drawings for reconstruction and Valadier used them to continue the work, as well as using the travertine elements that Stern had already commissioned, which suggests that he had already completed the project before he died; perhaps Valadier would have used his project, including Bosio's drawings.

Valadier (1822) refers in his publication of the project to the detailed removal of the remains of the arch that Desgodets had done in 1676–1677 (Desgodets, 1682), when the monument was measured very accurately, but due to the complexity of overlapping fabrics, some of the interpretations were incorrect. He makes an explanation about the identification of non-original elements, based on the geometry of the monument with respect to the original elements. In the publication also explains how he dismantled the upper two thirds of the arch and put them back in their correct position, but he calls this operation reinstatement rather than reconstruction. Valadier and Fea made a revised version of Desgodets (Fea and Valadier, 1822) in which they denied any possibility of previous reconstructions, as some critics of their intervention had proclaimed, noting that in the past it was usual to take the material from the monuments, not add it (Linstrum, 1982).

Although we would like to see the intervention in the arch as the architectural version of what was being done with the classic statues, in particular the Cavaceppi's approach we have talked about previously (Racheli, 2007), the operation was quite different. In his report, Valadier breaks the myth of the creation modern conservation criteria, and shows us that the simplification of the forms was due to reasons of economy, as Miarelli Mariani always mentioned in his lectures. However, the main objectives of the intervention were achieved: to return solidity and resistance, paying the utmost respect to the monument, finding its original quality after centuries of decline and ensuring its preservation over time.

Thus the Arch of Titus is considered as the first project in which two of the principles of modern conservation were used: the differentiation of materials (new travertine to reintegrate the lost parts of the original Pentelic marble) and the simplification of forms, limiting only to creating total volumes, without detail. For example, the original fluted columns were reintegrated as smooth.

Watkin (2011) considers this intervention a victory of archaeology over art, with the decision to celebrate, in his opinion, the temporal value of the restorer's skill, rather than the eternal vision of the original architect. This is a very valid point that touches on the centre of the debate about what conservation is. Watkin goes on to say that the incorporation of these principles into the 1964 Venice Charter had disastrous consequences, since only the conservation of some fragments is achieved, instead of the visual coherence of the monument.

This type of intervention is later developed into extreme reconstruction and will become at the hands of Eugène-Emmanuel Viollet-le-Duc (1814–1879) restoration, as his own definition demonstrates (Viollet-le-Duc, 1869): "Restoring a building is not maintaining, repairing or rebuilding it, it is restoring it to a complete state that may never have existed." Viollet-le-Duc performed restorations in French cathedrals, such as Chartres, Amiens, Vezelay and Paris, promoting the removal of recent interventions with the aim of reintegrating the building into its original unit and its stylistic purity. As regards the *lacune*, he considers that they must be rebuilt (or built for the first time) as they would be originally or as they should have been done. Viollet-le-Duc was the first professor of art history that reorganized the École des Beaux-Arts, and Vitet supported his curriculum reforms in 1863 with his emphasis on originality rather than emulation.

Prosper Mérimée (1803–1870) succeeded Vitet as an inspector of monuments in 1834, and his work was fundamental in the protection of French monuments. Stendhal, in describing the Roman ruins and the interventions that happened around 1828, including the Arch of Titus, criticized the reconstruction of Valadier and the its loss of authenticity (Stendhal, 1826, 1828, 1829; Linstrum, 1882). Stendhal's criticism was not unique: the intervention of the arch of Titus was controversial in its time. Cardinal Pacca wrote about his anxiety when he saw the dismantled arch, and Cardinal Consalvi believed that complementary studies would be needed and that the arch should not have been dismantled, because it was not anymore the Arch of Pius, but the Arch of Titus.

It was Quatrèmere de Quincy (1832) who gave the seal of approval to this method of conservation and established it as a model. A lawyer and theorist and historian of eighteenth century architecture, he was the leader of the French Academy in Napoleonic times. In 1815, he became Intendant Général des Arts et Monuments Publics. Quatremère's theories reflected those of the Académie, which considered that the Greco-Roman style is the only one suitable for architecture. But it also promulgated more modern ideas, such as the conservation of works of art in situ, against the conglomerate museums promoted by Napoleon. The voice 'Restaurer' of his Dictionnaire historique de l'Architecture (Quatrèmere de Quincy, 1832), uses the arch of Titus and the Pantheon as examples, but more from an environmental and contextual point of view, without going into the detail of how conserve the material. It has been since taken as a model, perhaps without enough scrutiny.

5.6 The Love for the Ruins and The *Grand Tour*

As we have already said, the tradition of the study trip in Rome as an obligatory part of the Grand Tour had already begun in the sixteenth century, and had its splendour in the eighteenth century. In the case of Goethe, Winckelmann, Lord Byron, Stendhal and Turner, it was a true cultural and sometimes physical appropriation of the object of study. During the nineteenth century, the opportunity for the trips was extended to a larger population.

Lord Byron was in Rome for four weeks in 1817 and describes the city in ruins. J.M.W. Turner (1775–1851), who had a great fascination and affinity with Rome, visits the city in 1819 and 1828 and paints the complex of the Temple of Venus and Rome—Santa Francesca Romana (González-Longo, 2015). His painting of the Roman Forum 'Modern Rome—Campo Vaccino' in 1839 is the last of his series on the city, based on the numerous sketches and notes of the Roman Forum from his 1819 trip. Turner represents Rome, the New and the Ancient together and is a testament to the political and cultural restoration of Rome after the Napoleonic Wars. In 1836, *Blackwood's Magazine* published criticism of Turner's exposed paintings that aroused the anger of his admirer John Ruskin. In the July-December 1839 issue, the magazine continued to criticize the artist. It is clear that Turner was breaking with the representation in use and Ruskin described him as the one that contained the light of nature (Ruskin, 1853)

Excavations at the Roman Forum were continued by Professor Antonio Nibby, who replaced his rival Fea in office in 1827, creating an appearance of chaos in the area, criticized by Louis I, king of Bavaria (Scherer, 1955). Unlike Fea, Nibby promoted and conducted in-depth excavations and demolitions of modern buildings and acknowledged that the one which was called the Temple of Peace was actually the Basilica of Maxentius. In 1827–9 he excavated and completely cleaned the Temple of Venus and Rome, whose excavations had begun in 1813–14, and discovered the seals of Hadrian on the bricks. A letter dated 13 April 1830 from Charles C. F. Greville (Greville, 1874) describes the environment in Rome among visitors to the excavations, and there was evidently a great degree of interpretation without much scientific evidence. In 1839 Luigi Canina succeeds Nibby as Commissioner of Antiquities.

Meanwhile, the winners of the Grand Prix of the *Académie Royale d'Architecture* and their successor, the *École des Beaux-Arts* de Paris and the pensioners of the Academy of France in Rome produced a series of detailed watercolour surveys of the main Roman monuments, in their present condition and as they would be originally, based on the works of Nibby and other archaeologists. In the 1860s students protested the rigidity of approach. In 1867 Julien Guadet (1834–1908), architect (winner of Grand Prix in 1864), professor and theorist, declared the absurdity of rebuilding monuments, similar to whether he wanted to complete the work of Cicero or Tacitus. He summarized his position with a brief aphorism: "Archaeology is the enemy" (Watkin, 2011). He published his theory in 1901–4 where he explains that architecture has only one reason to exist: to be built.

Émile Zola spent time in Rome in 1894 to write his novel "Roma" and calls the Roman Forum the 'cemetery' of the city. Artists continue to travel to Rome during the nineteenth century and to paint and write their impressions. Studies also progress; between 1855 and 1872 Ferdinand Gregorovious wrote his History of the City of Rome in the Middle Ages and Ettore Roesler-Franz created his famous paintings.

5.7 Architectural Conservation in the Second Half of the Nineteenth-Century: Restoration Versus Conservation

Despite the innovation of the restoration of the Arch of Titus, the discipline of conservation advanced in different ways. In England, the Catholic bishop John Milner (1752–1826) and his critique of the interventions of James Wyatt in Salisbury Cathedral is one of the first evidences of a debate on the conservation of churches, along with the Camden Society magazine 'The Ecclesiologist', since 1841. In 1846, Freeman publishes 'Principles of Church Restoration' making a distinction between "eclectic restoration" (when the building is returned to the oldest time) and "destructive restoration" (when this ancient period does not exist and has to be rebuilt) (Racheli, 2007).

The situation deteriorates in the nineteenth century when the formalism of architectural styles prevails, new buildings copy forms of the past and old buildings are restored privileging one of the phases of its history, usually the original. Pugin in his 'Contrasts' of 1838 declared himself against the arbitrary restorations of medieval churches, in which original elements were replaced, stating that it would be better to leave it in ruins. Ruskin continues this thought in 'The Seven Lamps of Architecture' (Ruskin, 1849) which will then influence the Anti-Restoration Movement and the Society for the Protection of Ancient Buildings (SPAB), founded in 1877 by William Morris, still active today and subscribing to the same manifesto. It considers architecture as a long decaying, and restoration a "strange and most fatal idea" and a "forgery" and reminds that buildings were conserved by changing them "in the unmistakable fashion of the time" making them "interesting and instructive and could by no possibility mislead" (SPAB, 1877).

Although Ruskin's famous controversy with Viollet-Ruskin was never direct and his real positions were not as extreme as historiography has led us to believe, this manifesto consolidated the idea in Britain that restoration was destruction. What is true is that Ruskin and Viollet responded to their context (Clark, 1964; Di Stefano, 1969). Ruskin rejected the dehumanization of industrial processes and proposed that the means to consolidate the building, as a moral position, should be rejected. Viollet sustained the use of materials and techniques as similar as possible to the originals, the revaluation of reason and the national identity, through a colossal work in search of a new architectural expression that will influence the next generations of architects in Europe.

Giovanni Morelli (1816–1891) (he had as pseudonyms: Iwan -or Ivan- Lermolieff, Nicholas -or Nicolaus- Schäffer and Johannes Schwarze) was an art historian who developed a method of knowledge consisting of identifying attributions through the study of characteristics of the artists. Morelli served in the *Risorgimento* movement of Italy in the 1860s, becoming Senator with the Italian unification of 1873 and directing many government commissions on art, and in particular those enacting legislation that prohibited the export of works of art and the standardization of conservation practices in the museums. The Morelli Method (Wollheim, 1973), called "scientific" art history during the nineteenth and early twentieth century, identified the artist's hand in its literal form and in the figurative sense, contrasted with the historical and documentary method prevailing at the time. His method influences not also art historians such as Bernard Berenson or Adolfo Venturi, but also others such as Sigmund Freud and Arthur Conan Doyle.

Camillo Boito (1836–1914) was an architect and writer. In 1856 his teacher, Pietro Selvàtico (1803–1880), called him to teach at the Accademia di Belli Arti in Venice, which would be followed in 1860 by a chair at the Brera Academy in Milan, where he would teach for 48 years. Boito was influenced by Selvàtico, historian and architect who was opposed to Neoclassicism and had a great enthusiasm for the Gothic. Boito tried a categorization by type of intervention. The conservation versus restoration debate, with Viollet-le Duc promoting the 'Stylistic Restoration' (*ripristino*) and John Ruskin the romantic treatment of monuments concluded with the proposal of Camillo Boito at the III Congress of Architects and Engineers in Rome in 1883, considered as the first Conservation Charter. This was based on the principles of minimal intervention and the clear distinction of the added parts, which would establish the so-called 'Philological Conservation' and would greatly influence the subsequent 'Scientific Conservation' of Gustavo Giovannoni.

Boito's proposal was based on eight points to take into account in the "honest" conservation of monuments to ensure their authenticity, clearly identifying the original material, and ensuring a scientific method in the works, including its documentation. The eight points were:

1. The differentiation of style between the old and the new;
2. The differentiation of materials between old and new;

3. The removal of mouldings and unnecessary decoration in the new elements;
4. The exhibition near the monument of the original disassembled material of the monument;
5. The inscription of the date or other symbol in the new elements;
6. Fixing on the monument a commemorative plaque describing the conservation work carried out;
7. Documentation of the conservation work through reports and photographs, documentation that must remain in the same monument or in another nearby public building. This requirement can be replaced by the publication of the material;
8. The conservation work must be visible.

Although, as we have seen, none of these points was truly new, Boito managed to gather them in the same document. We can recognize in these points the origin of the principles that since then will form the basis of the legislation in conservation in many European countries; Boito himself helped to shape the Italian laws for the protection of monuments of the early twentieth century, with international repercussion.

Boito had a great influence on the Italian architectural culture of the time, although he demonstrated contradictions between his written principles and his built work. He restored several buildings, including the Porta Ticinese in Milan (1856–61), which presents these contradictions, the church and campanile of Santi Maria e Donato in Murano (inspired by the theory and technique of Viollet-le-Duc) and the basilica of S. Antonio de Padua. He also made new work such as the *scalone* of palazzo Franchetti in Venice, the Palazzo delle Debite (1872–77) in Padua and the Civic Museum (1889) in Padua, the cemetery and hospital of Gallarate and the House of rest for musicians in Milan (1895–9), funded by Giuseppe Verdi (Boito was the brother of musician Arrigo Boito). He showed, however, a limited vision and certain provincialism with his opposition to iron architecture (Racheli, 2007).

5.8 The Transformations for *Roma Capitale* and the Monumental Complex at the End of the Nineteenth Century

The nineteenth century was a time of uncertainty for the church and monastery of Santa Francesca Romana, and started in a very intense way, as we have seen. After the Napoleonic era, Rome was dominated by Austria and declared a republic in 1849, but France restored, under its protection, papal power in 1850. The rest of Italy was under Austria.

Between 1828–1829, interventions were carried out in the church, and it was discovered that the core of the walls was composed of the marbles of the Temple of Venus and Rome. In 1831 Gregory XVI closed all the

Olivetan monasteries of the Pontifical State and donated the assets to the Cenobite Camaldolese. The monastery of S. Maria Nova remains as simple General Procure, with the name of "*Hospicio di S. Francesca Romana*" and the control of an Economic Administrator, agent of the Camaldoleses. In 1837 there was a period of plague in Rome and the hospice played an important role in the fight against the disease and its consequences.

Pius IX reintegrates the Olivetans into the monastery in 1846. Between 1856 and 1861 the Cardinal-Protector of the Order, Giacomo Piccolomini, lived and died in the abbatial apartment, composed of ten rooms and a chapel, oriented south, towards the Palatine. In 1866 the musician Franz Liszt rented this abbey apartment of the monastery, where he remained until 1870. Meanwhile, in 1860 the spaces of the old refectory to the north, and four rooms of the Celleraria had been rented, with their windows, four of which were blocked, to Giacomo Mazzetti, a merchant, for grain storage with access from the north; when the grain was beaten, a portion of the vault of the old Refectory collapsed. Since then the stability of this area has been compromised. Between 1867 and 1870 the architect Giuseppe Reibaldi repairs the church, expanding and decorating the underground area.

Although photography was invented in the years 1840–50, it was not extensively used for archaeological excavations until fifty years later. However, archaeologist J.H. Parker made a series of photographs between 1865 and 1877 that are a record of great importance in documenting the excavations of the time (Parker, 1879).

In 1870 Italy reunified and in 1871 Rome became the capital of Italy. Thus begins the time of the "Third Rome", after the old one and that of the popes. But the city was not fully prepared for it. A fever of works started in the brand new capital and, with these, strong speculation, and, as a consequence, demolitions. A restructuring of the centre of Rome was planned with the Royal Residence in the Quirinale, as main reference, with four main arteries: Termini-Piazza SS. Apostoli, Piazza del Popolo-S. Giovanni in Laterano, Corso-Colosseum and via Condotti-S. Giovanni dei Fiorentini. The Regulatory Plan of 1873, included a complex of main and secondary arteries, longitudinal and transversal, fragmenting the historic centre.

With the Reunification, the construction of the new capital is frantic and many demolitions of old monuments are carried out. With the Law of 19 June 1873, religious orders are suppressed again and the monastery of Santa Francesca Romana is suppressed for public utility; most of the building became part of the Ministry of Public Instruction. Buildings were demanded for collections of objects of art or considered precious because their antiquity, like all those inside the Roman and Palatine Forum; property and premises were expropriated. The Ministry, now called of Cultural Assets, still occupies the building. A minimum part was reserved for the monks (the rector and his assistants), who were granted a secondary income and continued to have a municipal shelter (hospice). A series of plans produced then mark the division of the property (González-Longo, 2015).

But only part was used for the collections; most of the monastery of Santa Francesca Romana was transformed into barracks and later into apartments for the families of employees and guards, arranged around the cloister, for which they blocked the arches and erected partitions for their domestic demands (González-Longo, 2015). The part towards the Arch of Titus, behind the facade of Valadier, including the abbatial apartment previously occupied by Listz was dedicated to housing of the Ministry staff. In 1875 the intention was to return the building to its original state, and in 1887 after 226 years, Leo XIII gives the church a presbyterial title. In 1890 part of the wall of the cella of Rome was conserved but the works had to stop (Boni, n.d.c).

The directional "New Rome", extended within the boundary of the walls, between the Esquiline and the Porta Pia, with the axes of via Nazionale and via XX Settembre, clearly delineated by the Quintino Sella Plan, which, with the Haussmann plan in Paris as reference, proclaims in the city the union of Science, Culture and Politics, in a bourgeois ideological model that denies the concept of periphery, thus preventing the eventual formation of large masses of workers that could create conflict. In the Regulatory Plan of 1883 a polycentric city is proposed, but with the crisis of 1887 the result was very different from the objectives of the Plan, with a city totally different from the proposed model. In 1909, Edmondo di Sanjust di Teulada elaborates the Regulatory Plan of Rome. The themes and contradictions of Roman architectural culture are found here again, at a crossroads of technique and politics. For the first time, in the Exhibition of the City of Rome at the 1884 Turin Exhibition, it appeared divided into 'ancient', 'medieval' and 'modern' sections, seeking to relate the city's architecture with its historical traditions. Medieval Rome is valued, with the position of Camilo Boito as starting point. The theme of "minor Rome" appears, recognizing the artistic value of small buildings, acknowledging their environmental value and their connection with historical and popular traditions.

The large number of proposals for the plan of the Historic Centre generally consisted of the layout of a road network, 'ordering' the traditional urban fabric, valuing some nodes through connections. From the pre-existing city, some buildings or complexes that retain a symbolic value, or to which a new function is attributed, were chosen and connected by means of axes. All this leads to the coexistence of elements on a different scale, with different design approached and with a great contradiction between the conservation of the picturesque character and the functional demands of the modern city. Since them this has been a problem to solve in each historic city.

With regard to the Forum area, Pietro Rosa excavated the Palatine for Napoleon III of France, and after the reunification, for the government of Italy. He was succeeded by Giuseppe Fiorelli in 1878–80 and then by Rodolfo

Lanciani until 1885. These were times of great activity in the Forum and the last remaining elms that flanked the avenue created for the entrance of Carlos V were cut. The dominant antiquarianism in the eighteenth and nineteenth centuries is transformed into a new archaeology. The extensive campaigns carried out, however, had a clear lack of overall integration of projects that would facilitate the final presentation of the excavations and their urban integration (Bianchi Bandinelli, 1961; Vlad Borrelli, 2006). With the clear antecedent of the French era, the common element of the urban culture of the period is public service as an element of prestige and the park as a monumental space, which reaches the point of proposing again the creation of an "archaeological park", achieving, through urban *sventramenti* (guttings), particular visuals.

Guido Baccelli (1830–1916), physician and politician was Minister of Education several times in the late nineteenth century. During his tenure the monumental zone or "*Passeggiata archeologica*" was valued urbanistically, beginning with an important excavation and presentation campaign of the Roman Forum, including the discovery of the House of the Vestales, excavated in 1882–83 by Rodolfo Lanciani. Bacelli's influence was so important that even Roman Forum tourist cards were made with his portrait (González-Longo, 2015). In part also as a reaction to the uncontrolled development of the first years of Rome as Capital, and with the intention of urban planning and artistic and cultural assessment of the monumental zone, Baccelli presented to Parliament in 1887 a plan for the monumental area, which became law in a few months. The law linked a vast area within the archaeological park: the Roman Forum with a small part of the Imperial Fora, the Colosseum, the Baths of Trajan, part of the Celio, Palatine, Forum Boario, Circus Massimus, Aventine, Terme di Caracalla, via Appia to the Aurelian wall. The complexity of the work and the planned expropriations meant that the ten years initially planned for the project extended over decades. Today a new structure is in place and Santa Francesca Romana and the Temple of Venus and Rome are part of the Archaeological Park of the Colosseum (*Parco del Colosseo*).

5.9 The First Vienna School, Alois Riegl and the *Kunstwollen*

There were other fundamental developments in the field of architecture, archaeology, history and architectural conservation and restoration at the end of the 19th century to consider. It is important to mention them in order to better understand the work of Giacomo Boni and his contemporaries, which we will discuss later on.

Franz Wickhoff (1853–1909), a historian of Roman and Paleo-Christian art, was one of the founders of the so-called first "Vienna School" of art historians. In 1879 he became an inspector of the Austrian Museum of Decorative Arts and since 1882 he also taught as a professor of art history at the University of Vienna. His method integrated the disciplines of art history, archaeology, philosophy and connoisseurship. He was interested in the Renaissance and its relationship with the classical era. He met Morelli, and his method greatly influenced him. A scholar also of the *Zeitgeist* in art, one of his fundamental contributions was to revalue Roman art-, which since Winckelmann had been considered a decadent art, copied from Greek art-, as well as the Paleo-Christian art, of which he highlighted his unique narrative and aesthetics. He also criticized as artificial the periodization of art history, the linear vision of art history and the predominant positivism that only appreciated what appeared as technical progress.

In 1895, the same year in which Wickhoff published his most important work, *Die Wiener Genesis*, with Wilhelm Ritter von Härtel, he left his work at the Austrian Museum of Decorative Arts and was succeeded by Aloïs Riegl (1858–1905). Riegl was a historian of medieval and late Baroque art, and an important figure in the new methods of art history. He later became head of the textile section at the Austrian Museum of Art. In 1894 he obtained a position at the University of Vienna, continuing his interest in 'minor' art objects and teaching Baroque art, seen at that time as decadent. He formed with Wickhoff the first "Vienna School" of art history, rejecting the existing conception of Roman and Paleo-Christian art as a degeneration of style. The success of this School was probably based on the combination of different ideas and methods: those of Riegl, the academic-intellectual, theoretical and abstract thinker and Wickhoff, a historian of the humanist tradition of great scholarship.

Riegl attacked in 1901 G. Semper's deterministic positioning and Wölflin's belief in the transcendence of all forms in Baroque art. Riegl developed the concept of *Kunstwollen*, or "artistic will" as the driving force behind the evolution of artistic styles in all types of art, deeply linked to time. His theory that the artistic representation is not the real, but the intentional, changed the vision of art and made it more understandable. The desire for the most spiritual, a combination between the "tactile" and the "visual", the subjectivity and multiculturalism in the history of art and the consideration of the viewer as the most important in the work of art, totally changed contemporary studies. Riegl (1927) indicated that in the imperial Roman figurative art, an optical impression, resolved in an 'illusionistic' principle must be observed, which contrasts with the total impression of the Hellenic and Hellenistic preceding art.

As regards to Riegl's contribution to conservation, his years at the Imperial and Royal Central Commission for Monument Research and Preservation inspired him to develop an approach about the respect for the object that still continues to this day. His concept of the value of aging (*Alterswert*) and the importance of the marks of the use appears in 1903 in his fundamental book "The modern cult of monuments: its character and origin" (Riegl, 1903). It is the work of a pioneer, standing against the nineteenth-century practices to represent objects to appear as new. Riegl considered that the objects should show the signs of their age. With the *Kunstwollen* the artistic value of a monument is always relative and it is necessary to talk about monuments and historical values. In this way the monument is recognized as a historical document and part of the need to preserve it as such. For Riegl this is reason enough to justify the conservation of the monument. It identifies time as a fundamental value and states two categories: the "cult of the value of antiquity" and the "cult of the value of novelty". The value of the Old is for him demonstrated in the eroded corners that show the passage of time. For the New, regular, complete and finished works are expected needing always a finished character of form and colour. For this reason, for any ancient monument the value of the New is unattainable, and this is irreconcilable with the value of the Old, where it is necessary to show the signs of the passage of time. He also distinguished between the historiographic method in the study of the monument and the action of protection and conservation. The thought of Alois Riegl had the novelty to consider the viewer, not just the creator of the work of art. It introduced the categories of "tactile" and "optical", which had a great influence on architectural conservation, although Racheli argues that his influence is more in the field of art history than of conservation (Racheli, 2007).

6 Conservation and Architectural Project
Giacomo Boni as Pioneer of the 'Critical Conservation'

6.1 Giacomo Boni: 'The Method', Instruments and Education

Giacomo Boni (Venice 1859–Rome 1925) was an architect, engineer, archaeologist, but above all a scholar of classical and medieval architecture and the conservation of monuments and materials. These varied interests started early on in Venice; he sometimes anonymously signed his articles in newspapers as "a Venetian" or "Monaco Bigio". He was not an art critic like Ruskin or Riegl; his production is based on his excavated, published and built work and in this sense with a profile closer to Semper and with the same interest in integrating theory, practice and different disciplines. He was already very clear about his ideas on how to intervene in monuments when he presented to the government in 1882 a paper on his concepts of preservation and conservation of monuments, signed by a group of artists. Boni considered that the main value of the monuments is the historical one and the method that should be used for its study must be historical. Nevertheless, it is historical in the sense of being based on real evidence: the remains of the buildings (Tea, 1952).

Minister Boselli called Boni in 1888 to Rome from his native Venice to deal with the reform of the Royal Calcography and the creation of the Royal Photographic Cabinet for the reproduction of works of art. After these commissions, the director of Fine Arts, Fiorelli, asked him, along with Adolfo Venturi and Natale Baldoria, to tour the Italian provinces to catalog the historic buildings and monuments as prescribed by law. His official reports, publications in the newspaper *La Riforma* and his contemporary correspondence with the English architect Philip Webb and others, give us an exceptional account of this work.

In 1894, Boni visits Greece for the first time, which is when he decides to excavate the Roman Forum, obtaining in 1898 the permission of Minister Baccelli. Shortly after, he would attract everyone's attention when he discovered in the Roman Forum—in the place where Romulus's grave was considered to be—the so-called *Lapis Niger*, an archaic inscription on a dark marble stone in which the word 'king' appeared. This discovery caused a sensation, since at that time the existence of the ancient kings of Rome was questioned. This discovery of the oldest vestige of their existence in Rome was undoubtedly the most exciting moment of his career. In 1907, the Minister Rava commissioned Boni to direct the excavations of the Palatine, although without abandoning those of the Forum.

Ugo Ojetti considered Boni as "one of the most unique and fascinating men of the twentieth century" (Ojetti, 1960). Each president and important personality who visited Rome had an appointment with him at the Roman Forum and Palatine. However, his figure has unfortunately suffered, until very recently a *damnatio memoriae* due to his relationship with Mussolini and fascism, and his support in consolidating the idea of the *Romanità*. We cannot deny the fact that in 1923 he is appointed senator and met Mussolini in the Ara of Caesar, and that there is an exchange of telegrams between Gabrile D'Annunzio and Mussolini at Boni's death. However, neither can we forget his socialist roots and his relationship with William Morris and his circle, who he visited at the 'Red House' in England. It is peculiar that, despite Boni's continuous efforts for international scientific exchanges, the next generation of Roman archaeologists shut out the world in their obsessive search for race as pure instruments of the Regime (Vlad Borrelli, 2006).

Already in 1906, Boni's rigorously scientific method was recognized, thanks to which the remains of the different epochs of Roman history were discovered, "superimposed as pages of a book" (Símboli, 1906). However, although his contribution is of great importance in the fields of archaeology and conservation, his figure is quite forgotten and, unfortunately, not all his works are published. A recent publication collects his great work in the archaeological excavation and valorisation of the Roman Forum, including his excavation diaries, notes and drawings (Fortini and Taviani, 2014). Boni was criticized for not having written enough about his findings, to which he replied that the best document was the very rigorous drawings he carried out. He left more than eight hundred drawings of the excavations of the Forum and the Palatine and hundreds of photographs (Tea, 1952).

World War I and its consequences interrupted the progress of the excavations in the Forum and Palatine. In 1915, Boni helped to provide winter protection to the soldiers; the same year he gives a lecture at the Athenaeum of Venice, with the presence of D'Annunzio and Missaglia. In 1916, he is paralysed on the right side, but he continues mentally lucid and, helped by his collaborators, continues with his intense work. He died on 10 July 1925, working on the *Lupercale* (the place where allegedly the wolf nursed Romulus and Remus), the Circus Massimus and the Curia. His obituary was published in many newspapers, including in *The Times* (11 July 1925). D'Annunzio asked Mussolini for Boni to be buried in the Palatine, where he lived and he lies now in the shadow of a large palm, his grave marked with a Roman altar. The intended inscription, not included at the end, was written by D'Annunzio, and was one of Boni's favourite phrases, (Consolato, 2006)

> *Non lasciarti guidare soltanto dalla ragione: nelle decisioni supreme segui gli istinti ereditari e il divino intuit.* [Do not be guided only by reason: in supreme decisions follow hereditary instincts and the divine intuition.]
>
> (Susmel, 1956)

As we will see later, Boni had British influences, but his education in Italy was much more important. Although he followed formal studies, Boni's training was mainly self-taught and related to non-academics. Boni followed the architecture courses at the *Accademia di Belle Arti di Venezia* between 1880 and 1884 under the direction of the architect Giacomo Franco, who had achieved the chair of architecture in 1871 with the support of Camillo Boito. Franco was a self-taught architect of great experience and worth; many of his projects were published in the magazine *Ricordi di architettura* (1878–83). He had carried out many restoration projects of medieval monuments of his native Verona, such as the basilica di S. Zeno (1869–71). These restorations included some additions 'in style' with no historical-philological foundation, which he justified by referring to the figure of the architect as an interpreter and custodian of what he called the 'character' of the monument, which would have existed and could recover an 'original state of perfection'. He followed the 'Lombard' style advocated by Boito as an expression of the identity of the nation.

For Boni, material evidence exceeded any theory and was suspect of those theories that needed too much defence. Boni explained his method of archaeological excavation and conservation in an article in 1901, in order to receive comments from other experts (Boni, 1901). It is an important document to understand his methodology and his position as a pioneer in archaeology, as well as its relevance in the field of conservation. In 1911 he participated in the archaeological congress of Rome, presenting again his method (Boni, 1911). This methodology was of great importance in the orientation of the new Italian archaeology and is still part of the bibliography of archaeology and conservation studies in Italy. Boni considered that intuition is not magic, but the result of careful observation: it becomes a habit in those who dedicate their lives to study. The archaeological strata were for Boni the continuation of the geological ones, and he considered that their study should follow the same scientific method that geologists follow.

The fundamental innovation of its method is stratigraphic excavation, reading and identifying each stratum, a usual method today but completely new then. His description of the excavation procedure of each stratum, how to avoid the contamination of archaeological evidence and how to document each step of the process was a great innovation and is still relevant today. Boni insists on the need for a scientific method that allows transmitting not only what can be interpreted in our time, but also the findings that may not be understood but that future generations may be able to understand. This is a fundamental principle today in conservation. Boni not only theorized about it but also actively practised it in the conservation of the monastery of Santa Francesca Romana, as we will see later.

Boni's innovations extended to the use of new technologies in the study of buildings and archaeological remains, integrated with traditional ones. For example, he explored the dating of ceramics from magnetic variation, a technique that precedes by decades studies in the field. He made extensive use of terrestrial and aerial photography, and although he had a great talent for drawing, he surrounded himself with excellent draughtsmen who produced documentation not only of scientific but also artistic value. His interest and talent for drawing lasted all his life, as denoted by some notes in which he reviews the ways of drawing of architects and treatises in history, analysing the different ways to represent architecture (Boni, n.d.d).

There is a misunderstanding about the influence of British archaeology on Boni's method, something of which there is really no documentary evidence. As his disciple and biographer, Eva Tea explains that he had no teacher in regards to the stratigraphic excavation method. Boni already used it when he excavated the base of the campanile di S. Marco in Venice when he was just twenty years old, making detailed sections. Then he did not know the work of others who used vertical sections such as Pigorini in Castellazzo and Dörpfeld in Hissarlik. However, he had read Parker's book (1876) on the Roman Forum, the first to be interested in Roman construction methods. The book encouraged reading the sources and confronting them with the remains of the buildings and making use of photography during excavations. He also read the work of Dörpfeld and Petrie (Tea, 1952). Upon Boni's death, and using his work to a great extent, there would be a breakthrough in the archaeological and topographical studies of Rome. In 1929 S. B, Platner and T. Ashby published the Topographical Dictionary of Ancient Rome, which would become a key reference.

Boni had a great interest in international relations and education throughout his life. He helped the students and scholars of foreign academies, such as the American, who had Rodolfo Lanciani as a contact before. Two of these students, Charles Rufus Morey and Esther van Deman would later become important scholars. Morey founded in 1917 the Index of Christian Art at Princeton University, which is still today a very important database of Christian art. Van Deman was a true pioneer as scholar and professor of archaeology, and her contribution to the Roman Forum studies is immense. She also became an excellent photographer, leaving valuable documents. Unfortunately, her initiative to publish a manual (handbook) of Roman construction techniques was not completed. This idea was based on Boni's scientific method, which related written sources to the analysis of buildings, their materials and construction techniques.

Boni also helped other students from other parts of the world, from Australia to Scotland. The Roman Forum was not only then an area of archaeological interest, but also of architectural study. Not only did he deal with foreign students, he was also involved in the education of Italian students. Minister Baccelli asked Boni to use the Forum as an experimental architectural 'cabinet' (Huemer, 2008). The architect Manfredo Manfredi, director of the architecture school of Rome, invited Boni to attend the opening of the academic year, and Boni asked him to take the best students to the Palatine to learn about the "grammar of Roman structures and decorations . . . to make a better school than those created in Rome by foreign governments" (Boni, 1924). Boni's influence spread throughout all these students and, therefore, archaeology and its methods influenced the architecture and art of the period.

Boni left a great deal of material at his death, including drawings and excavation diaries (written by his assistants) in the former *Soprindendenza Archaeologica di Roma*. However, her assistant Eva Tea looked after his personal papers and notes for publications, which she took with her when she moved to Milan. These documents are now in the library of the Istituto Lombardo—Accademia di Scienze e Lettere in Milan, deposited by Tea 45 years after Boni's death. This important documentary collection reveals the complexity of Boni's thinking, his multilingual ability and the incredible amount of work developed. Tea tried to reorganize the material, which is why there are many notes added (Guidobaldi, 2008, 2016; Paribene, 2008). Boni also left notes intended to be instructions for the technical offices of the Italian *soprintendenze*, which are of great documentary value.

6.2 Boni, Ruskin, Webb and SPAB

Boni spoke English and this gave him the opportunity to exchange ideas with the active British architectural world of the time. Continuous contacts with England since youth greatly enriched his studies. As Petrelli (2008) notes, his training was more similar to that of a British architect, trained in offices of experienced architects, although in his case it would be also through correspondence. Boni had Ruskin as a great intellectual reference and shared with him his interests in art and social aspects. In 1882, through Angelo Alessandrini, Boni went to help Ruskin in the survey of some buildings in Pisa. It was the first time Boni had left his native Venice. He had begun to work in architectural conservation at fifteen, working for the engineer Cadel and later for the engineer Annibale Forcellini—much appreciated by Camilo Boito—in the *Palazzo Ducale*

(1875–1888) (Scappin, 1997). In 1885 Boni appears domiciled in the Palazzo Ducale (SPAB, 1885); he probably met Ruskin there during one of his visits, and their friendship would extend until Ruskin's death in 1900. Ruskin very much admired Boni's drawings and commissioned him drawings and watercolours of Venice, such as that of the Palazzo Dario, now in the Ruskin Art Collection of the Ashmolean Museum in Oxford. Boni also sent Ruskin news about monuments and conservation works in Venice. The last time they would see each other was in 1888 on the occasion of Ruskin's last trip to Venice and shortly before Boni left for Rome.

Ruskin's thinking influenced Boni greatly. Ruskin believed that it is more important to understand the intentions behind the historic facts, rather than the facts in themselves. Boni looked in the ancient remains for the testimony of the thinking of its creators, studying the different layers of the forum as one would explore the pages of a book. Ruskin, as any innovator, made a radical change of thought concerning architecture: he forgets the rules, mathematics and treatises, moving interest to aspects of human effort in performing the work and the materiality of architecture, trying to understand the moral reasons and social conditions that had guided the realization of the architectural work. For both Ruskin and Boni, the important thing was neither art nor history, but the human being. Ruskin initiated this new approach about the relationship between history and art (Petrelli, 2008), which would be continued by Boni, who tried to apply the principles that Ruskin used in medieval studies to Roman antiquity, paying 'Ruskinian' attention to the "stones of Rome", an approach later followed by Cesare Brandi, as we shall see.

We also have to understand how radical was Boni's intellectual position regarding his contemporaries. Luca Beltrami (1854–1933), an important figure in architectural conservation and exponent of the so-called 'Historical Conservation', did not share his friend Boni's admiration for Ruskin. As we have seen, since the end of the nineteenth century, conservation principles were under debate, and the so-called 'Stylistic Conservation', based on the theories of Eugene Viollet-le-Duc that included the idea of the unity of the historic building, was questioned. Beltrami defended the architectural reconstruction on rigorously documented bases, which is also questionable considering that historical documentation may be inaccurate or misinterpreted.

Boni's relationship with English culture was not limited to Ruskin. He was also a friend of Philip Webb (Tea, 1940), William Morris and William Douglas Caröe, whom he visited in England—in Kelmscott in 1889—on the occasion of a conference given to the Society for the Protection of Ancient Buildings (SPAB). He was an honorary member of SPAB since 1885; in 1887 he was elected associate of the Royal Incorporation of British Architects (RIBA), in 1910 honorary fellow of the Society of Antiquaries of London and in 1911 honorary foreign corresponding member of the Royal Academy of Arts in London. He was also invested Doctor Honoris Causa by the Universities of Oxford and Cambridge in 1907. In 1913, he returned to London to give a lecture and gave also others in Vienna and Brussels.

The relationship between Boni and the SPAB circle has always been seen as one-sided, in the sense that Boni collected their ideas and used them in Italian monuments. The reality is much more complex than this. We have to consider that SPAB—founded by Morris in 1877 as a reaction to the damage suffered in medieval churches by inadequate interventions—was developing at the same time that Boni reflected and experimented with buildings, in a position of direct knowledge and intensity superior to those that SPAB enjoyed. The restoration of the Basilica of San Marco in Venice was also causing heated debates and controversies at the time (Zorzi, 1877) that prompted Boni and his circle, including SPAB, to concretize a 'theory' of conservation.

The exchange of ideas was undoubtedly important on both sides. SPAB was able to articulate in its manifesto some principles that Boni found easy to adopt, since it came from the same thought process and both influenced by Ruskin. The Manifesto, written by Morris, Webb and other founders of SPAB in 1877, was a response to restoration problems at that time in England, but has been extended to the present as conservation philosophy (SPAB, 1877). It denotes the paradox—which still extends to this day—that on the one hand the monuments attract great attention and are extensively studied, but at the time of intervention the original is destroyed to return to the building's illusory original state.

Boni cultivated a great friendship and exchanged ideas with the architect Philip Webb; both retained the practical aspect as fundamental. The material and technical aspects of architecture were for them a continuing concern as it was also in many of his contemporaries: Giuseppe Sacconi, Alfredo D'Andrade and Luca Beltrami, among others. Precisely to Webb he entrusted in 1891, perhaps for the first time, his opinion on the historical method in the study of monuments:

> The life of monuments does not last a generation only; they survive the races of which they are the only memory and their documentary value lasts as long as a fragment remains.
>
> (Tea, 1952)

In this way, based on the Ruskinian appreciation of the value of the original author's hand, Boni promulgated to go beyond mere description, understanding and interpreting the monuments that is, 'reading' the material testimony. Boni believed in the truth transmitted by tradition and enriched it in a great way, thanks to his excavations and studies, the knowledge of ancient Rome. Although he respected tradition, he also questioned it, in his search always to understand the origin of things.

The correspondence between Boni and Webb and some documents in the Boni-Tea archive indicate that Boni had a direct influence on the development of SPAB. In fact, he suggested that SPAB adopt the slogan:

> Authenticity is not the main value of monuments but it is a fundamental condition for every value that monuments may have.
>
> (Boni, n.d.e).

However, he said that it was necessary to interrogate the monuments and to imitate them "keeping silent". Another fundamental characteristic of his thinking was that the ancient and the modern were on the same plane (Tea, 1952), a thought very much in contrast to his contemporaries. Despite some more rigid statements in the Manifesto, both Boni and SPAB believed that buildings should be allowed to evolve, as had happened until the nineteenth century (Boni, n.d.e). The transformations of buildings gave them new life, and, unlike the restorations in use then at that time, they did not deceive about their age.

Nevertheless, Boni's influence would not remain only in theoretical aspects: it would have also influenced SPAB with its scientific way of documenting and analysing monuments. Proof of this is its exquisite and rigorous drawing of the foundations of the Basilica of San Marco, showing dimensions and materials and including a small envelope with a sample of the oak wood of the piles, which is found today in the SPAB archives.

Perhaps, due to Ruskin's influence, and later his interest in Eastern religions, Boni loved the ruins and their natural context. He considered that the ruins had to be preserved as such and that the vegetation contributed to its picturesque aspect, where nature acts on the hand of man, and where the old age of the building is its most beautiful age. In Boni, the picturesque had the scientific value of the authentic, prevailing over the romantic (Tea, 1932). Ruskin undoubtedly also inspired his interest in flora. Boni tries to bring beauty to the 'wounds in the earth' opened by the excavations, planting trees, flowers, shrubs and plants around the ruins to protect and beautify them, carefully choosing those that will not damage the fabrics and sometimes at his own expense.

6.3 The Innovation in the Conservation of the Cloister of the Monastery of Santa Maria Nova: from *'com'era, dov'era'* to Scientific 'Stratigraphic Architectural Conservation Design'

Boni's work is normally analysed concerning his activity as an archaeologist. Nevertheless, while he was carrying out the large excavations of the Roman Forum, he extensively intervened in the monastery of Santa Maria Nova, with the help of the architect Guido Cirilli (1871–1954). This work is however quite unknown and very different from the one carried out at the Forum. We have already published some details of this important conservation design project (González-Longo, 2006), discussing how Cirilli and Boni followed at the same time a rigorous methodology and an "open" and flexible way of conserving the building, all well-integrated in the architectural design project. To understand the scope and innovation of this conservation work, we should just consider some contemporary projects such as the reconstruction in 1902 of the campanile of San Marco in Venice after its collapse. Gaetano Moretti (1860–1938) rebuilds it "as it was and where it was" (*com'era dov'era*), that is, according to the so-called 'Historical Conservation', the common approach at the time.

However there had been other more innovative experiences. The *Associazione Artistica tra i Cultori di Architettura*, created in 1889 under the example of similar English associations of "Friends of the Monuments", assumed a decisive role at the end of the nineteenth century in Rome. It was born from the movement that discovered the value of the pre-existing city and the link between building and tradition, theorizing about a form of intervention in the historic centre. Its flagship project was the conservation of the church of Santa Maria in Cosmedin in 1893, were they have undertaken a 'Scientific Conservation'. The intervention came from the analysis of the monument's formation, choosing the most significant stylistic era in the history of the monument, and reconstructing it according to the ways of the chosen period, eliminating the baroque phase and returning to what was considered was its medieval appearance. The *Associazione Artistica tra i Cultori di Architettura* also proposed in 1900 the differentiations in the building typology, one of the novelties of the subsequent Regulatory Plan of 1909. They found their cultural manifesto with the translation of '*L'Esthetique des Villes*', published in 1893 by Charles Buls, who gave a lecture in January 1902 at the Capitoline Hill (Buls, 1903).

Boni intervened in the monastery between 1900 and 1907, turning it into a Museum of the Forum and offices of the Roman Forum Directorate. For this, he had to unearth the northern part of the monastery, moving a large amount of material, as it appears in the photographs that Boni took to document the works. As we have seen, the building had suffered great damage because of the suppression of the monastery and its transformation into barracks and flats at the time of the Italian reunification. The building was carefully surveyed, investigated and monitored, establishing its condition and the necessary work. It is important to insist on the importance that Boni gave to drawing as an instrument of conservation and the attention to detail, as well as, technology and materials, also shared by Cirilli. We must also highlight the serious economic restrictions of the period, the unstable administration and the strong leadership role, integrity and personal and professional courage exhibited by Boni in the realization of this project.

In 1903, on the occasion of the *Congresso Internazionale di Scienze Storiche*, a visit to the cloister was organized. The architect Guido Cirilli, who had carried out the project with Boni, showed the congressmen photos and drawings of the conservation of the building and its conversion to the Museum (Atti, 1903). Boni proposed, designed and carry out the works for a museum to display and interpret the contribution of Roman culture to the world, but only with dispersed original artefacts or copies, because he always defended the conservation *in situ* of historic artefacts. The intention was to incorporate in the project a library that collected all that has been written about Rome, along with photographs and casts of the main Roman monuments, buildings and public works in the empire. In this sense, Boni wrote in 1905 to the '*cultori*' (lovers) of Roman civilization throughout the world. On 22 July 1908, eight years after the first proposal by Boni, the Museo Forense was formally instituted. The project was contemporary with Boni's major discoveries in the Roman Forum, so he never had enough time to complete it as he intended. After his death in 1925 further archaeological fragments from the Roman Forum were located in the ground floor, forming the *Antiquarium Forense*, inaugurated by Mussolini in 1935 and in existence until recently (Figure 6.1).

Thanks to the generous help of his friend Beltrami, Boni was able to place in the monastery of S. Maria Nova some of the archaic tombs and *sepulcreti* found in his excavations at the Roman. Boni arranged the tombs as he had found them, for which he had to excavate part of the museum's pavement. In his eagerness to document and contextualize these important findings, Boni placed around the graves the drawings and photographs made during the excavations, also illustrating the stratigraphy of the area.

Figure 6.1 Antiquarium Forense, now disappeared (A.)

138 *Conservation and Architectural Project*

These tombs were until recently still in the same position, but unfortunately they have been removed together with the whole *Antiquarium Forense,* as the building is currently being converted to a new museum and offices for the *Parco Archeologico del Colosseo*. It is expected that the new museum will incorporate the remains of Boni's museum, the original drawings of Boni's project of the monastery, photographs during the works and his diaries, preserved at the former *Soprintendenza Archaeologica di Roma*, which we have been fortunate to copy and study (González-Longo, 2006, 2015).

Cirilli, under the direction of Boni, also exposed the apse of the Temple of Venus and Rome, the foundations of the columns of the portico on the Forum side and those of the wall of the Rome cella, as well as part of the marble floors (Boni, n.d.b). The temple would be restored again in 1932, as we will see later. In the cloister, Boni discovered the previous phases and decided to leave them in view, despite the technical difficulty, since he had to alter the structure, creating openings where the later columns were encompassing the first phase of the cloister (Figures 3.12, 4.3, 6.2).

Ruskin's teachings are evident in this intervention, in which all the architecture, history and times present in the cloister regain prominence, apart from the last additions. There were however removals of existing fabric due to the abusive nature of the works of the barracks and the need to choose between preserving fabric of the eighteenth century or returning the cloister to all its medieval design and character. Boni found the original columns of the upper level of the cloister within the walls of the eighteenth century and decided to uncover them (Figures 6.2, 6.3, 6.4), as Stern before had wanted to do in the Arch of Titus, preserving all the original elements

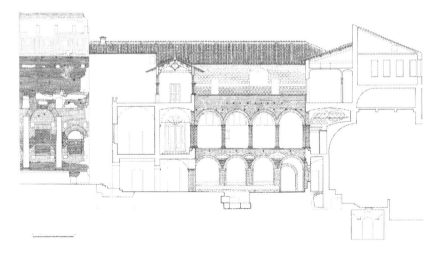

Figure 6.2 Cross-section E-W through the cloister and crypt area

in situ, instead of disassembling and rebuilding them, sometimes with great technical difficulty.

The works also extended to the areas adjacent to the monastery, including the cryptoporticus at its northwest corner, of which we have spoken previously. In a 1907 report, Boni also declares that, to create the entrance to the *Museo Forense* to the southwest, he emptied the corridor from the time of Hadrian located below the section of the monastery demolished, adjacent to the Arch of Titus, and the steps of the stereobate of the Temple of Venus and Rome (DG AA.BB.AA. 1907). This corridor of brick walls and tuff vault was full of medieval material that served as the foundation of the section of the monastery that joined the arch of Titus, demolished by Valadier, as we have seen, at the beginning of the nineteenth-century. Some of these remains were carved marbles belonging to the cornice, corbel, architrave, pediment and columns of the arch of Titus. Under the bipedales that constituted the pavement of the corridor, Boni found remains of buildings that were on the edge of the August Sacra Via, before Hadrian modified his trajectory. Beside it, he also found a medieval round well (Boni, n.d.b), possibly used for the elaboration of lime, using the temple stone.

Judging by some drawings of the original project, Boni also explored the idea of restoration (*ripristino*), bringing the cloister to a certain original state, exposing the apse of the church and building a new staircase (González-Longo, 2006). Ongoing works at the cloister have exposed original drawings and paintings adjacent to this apse, already found by the architect Claudia del Monti in 2016, which confirms Boni's interpretation of the original configuration of the cloister, with arches only in three parts and the wall of the church and apse exposed. This configuration is clearly represented in Etienne Du Pérac's view (1577), where, as mentioned before, the cloisters demolished by Valadier can be clearly seen (Gonzalez-Longo, 2012, 2015).

In the end, Boni's intervention exposed the oldest medieval phases and the new design was limited to simple forms of arches to consolidate the structure and a new pavement, recreating that of the temple, a very effective way of indicating the scale and extension of the temple, with a minimal intervention (Figures 4.7, 6.3). Boni also made a great effort to make underground areas accessible to facilitate investigations by future researchers. To do this, he executed excavations and removal of debris and built a series of vaults under the cloister floor. In short, Boni and Cirilli applied a method that we could call 'stratigraphic architectural conservation design', which allows displaying the building fabric from different periods without disturbing the overall image of the building and making clear what is new and old. These innovations are of great importance, internationally, and we consider that Boni was the pioneer of architectural conservation as we understand it today.

Boni and Cirilli's methodology of documenting all work with diaries, photographs and drawings demonstrates also pioneering conservation practice (Boni, n.d.b.). Their intention was also modern in the sense

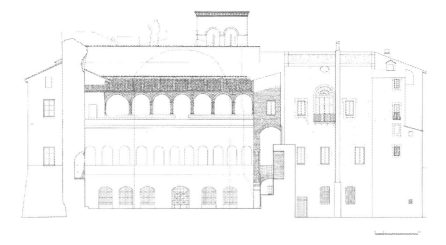

Figure 6.3 Section S-N through the Roma cella (A.)

of wanting to keep the original fabric as a document but at the same time reuse the building and create a new architecture of quality (Cirilli and Boni, 1909). The intervention undoubtedly followed a historical-critical method and as such precedes in years the theory of conservation of Cesare Brandi and the *Restauro Critico* ('Critical Conservation') to be discussed later.

Nevertheless, this approach and method was perhaps too innovative to be understood by its contemporaries, who, on the other hand, were more interested in the work of the Forum and Palatine. It also required extensive education and training that, as in the case of Boni, allowed 'to read' the monument in all its complexity, from historical to tectonic aspects, and an interest in contemporary design and culture. Boni had a deep knowledge of medieval art and architecture, accumulated in years of experience in Venice and southern Italy as inspector of monuments, which certainly helped to decide how to conserve the cloister. It was not an easy task with the complex addition of medieval and later fabrics from different eras, built above the remains of the Roman Temple of Venus and Rome and Nero's vestibule.

6.4 Giovannoni and Mussolini: *Romanità* and Modernity

In 1910 Gustavo Giovannoni (Rome, 1873–1947), architect, engineer, urban planner, historian and architecture critic becomes president of the *Associazione Artistica tra i Cultori dell'Architettura* and exponent of the 'Scientific Conservation'. He was Professor of Architecture at the Faculty of Engineering of the University of Rome, where he had trained as an engineer and then as an art historian with Adolfo Venturi. He believed in the concept of 'integral architect', capable of dealing with both technical and artistic aspects, practised by Antonio da Sangallo, one of his main subjects of study, which combined archaeological and architectural knowledge. In this spirit, he was instrumental in the creation in 1919 of the *Scuola Superiore di Architettura di Roma*. Where he influenced the curriculum and taught architectural conservation. Giovannoni made a great contribution to the field of architectural and urban conservation, which he considered to be united.

Giovannoni established modern ideas on architectural conservation and, following Boito's line, classified consolidation, recomposition, completion and innovation as different ways to conserve (Giovannoni, 1929). He describes the process of developing his thinking at the First International Congress of Architects and Technicians of Historic Monuments held in 1931 in Athens, opening the possibility to the "judicious use" of modern techniques, such as reinforced concrete (Giovannoni, 1932). Unfortunately, the interventions of those years by N. Balanos in the Acropolis of Athens, which are being corrected now, show that their use was not as judicious, durable and reversible as Giovannoni expected. He was attentive to everything that was happening in Europe and his influence in the field of conservation was enormous, internationally, as is the case of the influence in Torres-Balbás and its conservation of the Alhambra in Granada (1923–36).

Perhaps, Giovannoni's greatest contribution has been in urban conservation (Giovannoni, 1931). He enunciated in 1913 the concept of *diradamento*, which consists of an assessment, case-by-case, of the opportunity or not of small interventions of demolition in buildings, or of widening of streets, to add value to buildings or parts of an old urban fabric of value, in a conception around the theme of taste. This theory, which could have as a precedent the "conservative surgery" of Patrick Geddes, was applied in many parts of Rome: he proclaimed the need to take the activities of the public administration out of the historic centre, to counteract its densification, adapting in turn the old buildings to the new hygienic and residential requirements. It becomes an economic intervention with a progressive elevation of the social class of its inhabitants, corresponding to the improvement of the hygienic and comfort conditions of the homes, but without radically mutating the destination of use.

With the March on Rome by Mussolini in 1922, and the beginning of the Fascist Era, the new interventions are designed to make Rome, again, the Capital of an Empire. A century after the Napoleonic invasion of Rome, Mussolini, without at any time making a direct allusion, collects and carries out many of the proposals enunciated in that period, and in that of Sixtus V, seeking to restore the city to its imperial *Romanità*. Mussolini declared that the past is a source of education and encouragement for the advancement of the nation. However, for Mussolini everything was based on the "greatness" of the city, on its monumentality, eliminating, with *sventramenti* (cutting open the historic city) everything that, according to him, disturbed it. In a second time, the intention was to make a modern Rome, from the hills to the sea, a unique city in the world.

At the base of all this was the old idea that the monuments and historic buildings had to be isolated in order to be better admired, thus turning the city into a desert with specific monuments in a vacuum that, as L. Benevolo has written, was nothing other than the physical equivalent of the mental emptiness in which it was conceived. As we have already seen, this idea of isolation of the monuments had already been enunciated by the French during their occupation of Rome a century earlier. Mussolini orders large excavations in order to isolate some monuments and expose Imperial Rome. As we have discussed previously, he opened the *Via dell'Impero* (*Via dei Fori Imperiali*) and the *Via dei Trionfi* (*Via di San Gregorio*). In the fifteenth year of the Fascist Era (1937), the *Duce* gives the first peak blow for the demolition of the *Spina dei Borghi* in the Vatican, something which was proposed in 1811 under French rule.

The case of the *Piazza della Colonna Traiana* is emblematic. The similarity between De Tournon's proposals for Rome and those made after Italian Reunification is not a coincidence, especially in the fascist era, despite what some characters of the time declared. An article of the time (Bianchi, 1937) indicates that the French program was known by the professionals who were acting at that time, and Giovannoni (1927) had published an article on the Program for Rome of Count De Tournon.

One of the aspects of the *sventramenti* was its character as an "urban sanitation" plan. This consisted of the integral demolition, very different from the principle of the *diradamento*, where the demolition of degraded houses of the old city created opportunities for the creation of new squares or public buildings. For the people stripped of their houses, *borgate* were built outside Rome. There is something pejorative in the term: subspecies of *borgo*, a piece of city that does not have the organization or the sufficient equipment to be called a neighbourhood.

Unlike Giovannoni, who proclaimed the rational analysis of the structure of the urban fabric and the possibility of a continuity of reading the stylistic values of the past, the regime's architect, Marcello Piacentini, author in 1916 of a Plan for Rome, believed there should be a distinction between the intervention in the new and old city (Piacentini, 1925). Between 1924 and 1926 Giovannoni and Piacentini collaborated in the drafting of the Reform of the Urban Regulatory Plan of 1909, all full of ambiguity and inconsistencies: after deciding in favour of "leaving the old city as intact as possible", *sventramenti* were proposed. Between 1925 and 1940, large areas of the historic fabric of Rome were demolished.

The project for the Imperial Fora area was drafted in 1929 by the group '*La Burbera*' of which Giovannoni formed part. At the same time, it was presented the Plan drafted by the GUR (Roma Urbanist Group), of which Piacentini (who strongly attacked Giovannoni) was also part. A young architect, Luigi Piccinato, emerges also here, who would later comment on the paradox of that time, in which the greatest devastators of Rome are the most exalted by the *Romanità*, the tradition and the ancient civilization.

But the biggest operation of *sventramento* carried out by the fascism was the isolation of the Capitoline Hill and the "liberation" of the archaeological zone around it, with the creation, around the monument to Vittorio Emanuele, of the *Via del Monte* (or *Via dell'Impero*), and the *Via del Mare*, which collected traffic from the southern and southeastern districts of the then recently created periphery, as well as being a perfect set for frequent military marches. The two routes joined in the *Foro Italico* (as they called then the *Piazza Venezia*). Corrado Ricci devised in 1911 the "liberation" of the entire Imperial Fora complex, as well as the construction, once the excavations were finished, of a road that sacrificed the least possible archaeological elements in situ. But the result would be very different. While decentralization was sought in all the cities of the world in that period, in Rome, a city that had always distinguished itself by not having a single centre, these large traffic arteries were opened, leading all to a single centre.

On the other hand, the "archaeological criterion" used in Rome was anachronistic: while in France, for thirty years, archaeologists had recognized the importance that the whole past had in the formation of our present, constituting something irreplaceable in our spiritual and cultural formation, some Italian archaeologists had stopped in time. With a purely stylistic and monumental conception, people's houses were only important if they were of the classical era, and not even in some cases. It seems that Boni's efforts had been forgotten and archeology became a political instrument rather than a scientific and cultural one, with devastating effects to the city.

6.5 The *Via dell'Impero* and the Destruction of the Velia

The wildest *sventramento* of fascism and its emblem was the creation of the *Via dell'Impero*, already mentioned. A concern from the time of the Roman Empire, was the connection of the Capitoline hill with the area of the Flavian Amphitheatre. In the Napoleonic Era, as we have seen, the connection had been made as originally, that is, through the Roman Forum. In the Fascist Era, the old fixation that existed since Unification would reappear: to connect the southeast neighbourhoods with the Piazza Venezia, which would also constituted a political function.

144 *Conservation and Architectural Project*

Despite the great Neronian and Hadrianean transformations that we have already discussed, the Velia maintained its presence and almost all of its integrity until 1931, when Mussolini created the *Via dell'Impero*. With its 900 metre length and 30 metre width, this new artery communicating Piazza Venezia with the Colosseum radically modified the natural topography with an imbalance of masses built along its trajectory. A large cut (60 m long and 18–20 m deep) was made across the Velia hill (Pisani Sartorio, 1983); 50,000 square metres of land were excavated, in the area of archaeological and paleontological interest. With this operation the hill was destroyed as such; a Neronian retaining wall, formerly covered by the Velia terrain, still reveals today the scale of the operation (Figure 1.5). The works lasted only eleven months and on 28 October 1932 the new *Via dell'Impero* was inaugurated. This colossal work gave the opportunity to investigate, although at an accelerated rate, the area (Colini, 1933; Barosso, 1940; Colini, 1983; Insolera, 1976). It is curious that Maria Barosso was commissioned to carry out watercolours of the works, perhaps to soften the trauma that the area and the community that lived there were actually suffering. Some key people were in office at the time: A. Muñoz was then Director of Antiquities and Fine Arts, and A.M. Colini was Inspector of the Archaeological Services of the Government of Rome (Bellanca, 2003, 2004).

Never had a *sventramento* been carried out in this way, despising and destroying any element, whether they were churches, archaeological remains of Republican Villas or sixteenth-century gardens such as that of Villa Rivaldi—and all this in the record time of one year. On the other hand, instead of, as intended, improving the knowledge and understanding of the area, it was divided in two by a real traffic barrier. Subsequently, the *Via dei Trionfi* was inaugurated, which ran from the Arch of Constantine to the *Circus Massimus*, for which the remains of the base of the *Colossus of Nero* and the *Meta Sudans* were demolished, because it was a problem for car circulation.

6.6 The Restoration of the Temple of Venus and Rome and the Athens and Italian Conservation Charters

The opening of the *Via dell'Impero* greatly affected the monumental complex of the Temple of Venus and Rome—Santa Francesca Romana. The complex appears now in an elevated position and what had been until then the rear facade of the monastery, is now an open facade towards the new road: the entire complex lost its direct connection and relationship with its surroundings. This is a difficult conservation and design challenge to undertake, which in fact has not been carried out since and it should be confronted.

The Temple of Venus and Rome was restored in 1932 (Lugli, 1935). Due to the different competencies, the works were carried out by two different architects and organizations: A. Bartoli restored the cella of Rome for the Ministry of Education (Figures 2.10, 6.3), and Antonio Muñoz restored for the *Governatorato di Roma* that of Venus, towards the Colosseum (Muñoz, 1935a; Bellanca, 2003, 2004). Muñoz published a book about his intervention in which he states how rushed the works were (Muñoz, 1935b). The situation of different competencies for the same monument reflected the problem of ownership and protection of the monuments mentioned in the 1931 Athens conference and the difficulties encountered by legislation in this area, especially when it comes to property. Unfortunately, this is still the situation today with regard to the church and monastery. In the Conservation Charter created at this Athens conference we find the principles that seem to have guided part of the conservation of the temple: *anastylosis* making the new materials recognisable, picturesque perspective treatment and ornamental vegetation to preserve their ancient character.

In this way, the remains of the scattered columns in the immediate vicinity were placed in the columns using a mortar that clearly distinguishes the original material from the modern one (Figure 2.4). However, the rush with which the works proceeded and the lack of a scientific study for a correct *anastlylosis*, meant that the columns were erected more in accordance with the intention of creating the picturesque view that the Athens Charter mentions, rather than a scientific reconstruction. This picturesque view was completed with the placement of a cylindrical pruned hedge in the position of each missing column, a gentle way to recreate the original form of the temple (González-Longo, 2015). Later archaeological excavations were forced to remove these elements, making the building inaccessible to the public for a very long time. There has been a recent conservation intervention at the temple, making it accessible again, but with the ongoing works for the construction of another underground line, the area has been made once again inaccessible and its stability seems to be compromised.

Based on the Athens Charter and extending its principles with the practical experience of the first thirty years of the twentieth century, and for sure the experience of conserving the temple, the *Consiglio Superiore per le Antichità e Belle Arti* updated the Italian Conservation Charter in 1932, the same year that the temple was restored, with the following general principles established for the conservation of monuments. Because of its relevance we have translated it here:

1. Give maximum importance to continuous maintenance and consolidation, in order to give back to the monument the structural integrity and durability lost;
2. That the restoration be made only for artistic and architectural unity reasons closely linked to historical criteria, and when based on original

evidence and not on hypotheses. On existing notable elements and not on predominantly new elements;
3. That ancient monuments, far from our uses and civilization are not completed, and that only *anastylosis* be used, that is, the recomposition of existing parts dismembered with the addition of the minimum number of neutral elements necessary to ensure the recomposition and conservation of original;
4. That in 'live' monuments be admitted only similar uses to the originals so as not to alter the building too much;
5. That all elements of an artistic and historical nature be preserved, regardless of the era to which they belong, without the desire for stylistic unity or return to the primitive form to exclude some of these and that this operation is based on rigorous judgment and not on personal opinions;
6. That, together with respect for the monument and its phases, that of its environmental condition is also taken, avoiding inopportune isolation, construction of large dissonant fabrics due to colour, mass or style;
7. That in the necessary additions, in the consolidation, in the operations of total or partial reintegration or in those necessary for the use of the monument the essential criterion to follow, in addition to limiting the new elements to the minimum, is that these have a character of naked simplicity and in accordance with the construction scheme and that only the continuation of existing lines be admitted in a similar style, when it comes to geometric expressions, without decorative individuality;
8. That the necessary additions must be well designed and must be distinguished from the original, and must be made with material other than the primitive or with lines of separation between the old and the new (*cornici di inviluppo*) simple or with symbols or inscriptions, so that deceit does not occur to scholars and represent a falsification of a monument
9. That in order to reinforce the structure of a monument or to reintegrate the mass, the most modern construction materials can be precious aids and it is appropriate to use them when the adoption of constructive methods analogous to the ancients does not reach the objectives; and that also the benefits of experimental sciences should be called upon to contribute in minute cases and complex conservation of deteriorated structures, where empirical procedures must give way to strictly scientific ones;
10. That in the excavations and explorations that bring to light old works, the uncovering work must be methodically performed and proceed immediately to the presentation of the ruins and the permanent protection of the works of art found, which can be preserved in situ;

11. That, as in the excavations, also in the conservation of the monuments must be an essential and obligatory condition, that the works be accompanied with analytical reports collected in a conservation journal illustrated with drawings and photographs, so that all the elements in the structure and form of the monument, all phases of the recomposition, uncovering and finalization work are permanently and safely recorded.

The *Consiglio* also recognized the complexity of the monuments and historic buildings and thus the need to complete the general principles with the discussion of specific cases, and therefore states:

a. That the opinion of the *Consiglio* be requested before beginning the conservation works of monuments outside the ordinary preservation activity, both those promoted or carried out by private as by public entities or by the *Soprintendenza* itself;
b. That a friendly congress be held every year in Rome (whose minutes can be published in the "*Bollettino d'Arte*" of the *Ministero dell'Educazione Nazionale*) in which the *Sovrintendenti* expose the cases and problems that are presented to them to attract the attention of colleagues and expose proposals for solutions;
c. That the compilation and methodical conservation of the Conservation Journals be forced, and, if possible, that a scientific publication be made with the data and analytical news in a similar way as in the excavations.

Although some of these points were consistently followed in the intervention at the temple, as we have said, Antonio Muñoz recomposes the remains of columns, but more than a scientifically performed *anaslylosis*, he made a picturesque composition, and not all the columns were erected. Documentation aspects are also scarce, motivated by the speed in which the work was carried out. We can only speculate that the project's shortcomings somehow informed what the Conservation Charter promoted.

The intervention of Bartoli shortly after focused on the first section of the Charter, that is to say in the consolidation, but unfortunately too much: a new brick 'sheath' was added to the walls of the cella, which makes difficult the study of the original building (Figure 2.10). The reversibility was not then taken into account.

The idea of *Romanità* still presents a lot of distrust among historians; it undoubtedly was an identity that helped save and restore many ancient monuments but deprived us of the richness of many later ones. The adoration of the imperial past did forget the later history. If the same operation as that at the temples of *Largo Argentina* had been executed in the Temple of Venus and Rome, or the area around the *Capitoline Hill*, the result would be very different. Many later buildings, in the Imperial Fora and the Roman Forum, built on top of the republican or imperial ones were demolished, creating a historical void of twenty centuries, unrecoverable.

6.7 Theory of Conservation: Cesare Brandi on Painting, Sculpture and . . . Architecture?

A little forgotten, like Boni, is also the figure of the architect Ambrigio Annoni (Milan 1882–1954), a disciple of Camillo Boito. He was *Soprintendente* of Ravenna until 1944, when he became a professor at the Technical University of Milan. At the same time, he continued an intense professional conservation activity, including the tomb of Dante and the churches of S. Francesco and S. Giovanni Evangelista in Ravenna and several projects in Milan such as the Vinciana Hall of the Ambrosian Pinacoteca (1936–1938). He also wrote about these conservation projects, demonstrating an integrated knowledge of history and techniques. Annoni refuses to accept standardized methods or theories, referring to each project 'case by case' and the need to adapt the method to each project, an approach that we can also attribute to Torres-Balbás in Spain: it is the approach of the architect-designer. Like Boni, Annoni insists on the importance of surveying and drawing the monument, preserves and puts into view all the stratifications of the building and considers architectural conservation a professional act, but also of culture and love (Annoni, 1946).

However, there was at the time a desire to standardize theories and practices. Cesari Brandi (1906–88) worked from 1933 in the Directorate of Antiquities and Fine Arts. He travelled in 1937 to Rhodes to see the reconstructions that were carried out there and in the Dodecanese and Africa during the Italian occupation, with a clear lack of criteria; this experience made him reflect on conservation, which was performed similarly in many other places (Vlad Borrelli, 2006). Brandi's work is not only important for his theoretical proposal, but because it was based on an intense practical, interdisciplinary activity, as head of the *Istituto Centrale del Restauro* (ICR). The Institute was created in Rome 1938 by Giulio Carlo Argan (1909–92), art historian and Minister of Fine Arts, promoting conservation as a critical reading of the work of art and putting his friend Brandi as the director. Here Brandi develops his Theory of Conservation published in 1963, four years after he retired from the ICR. Brandi did what Toesca and Argan considered impossible: to establish a theory of conservation. His definition is still valid today:

> Conservation constitutes the methodological moment of the recognition of the work of art, in its physical consistency and in its double aesthetic and historical polarity, with a view to its transmission to the future.
>
> (Brandi, 1963)

As in the case of Boni, we have to understand the context in which Brandi worked. Important contemporary historians like Berenson promoted the *ripristino* of the monuments destroyed during the war in Florence, following the "*dov'era e com'era*" motto of the San Marco campanile. On the other hand was the practical experience accumulated during the first half of the twentieth century in the conservation of paintings, which Brandi collects and formulates in his Theory of Conservation. Just look at the way in which the reintegrations and *anastylosis* were executed in the Imperial Forums, with a strong concern to distinguish the additions through the use of materials very different from the original ones, which in most cases disturbs the perception of the monument. Brandi promoted a better chromatic and figurative continuity. He understood conservation as the expression of the third time of the work, distinguishing in each work of art the historical and aesthetic instance and allowing the conservator the ability to give one or the other more importance and to see the conservation as a continuation of the original creative process. It is the unrepeatable work of art that determines the conservation, establishing fundamental principles of conservation:

1. Only the material of the work of art is conserved, where its image is manifested, ensuring its transmission to the future. Despite considering the closely related support (structure) and image (aspect), it is legitimate to sacrifice, if necessary, part of the support to preserve the image;
2. The conservation aims to reinstate the potential unity of the work of art, not only its functionality, avoiding its falsification (historic or artistic) and without erasing the trace of time on the object.

As for the principles of action:

1. The reintegration of missing fragments must be recognizable, but invisible at a distance, so that their visual unity is achieved;
2. The matter of the structure can be substituted (always taking into account the historical instance) but not its appearance;
3. The conservation should not prevent future interventions.

With regard to the problem of *lacune* (gaps) in works of art, he is against analogue reintegration, but insists on the need to maintain the figurative unity of the remains. Brandi offers three solutions to the problem:

1. Neutral colours to prevent the *lacuna* from highlighting over the work;
2. Archaeological treatment, so that it differs from the work in tone and luminosity;
3. Move the *lacuna* back to a lower physical level.

150 *Conservation and Architectural Project*

The most widespread solution today is "chromatic abstraction" using in paintings techniques such as the *rigatino*. Umberto Baldini (1921–2006) establishes a theory and practice of painting conservation, in particular the treatment of the *lacune* (Baldini, 1978), and considers the intervention of conservation as restitution of the *Eros* of the work. Baldini, like Brandi, considers that a work of art has three times: 1. the creation of the work, 2. the interval between the end of the creative process until it is seen by a spectator and 3. the recognition of the value of the work by the observer when the consciousness updates it. This is the time to conserve "as and where it is".

Brandi says that it is a mistake to try a "Conservation of Reinstatement" (Restoration), restoring the work to look like the first moment when it was created, trying to eliminate the passage of time: history cannot be deleted. For him the only legitimate moment to intervene is the present, practising 'Archaeological Conservation', respecting the *patina*, the "sedimentation of time".

As a method, Brandi states that in conservation each work is a separate case. The first stage is to make a critical study (historical—artistic and well documented) in order to choose the appropriate treatment. In conservation there are two phases: the reconstruction of the authentic context of the work and the intervention on the material of the work; these phases are not consecutive, they are integrated.

Brandi also discusses preventive conservation (*restauro conservativo*) in view of his definition of Conservation. It is necessary to examine the work from two points of view: the effectiveness of the image it transmits and the state of conservation of the materials. It is necessary to begin by determining the necessary conditions (including changes of legislation) for the enjoyment of the work as an image and as a historical fact, in its spatial scope, to continue with the investigation on the condition of the materials and the conditions of the environmental factors that determine its conservation.

Brandi's Conservation Theory has been widely discussed when it comes to architecture. But we sometimes forgot that Brandi also wrote specifically about architecture and in particular on the critical subject of the insertion of the new into the old (Brandi, 1967). Brandi tells us that "new artistic expressions cannot be inserted in an old context, even if this same context is the result of stratifications from different eras". Brandi considered it impossible to have modern architectural interventions in the old fabric of the city, which he criticizes continuously through articles in the newspaper *Corriere della Sera*. When he talks about examples of architectural transformation, he opposes 'creation' to 'conservation' and is right to say that when the building is transformed, a new image of it is made. However, he recognizes that his Theory of Conservation could not deal extensively with insertions, only those necessary for the stability of the building or the continuity of reading the figurative text. Brandi believes that each modification of a work of the past represents the critical consciousness of the time and has to be justified in the face of universal consciousness, which presents a great responsibility.

Brandi puts as an example the *Pantheon*, a monument of the second century AD that has reached our days thanks to its continuous use, since the seventh century as a church, including additions such as Bernini's 'ears' (bell towers), later demolished. He considers that since the recent birth of the historic consciousness of the monument, this attitude is not acceptable. He justifies that additions can be removed on the most recently made monuments, about a century and a half ago, when they were subjected to *ripristino* operations. Brandi himself acknowledges the aberration that scientific conservation was born from the *ripristino* interventions of Viollet-le-Duc (Brandi, 1967).

Brandi considers that it is impossible to go back and invalidate this historical awareness of the building, from the moment that it is a scientific attitude of our time, in the same way that one cannot go back from the theory of relativity and quantum mechanics to determinism. Thus, the fact of not being able to intervene in a building, only consolidate and safeguard it, is not due to the lack of confidence in contemporary architects, but to this historical conscience, which must absolutely prevail and must be conserved and genuinely transmitted to the future. According to Brandi we owe what we are to the historical tradition.

Like Boni, Brandi also discusses the case of the ruins. Considering the historical instance, the ruins are only those works that testify of a human time, of the history of man, but with a quite different and even unrecognizable aspect compared to what they had at first. Therefore its conservation should be limited to consolidation and preservation, otherwise it would no longer be such a ruin and its environment. According to the aesthetic instance, a ruin is any remainder of a work of art that cannot be returned to its potential unit without the work becoming a copy or a forgery of itself. If the ruin is integrated into a certain environment (monumental, environmental or landscape) that conditions it and that gives it a different meaning does not alter the terms of its conservation, because if it is a new work of art that has reabsorbed to ruin, it is already the second that has the right to prevail. A ruin is recognized as complete in the conscience of those who know how to recognize its value, which derives precisely from its "current mutilation" and not from the integrity it may have possessed at the beginning, so it is a mistake to want to rebuild it; the intervention must be limited to its preservation and consolidation.

Brandi raises the problem of the conservation or elimination of the "additions" and the "reconstructed parts". The additions, including the patina, are new testimonies of history, testimony of the passage of time on the work of art, so they have the same right to be preserved as the original part. Its elimination must always be justified, and in any case it must leave its mark on the work itself. The reconstruction tries to intervene in the creative process, to recast the old with the new without distinguishing them, trying to make a period of time disappear. Therefore, the addition will be more acceptable when trying to create a new unit over the old one.

For a good understanding of Brandi's theory, we must also understand his attitude of continuous search for new methodologies of study to apply to art history, which led to exploring the emerging field of semiotics, helping him to give a new vision of art (Eco, 1968). Brandi said that to conserve one must know. From the other hand, Brandi dedicated his life to unifying conservation systems: through the ICR (which was intended to extend to all regions, although it did not happen that way) and through the 1972 Italian Conservation Charter. He recognized that although the principles for painting, sculpture and architecture must be the same, the methods cannot be the same. He regretted that this Charter has not been used more strictly, but 'elastically', in architectural conservation. He was publicly very critical of architectural conservation projects, which he said are usually mediocre, often bad and sometimes appalling.

G. Morganti (2006) considers unlikely that Brandi's theory was informed by Boni's work, as it is not documented in any way. However, as Morganti himself explains in detail, most of the issues that Brandi includes in his theory already appear in Boni's thought and experiences: ruins, *lacune*, *patina*, authenticity, *in situ* conservation and preventive conservation. The similarities of the lexicon used by Boni and Brandi cannot be ignored either. But there are also differences of opinion. While Boni strongly attacks the reconstructions in the style of buildings, considering it a worthless operation, Brandi avoids generalizing, insisting on the need to judge on a case-by-case basis, and says that "not every stone that replaces the old one is a false one." Like any theory, it is interpreted in different ways. Brandi's premises of pure preservation and consolidation led to inadequate works, in which buildings were drilled to avoid disturbing their appearance, but their structure was forever altered with irreversible consolidation operations (Morganti, 2006).

This difference of opinion is of great importance, and denotes Brandi's most preservationist attitude towards Boni's creative and architectural one. However, Boni made reconstructions, although simplified, in Santa Maria Antiqua due to the need for protection. This way of rebuilding, reconstructing volumes and proportions, is in line with that executed in the cloister of S. Maria Nova that we have already seen, although in this case of the cloister, rather than a reconstruction, it is a true architectural project of the new over the old, incorporating the original elements.

The, say, spirituality and also Ruskin's romanticism, as well as Boni's interest in India and Japan, become in Brandi pragmatism and interest in material aspects, undoubtedly also due to the very different formation of the two: Brandi as a lawyer and Boni as an architect-engineer and archaeologist. Unfortunately Boni did not articulate any explicit theory, but without a doubt Brandi collected a large part of his thought and work in his theory, which, on the other hand, are notes collected by his students. He most probably had read Boni's detailed biography by Tea and the multiple documents that Boni left and his extensive correspondence with the *Antichità e Belle* Arti Administration, where Brandi worked from 1930 to 1960. To reinforce this theory, Russo (2006) has noted Brandi's tendency to 'cannibalize' the authors of whom he nourished, making his own concepts, and to continually develop his thinking. Russo encourages, following the example of Brandi himself, to develop from Brandi's aesthetics new models tailored to us and according to our time, the only way to continue the life of thought (Russo, 2006). On the other hand, theory and practice cannot be separated in Brandi (Parlato, 2006). In the case of *lacune* in painting, the work of P. Toesca is also a clear pioneer of Brandi's theory, as Boni is in the case of architecture.

6.8 Boni, Cirilli, Scarpa, Brandi and Venturi

Before the well-known intervention of Carlo Scarpa in Castelvecchio (Verona), a historicist restoration had been carried out in medieval style in 1924, 'enhancing' the towers, rebuilding the walls and decorating the interiors in medieval and Renaissance style to convert the building into a Museum. In 1945, during the Second World War, Castelvecchio was bombed, and in 1954 Scarpa was commissioned to conserve the building and design a new museum within it, with the help of architect Arrigo Rudi and engineer Carlo Maschietto, all under the supervision of the sovrintendente Pietro Gazzola, who, as we shall see, wrote during the middle of this work, together with Roberto Pane, the Venice Charter. Museum employees, the technical office of the city council with engineer Rocco Nicolò in front and craftsmen who worked in the conservation works contributed largely to the success of the project. The ongoing dialogue on conservation issues between Scarpa and the museum's director, Licisco Magagnato, was also very important.

Carlo Scarpa's project unites conservation and musealization; it is an integrated and creative architectural project, which includes extensions, redistributions of spaces and new itineraries. His masterly treatment of old and new materials has made him and this project a reference for architectural conservation. This intervention has been linked to modern painting, such as the De Stijl movement and its greatest exponent Piet Mondrian. But there is a clearer and more direct reference: Guido Cirilli and his work as a conservation architect in Santa Francesca Romana. We recognize in the cloister of S, Maria Nova a clear intention to distinguish the new from the old, but also to integrate it, through the manipulation of forms and materials (Figure 3.12).

In our opinion, this way of acting, and, perhaps, aesthetic, came to influence Carlo Scarpa through what would be his teacher and employer in Venice, Guido Cirilli, despite the fact that his work was loaded with

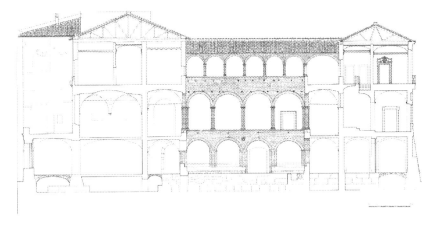

Figure 6.4 Cross-section N-S through cloister and old refectory looking towards the Colosseum (A.)

a strong eclecticism. Scarpa's work of superimposed layers creating an authentic contemporary stratigraphy, always appears as it was the result of conservation works and precedes the thought of Vittorio Gregotti and Franco Purini in their consideration that each construction is actually conceived as a reconstruction, and in this way a language of the modification of the existing architecture must be developed (Carbonara, 2011).

In addition to this characteristic stratification of materials, we also find other precedents in the project of the cloister of S. Maria Nova to the work of Scarpa, such as the composition and the play of textures and lights. The roughly dressed masonry walls that Boni and Cirilli use for the new construction obtain an effect very similar to the textured concrete used by Scarpa, and both exhibit the archaeological artefacts through a set of lights and textures, creating a real scenery. However, in the case of the cloister, old photographs seem to indicate that the carved wall was intended to be covered by ivy, most likely considering Boni's interest in combining flora and monuments (González-Longo, 2015).

Scarpa recognizes its roots but also the constraints:

> I descend, by cultural tradition, from the monument to Vittorio Emanuele II in Rome [where Cirilli was working before Santa Maria Nova]. I was, in fact, the best pupil of my professor [Cirilli] at the *Accademia*, who in turn had been the best pupil of the author of that monument. . . . The spiritual poverty of that time was due to the fact that the teachers of the academies of fine arts shared the eclectic taste of the nineteenth-century. This is why we had to make some effort to free ourselves from our school education.
>
> (Scarpa, 1976)

Perhaps inspired by the Castelvecchio project, Bruno Zevi felt that architectural conservation should be controlled more. He proposed that the projects were reviewed by a panel of scholars and the *Sovrintendente* of monuments, and that the best 'modern' architects be commissioned (Cristallini, 2006). Zevi's proposal to form a panel goes ahead and a commission is formed in which he himself participates. A debate on the safeguarding of works of art and natural beauty is also opened in its magazine '*L'Architettura-cronache e storia*' in 1957. In opposition to Brandi, Zevi held the thesis of the possibility of including new quality modern architecture in historic centres, creating language dissonances. This created a great controversy with Brandi, who in 1956 gave a lecture at the Italian Cultural Association called: "The old and the new in the historic Italian cities" declaring against new constructions in historic centres.

Brandi tells us about a code present in architecture (as in music), which appears clearly if we look at Roman, Byzantine, Romanesque and Gothic architecture (Brandi, 1967). He invents the term *astanza*, which constitutes the current presence of the art object. In the case of architecture, Brandi believes that when there is no fundamental articulation of the interior with the exterior, this *astanza* of the work of art will not occur. This is a critical point, considering the disarticulation that exists in so many buildings between the interior and the exterior. Brandi notes in his Theory of Conservation, written in 1963, this interior-exterior articulation of the architecture. Interestingly, in 1966, Robert Venturi in his book *Complexity and Contradiction in Architecture* includes two final chapters: 'Inside and Outside' and 'The Obligation Toward the Difficult Whole' (Venturi, 1966). Remarkably, he deals here with issues discussed by Brandi in his theory: the interior-exterior aspects and the unity of the work of art. This similarity is not accidental: Venturi was between 1954 and 1956 at the American Academy in Rome, years in which Brandi was the director of the ICR in Rome, and when was very active. Although Brandi extensively uses Italian examples and Venturi's bibliographical references do not include Brandi or any other Italian author, a clear reference to contemporary Italian thought cannot be denied. A further clue is the presence in the book of a photograph of Piero della Francesca's 'Flagellation of Christ' from the ICR; Brandi published in the years in which Venturi was in Rome an article about the conservation of this painting. These similarities between Venturi and Brandi discussions about architecture as a meeting place between interior and exterior, space and function, as well as their concept of artistic unity should be further researched.

6.9 The Roman School of Conservation, the 'Critical Conservation'

The founder and first director of the *Scuola di Specializzazione per lo Studio ed il Restauro dei Monumenti*, at the Università degli Studi di Roma

"*La Sapienza*", Guglielmo de Angelis D'Ossat (1961) proposed the separation of the architectural intervention (when the building has to respond to a certain use and program) and the preservation-repair operation, from a conceptual and operational point of view. The following directors of the Roman conservation school, Renato Bonelli, Gaetano Miarelli Mariani and Giovanni Carbonara, continued the reflection. With Brandi as a major reference, they have maintained continuity but at the same time the evolution of the discipline, with a great influence internationally.

The methodology of Professor Roberto Pane (1897–1987), a student of Giovannoni, can be deduced from the attack he makes on Rudolf Wittkower's book 'Architectural Principles in the Age of Humanism' at the 18th International Congress of Art History in 1956 in Venice. S. Casiello (2010) reminds us of the psychological instance that Pane encourages to keep in mind, "in the name of the attributes of memory and according to our inner life", in addition to the historical and aesthetic instances. In 1945, Bonelli, a follower of the philosophy of B. Croce, and as such separated the aesthetic implications of the practices (Croce, 1920), already framed the concept of architectural criticism as art criticism (Bonelli, 1945).

Along with Pane's argument, Bonelli established that the historical value of the work of art is identified with the expressive, while its understanding is entrusted to criticism and not to the practical principles from which the creative act has resulted, thus laying the basis of 'Critical Conservation' (*Restauro Critico*) (Bonelli, 1945). To Bonelli, conservation does not belong to the practical sphere but to the theoretical one. Accordingly, the conservator sees the final work not only as a historical or critical one but also as an artist who takes the work to its original expression. The need to identify the added parts loses importance; the important thing is the final result. The task of the conservator is to reinstate the "intimate and robust coherence of beauty" to the work of art. This is a beauty in Croce's sense, not in nature, but in the spiritual energy of human activity. In this way the work will never be false, but original in its value of universality (Bonelli, 1945).

As we have seen, Brandi's theory is focused on the subject of the work of art, the only one to be preserved, with the aim of conserve the potential unity of the work of art and without cancelling the traces of history (Brandi, 1963). The 'Critical Conservation', as formulated by Bonelli (1963), once again considers the architectural conservation as a creative act, in which the original (the building as a document) and the intervention that increases the value of the building (taking possession of it) are respected at the same time, in an effort to merge the new with the old. At the beginning of the twentieth century, there was a strong connection between conservators and art historians, antiquarians and collectors and the discourse on authenticity was intense, as we have seen in the case of Boni.

This theory is influenced by the two preceding centuries. As we have seen, since the eighteenth century, architecture has been exposed to historical judgments, and the present separated from the past with the consequent loss of continuity. The archaeological value of the building increasingly prevails and monuments became bearers of ideal images of the past, anecdotal documents or scenery that only contribute to the urban context, losing identity as individual buildings, and in the end the true nature of its architecture was not understood. As we have also seen, the definition of conservation as a discipline appears in the nineteenth century, but the great evolution occurs during the twentieth century, as reflected by the definition of conservation (*restauro*) in the *Enciclopedia Italiana* (Giovannoni, 1936) and the *Enciclopedia Universale dell'Arte* (Bonelli, 1963).

The practice promoted by the Italian Conservation Charter and by Giovannoni (1936): "the reinstatement of existing fragments with the eventual addition of neutral elements, necessary for the reintegration of the whole and to ensure future conservation", is called by G. Miarelli Mariani (1999) 'Theory of Substitutes'; he also believed that the ways in which architectural conservation is carried out today do not respond to contemporary sensibilities and the current way of understanding the past. He blamed the philological or 'Scientific' approach of the interwar period of the twentieth century for the progressive separation of the conservation from the architectural debate, which he thought it has been recently increased, separating conservation from the *Zeitgeist*.

6.10 Rebuilding the Velia: Reflections on Architectural and Urban Conservation in the Second Half of the Twentieth Century

Perhaps all the early developments of the twentieth-century we have seen in urban archaeology in Rome influenced S. Freud (1930) when he speaks of the 'preservation of mind'. Freud, who was very interested in archaeology, made the architecture of Rome a metaphor of the mind, representing its history the same that represents the psychic life of each person, a true 'historic city of the mind'. In this way, an early experience remains in memory and inhabits psychic structures, in the same way that in Rome new buildings occupy the structures of the previous ones and all epochs coexist.

The French influence was fundamental in the city project. Until their arrival, the only action had been to dig up the monuments. In Rome, unlike in Paris, the works were small and poorly connected. The French, in addition to a large dose of method, contributed the idea of creating an appropriate framework, giving an urban dimension by joining them through tree-lined walks. In this way they also influenced the development of the ideas of urban conservation of Giovannoni. In the fascist era, speculation and meeting traffic needs were the only objectives. The aim was to satisfy the new functional requirements with the help of an aesthetic sometimes unable to understand the new situation. The central monumental zone was for a long time, with the exception of the *Vittoriano*, without new monumental architecture. The 1938 proposal of the *Danteum* by G. Terragni, in the immediate vicinity of the Temple of Venus and Rome, was going to be presented at the planned universal exhibition (EUR) in 1942, which never took place due to World War II.

During the Mussolinian era, the debate and the actions at the urban level were continuous and Giovannoni tried to establish a relationship between the conservation of monuments and urban conservation, between the monument and its context. Racheli (1995, 2007) considers that architectural conservation has no meaning unless it is related to its context and the city, which are what give it semantic and figurative values. Undoubtedly, the origin of this must be found in the architect and urban planner Camillo Sitte (1843–1903) and its publication in 1889 'The art of building cities', where he promoted an organic and three-dimensional construction of cities, with squares and nature. Patrick Geddes (1854–1932) also develops similar concerns, but adding social aspects, following Ruskin's idea of the relationship between social progress and spatial forms. He intervened accordingly in the Old Town of Edinburgh, also creating historical associations with local characters.

As we have seen at the monumental complex of the Temple of Venus and Rome and Santa Francesca Romana, history is a fundamental part of its architecture and its conservation cannot be carried out without a deep understanding of this history, to be used as one more instrument of the project. We know the extensive use of history that architects have made in their projects (Garnham, 2013), however, as C. Varagnoli (2004) notes, contemporary designers in general do not investigate history, discarding the fundamental phase of knowledge at the time of the creative process. In this way, the project becomes self-referential and without dialogue with the existing (Varagnoli, 2004). P. Torsello (2005) also warned us of the fact that architectural conservation is almost always a design pretext, avoiding a true dialogue with the old building. The existing building is just an excuse for the new design, which is immediately attractive due to the material contrast.

That history serves to design and reflect on the contemporary architectural project has already been demonstrated by Robert Venturi, with his elaboration of a theory of architecture through the analysis of Mannerist buildings, precisely during a stay in Rome in 1956, as we have mentioned previously (Venturi, 1966). Manfredo Tafuri (1935–94) understood the need, above all, to understand the mentality and culture of each historical period, entering the intellectual spirit and the cultural context of the work (Tafuri, 1986). He became a defender of the conservation carried out by qualified architects, getting involved himself in the conservation of Giulio Romano's Tea Palace and helping to prevent the intervention of Renzo Piano in the Palladio's Basilica. For Tafuri, criticism does not exist: it is simply history. He accuses the critics (Zevi, Portoghesi) of exercising instrumental architectural criticism, using it for their benefit as practising architects. Crucially, Tafuri claimed the need for architecture to have autonomy as a discipline and his interest was in the project, as specific to the discipline (Pane, 2009).

Carlo Aymonino- perhaps inspired by Terragni's *Danteum* designed for an adjacent place-, proposed in the 1980s to rebuild the Velia hill using the space as a museum, and even to build a new colossal statue, recreating that of Nero. The late 1980s and early 1990s revives the debate on archaeology of the central area of Rome and its relationship with the city, which is reflected in initiatives of international competitions of ideas and publications of the City Council, such as *Romacentro*. The Forum area is recognized as the cultural root of Rome, but also a historical problem in relation to the city, and a review of the situation was carried out. It is interesting to note that the ideas competition was for the areas bordering the Central Archaeological Area; some of those, such as the Velia or Piazza Venezia, were empty spaces created by previous drastic interventions in the city. The fear of occupying the monumental zones is latent. The commission for the elaboration of the competition brief was constituted by the City council, the *Soprintendenze*, the professional incorporations of Architects and Engineers and the University.

G. Carbonara (1990) made a lucid exposition of the five fundamental criteria for the protection and conservation of cultural heritage, that any project 'on' or 'of' the pre-existence must consider:

1. that the functional and practical problems are 'medium' and not 'end' of the intervention; the end is the transmission to the future, in the best conditions of a historic-artistic heritage, "material with the value of civilization" (Commission Franceschini, dich. 1st);
2. that the guiding criterion is always the "minimum intervention", and that everything that is proposed or done finds, before, cultural/preservation justification and, only in a subordinate way, of another type. That the creativity of the architects be used to "maximize" the effectiveness and "minimize" the weight of each intervention, pursuing quality and not quantity, as unfortunately often happens;
3. that the most noble and grandiose testimonies, as well as the smallest and poorest, be taken care of in the same way, as "monuments" (by their same antiquity), in all cultural property. It is a point that has been clarified for some time, on which it would be superfluous to return, if some frequent misunderstandings about the concept of monument, still understood as an emergent structure and "protagonist", did not

make it useful to specify, which finds confirmation in its etymology, which refers to the meaning as "document";
4. that conservation, dealing with historic, artistic and "authentic" material culture testimonies, resembles, by criteria and method, philology and the critical edition of texts; that in this way all temptation of *ripristino* should be banished, which would only confuse—except, perhaps, few elected connoisseurs—the documents of history and that it would use philology surreptitiously, making it return "certainties" (based on which reconstruct and complete) that by definition can never be anything more than, to the maximum, pure "critical hypotheses";
5. that by such a hypothetical nature, then, the indispensable additions must always be modern, with an effective expressive actuality, so that the new and the old are really such and not forgeries. There is nothing more painful than seeing, for example a plastered wall painted again—most of the time without need—and then aged artificially, trying to recover the patina just sacrificed; in this respect, the damage that an eventual "colour plan" of Rome could cause, in the absence of clear and shared theoretical and methodological references, can already be foreseen. (Carbonara, 1990)

Carbonara also gives there a good definition of 'new':

> 'New' does not mean 'dissonant', but means something thought, reinterpreted and invented, in relation to the specificity of a place (or an object), to solve, respecting the old and following critically the suggestions, the problems that it presents.
>
> (Carbonara, 1990)

He continues noting how positive the normative restrictions may be for the project and the absurdity of the "continuous evolution" of pre-existence, acting as the architects of the sixteenth and seventeenth centuries would do. The modern historic and historic-artistic conscience, configured from the eighteenth century, make another attitude necessary that is conservative on the one hand, defending the historic-artistic testimonies, but, on the other hand, strongly innovative, in all those choices that, more than conservation, we can define as protection, preservation or prevention. Therefore, the need to look at the urban environment.

As base material for the competition, some schedules were made by zones. Area 3 was dedicated to the Velia area and denotes lack of interest or perhaps ignorance of its history and significance, and its value was presented as subject to neighbouring monuments such as the Colosseum. As we have mentioned, the proposal was to reinstate part of the Velia's volume with a museum. The ideas were confusing and the conservatism and weight of history predominate in the proposals.

Carbonara has, most recently, summarized the development of architectural conservation in the second half of the twentieth century, with some pessimism due to the reduction, since Brandi's work, of the theoretical debate on conservation and the reductionism, between 'preservation' and 'restoration' (*ripristino*) (Carbonara, 1995, 2012). Although he does not name them, the identification of the leaders of these two trends is clear: Marco Dezzi Bardeschi of the 'preservationists' and Paolo Marconi of the 'restorers' (Racheli, 2007; Dezzi Bardeschi, 1991; Marconi, 1993).

Marco Dezzi Bardeschi considers conservation as a science of preservation and with the objective of not subtracting material from the fabric, but to add, increasing the historic stratification and the consequent global dialogue between elements (Dezzi Bardeschi, 1991). Amedeo Bellini, also in the group of 'preservationists', considers that conservation cannot mean anything other than the search for a regulation for the transformation, reinterpreting without destroying. But also disregarding a system of a priori ideas or theories and based on conditions concrete and on the use of the building's past for the conservation project (Bellini,1997). In this sense, he seems to be oriented more towards the 'Critical Conservation'. Marconi's work and legacy has recently been discussed by J. García-Gutiérrez Mosteiro (2014) and C. Varagnoli (2015, 2016), making clear that his approach of restoration was not that of Viollet-le-Duc, but a more substantiated and complex one.

6.11 Old and New: The Contemporary Discourse

The topic of new architecture in historic places and buildings has generated a great deal of literature in recent times, but already in 1965 the great Italian architects of the time met in Venice to discuss the issue, concluding that it was possible to preserve and incorporate new architecture at the same time (Pane, 1965). Carbonara makes an excellent review of the latest publications on the theme of the Old and the New in the historic city, including a proposed classification regarding the possible intervention approaches (Carbonara, 2011). As Carbonara mentions, there is an incomprehension of the archaeological remains and monuments as well as a palpable poverty in the proposals of new architecture on these (Carbonara, 2011).

It is complex to respond to the question about why architectural conservation discourses are not followed up, starting from the positioning of the discipline, and architecture in general between the Arts and Sciences. Language barriers have also been determinant in the lack of a wider discussion on the subject. The terminology in the field of architectural conservation seems to be as confusing as the criteria that different institutions and professionals apply today, even within the same country. The difference between conservation, restoration and preservation, words used continuously, interchangeably, is not usually clarified. The fact that different countries have different terms make things even more complicated. The British 'Conservation" is in the United States 'Preservation', in Italy '*Restauro*' and in Spain '*Restauración*'. The translations of texts have sometimes caused also confusion, such as the English translation of Brandi's '*Teoria del Restauro*' as 'Theory of Restoration' instead of 'Conservation' as would be more appropriate. In Spain, the term '*Rehabilitación*' (reuse) is used extensively and in the United Kingdom 'Retrofitting' (upgrade, normally concerning energy issues), are inappropriate terms as they may indicate not enough respect for the existing architecture and its fabric.

As well as, method, it is a matter of conservation criteria and architectural culture. For example in Spain there is a unique tradition of architects who do both new work and conservation while in the United Kingdom most of the time these are considered two different activities. Antón Capitel (2009) has reflected on interventions through history to develop a methodology of intervention by analogy. For Enric Miralles, new and old were the same, in the same way it was for Boni, for Alberti and many more, although the method and approach of their projects was very different. At the beginning of Carbonara's book '*Avvicinamento al Restauro*' (1997) he includes a revealing quote from Plutarch:

> That is why the works of Pericles are even more admired, born in a short time to last a long time. Each one in fact for its beauty was then immediately old and until today it is, by force, current and new.
> (Plutarco, *Vita di Pericle*, XIII, 4–5).

Francesco Dal Co recognizes the variability and instability of value judgments in regard to intervention in built heritage and the fact that there are no shared values or theories to refer to (Dal Co, 2007). Carbonara (2011) picks up the answer G. Cristinelli (2008) has given: just as there is no singular theory of art or architecture, there should be not one for conservation, which is a branch of architecture.

With the starting point (sometimes unconscious) of the classification of Giovannoni into categories (consolidation, anastylosis, liberation, completion and renewal) people still try to define today the different forms of intervention with the aim of reaching a classification: total demolition or partial, total or partial reconstruction, extension of the original project, etc. Also, as we have seen, there is the tendency to develop theories focused on one aspect only: style, philology, science or history. However, classifications, although helpful to clarify the interventions, are unsuccessful in defining them in full, since the architectural work is too complex to be inscribed in a single operation.

Architectural Review dedicated its November 2007 cover to the project of the Diocesan Museum of Peter Zumthor in Cologne, calling it 'Layers of Meaning'. Despite such a promising title, it covers only with superficial, ornamental, material and detail aspects, although recognizing that this is not the only language. The criticism of the Zumthor Museum, built on the Gothic church of St Kolumba, destroyed during World War II, is focused on formal aspects, without any reference to Zumthor's interpretation of this historic place (Davey, 2007). The lack of a historical-critical approach to architectural criticism is made even more evident in another article of the same journal about the project by Edouard François in which he copies a nineteenth century building in Paris, in concrete (Slessor, 2007). The journal includes one article after another confusing the anecdotal, the picturesque and literal with the actual use of history in a project. There are more substantial issues that could have been discussed, such as the preservation in Zumthor's project of the 1950s chapel within the ruins. Unfortunately, current architectural criticism seems to be largely incapable of discussing such an intervention.

On the other hand, this project in Cologne is an unusual one in Germany, where restoration seems to be the usual norm, more extremely in the case of Dresden Cathedral. Curiously, at the Neues Museum in Berlin, we find the 'import' of the typical British situation of two different type of architects: one that deals with the 'New' (D. Chipperfield) and the other with the 'Old' (J. Harrap), with the result of two different criteria operating at the same time, as it will happen to any building with two different architects. While Chipperfield mimics the facade in the *lacune* situation and adds new elements in a simplified way, Harrap just consolidates the ruin, leaving the *lacune* without any treatment, disfiguring the appearance of the whole and making the *lacune* very evident. However, both masterful executions managed to achieve a project of high interest.

These projects in Berlin and Cologne follow contemporary trends, but also some of the internationally recognized conservation principles of minimal intervention and distinguishability. In the case of the Neues Museum, Chipperfield refers to the Venice Charter for his intervention.

Among others, the architects F. Minissi (Vivio, 2010), F. Venezia, F. Cellini, G. Bulian and F. Scoppola in Italy have tried to act as designers in the architectural conservation projects, but have also encountered many controversies. More recently, a simple, neutral architecture has been chosen, subject to the identity and character of the monument which is conserved with great care. The work of the architect Guido Canali has shown that there is a quieter way to conserve and make new architecture, creating a continuous dialogue with the old building, an option that Carbonara calls 'critical-preservationist' (Carbonara, 1996).

Spain is where we could say that a more "free" attitude is cultivated with respect to monuments but a greater historical-critical interpretation is needed to avoid the homogenization that monuments

164　*Conservation and Architectural Project*

often have to endure. The acclaimed 'Caixa Forum' building in Madrid by architects Herzog and De Meuron is an example of false heritage preservation, its use as a design pretext, and old-fashioned modern-old collage, as Capitel has noted (Capitel, 2008).

There is a real division between those who believe that historic centres should be preserved as they are and those who believe that new architecture should be added. In consolidated historic cities, such as Edinburgh, declared World Heritage by UNESCO, the debate is ongoing but somehow fruitless. The case of the new Scottish parliament, in which the seventeenth-century Queensberry House was the only building saved from demolition (González-Longo, 2008), is an example of actions on historic centres in which the new prevails over the old. At least in this case the quality of the new building far exceeds what it was in the place and the city has improved as a result, although it is true that more layers of the area's rich history could have been preserved. The ongoing new building in St James Centre also in Edinburgh is an example of the commercial values prevailing above the architectural and wider cultural ones.

On the other hand, the management of architectural heritage begins to be invaded by the big operators of the consumption, and at the same time the universalization of heritage extends, especially with the declarations of World Heritage by UNESCO, as already predicted J. Rivera Blanco (1999). An example of tensions between consumerism and heritage protection is the 'Cronocaos preservation tour' installation in 2010 at the Venice Biennale of Rem Koolhas (OMA), making a call for an unified theory, which shows the topicality of this issue as well as the great ignorance about architectural conservation within the architectural profession. Despite Koolhas's basic knowledge of the subject, limited to the theories of Ruskin and Viollet-le-Duc and ignoring the great developments in conservation afterwards, and in particular during the twentieth century described previously, the exhibition has been displayed all around the world.

Our discourse may seem too focused on Italy, but it is inevitable because that is where conservation theory has developed during the twentieth century and today. B. Paolo Torsello published in 2005 a small book confronting nine contemporary scholars on the subject: A. Bellini, G. Carbonara, S. Casiello, R. Cecchi, M. Dezzi Bardeschi, P. Fancelli, P. Marconi, G. Spagnesi Cimbolli and Torsello himself, to whom he gave a maximum of 9,000 characters to develop their individual position (Torsello, 2005). G. Miarelli Mariani was the tenth, but unfortunately his passing has deprived us of his contribution. Torsello notes that only Viollet-le-Duc and Brandi have given a definition of restoration and conservation and that the reflection on conservation theory has been circumscribed to Italy, while other European countries have developed studies only from a technical point of view, taking care more of how and not why we conserve. A. Bellini says that conservation is the execution of an architectural project that actively helps preserve and prevent degradation. For G. Carbonara, it is any intervention to preserve and transmit to the future, facilitating reading without cancelling the signs of the past, the execution of an act of critical interpretation, a modifiable critical hypothesis that does not irreversibly alter the original. He insists that conservation is not the sum of individual specialized operations, but also needs an architectural solution. Carbonara also points out that there is no difference between conservation in general and architectural conservation, only in terms of object consistency. He also clarifies the distinction between 'conservation', that is to say the direct intervention and modification carried out under a rigorous technical-scientific and historical-critical control, and 'preservation', as a prevention and protection work to be carried out to avoid the restoration intervention, which constitutes always a traumatic event for the 'cultural asset'.

It is necessary to stop in these definitions, since many of the mistakes and the current 'pollution' in the field of conservation are due to the fact that it is not understood exactly what it is. Italian scholars have already clarified for some time what conservation means, but it seems that in the Anglo-Saxon world it should still be done, since at this time very different practices take place. Carbonara clarifies it (Torsello, 2005): in spite of similarities, since they all deal with monuments restoration is not conservation, as neither are the functional 'repair' of an object, the 'reinvention' or 'reconstruction' of an object, since it is about a new project that does not respect the values and the original matter. Conservation is not the 'reuse', the 'rehabilitation', the 'recycling', 'regeneration', nor the 'safeguard' and 'maintenance', which are 'preservation' operations. 'Conservation' goes beyond 'preservation'; it implies an interpretation of the work, in a critical and creative way, and where 'preservation' and 'innovation' are closely linked. In short, the project intervention is directly linked to the historical-critical understanding (always with a hypothesis value) of the object to be conserved. And this understanding requires the guiding criteria (distinguishability, reversibility, minimal intervention and respect for the authenticity of the work), historic-philological and technical competence, conceptual clarity, prudence and knowledge.

S. Casiello defends in the same book the need for the architect-conservator to be competent in the historical-critical aspects and able to decipher the complexities of the various stratifications and decay over time. He refers to Miarelli Mariani: "The quality of the results, rather than the rules, depends on the culture and finesse with which they are interpreted, in addition to the ability of the team leader of the conservation project and those who execute it." (Torsello, 2005). Along these lines, Carbonara (2011) reminds us that Saverio Muratori argued that the conservation architect must be 'even more architect' in order to have the capacity for dialogue with the past, until the conservation project becomes an architectural project.

As C. Ceschi (1970) noted, the great Roman tradition in the field of the conservation of ancient monuments and archaeology had already allowed to execute scientifically correct works, without relying on any 'conservation charter'. However, Charters were quickly popularized in Italy and globally, however, we would argue, they have not been critically used in conservation projects (González-Longo, 2015). The Venice Charter (1964), written, as mentioned before by Pane and Gazzola during the conservation of Castelvecchio, is perhaps still the most substantial and specific to architectural conservation. It actually specifies the differences between 'conservation' and 'restoration', but we believed it was not correctly translated to English as it should have been 'preservation' and 'conservation' instead. It is curious that this has not been corrected. From our point of view, there have been an excessive number of Charters since then, which create confusion: Charters should be revised or made obsolete rather than creating new ones and leaving the previous ones. Superseded charters should be clearly marked and placed in a repository for historical reference only. There should be also a hierarchy, from the most generic to specialized ones, such as the recent and excellent one on the conservation of wooden-built heritage.

7 Conclusions

The Architectural Conservation Project: Preservation and Transformation

7.1 The Continuous Architecture

Until the seventeenth century, conserving, restoring, preserving or repairing was not a different cultural activity than building new. In addition to the monumental complex studied here and others in Rome, this fact can be seen in many other sites, and we would almost say that there is always an element of pre-existence in any given site. However, the objectives and degree of intervention were different: sometimes it was a daily practice of the art of building, from the sublime to the simply dictated economically. Other times the reuse of *spolia* (Bernard et al,, 2008) or entire buildings had explicit ideological and symbolic content for owners, architects and operators.

Emperor Hadrian had different approaches depending on the place—the material element he valued most—and the public. His political message evoked and commemorated the past, but also called the present, from the extensive design and conservation of existing structures and places on his new buildings, as in the Temple of Venus and Rome and the Pantheon, to conservation projects (as it is the case in his intervention the Olympeion in Athens), retaining the original material and forms.

During the Middle Ages, buildings and ruins were constantly reused and transformed in Europe, almost always for practical reasons. Monasteries, churches and castles were built on the foundations of previous constructions and ruins (usually Roman) and later they were transformed and extended. But this was at the expense of many others that were 'sacrificed'; Roman buildings, even of value, constituted true quarries of material, extending during the Middle Ages to the practice of burning marble to obtain lime. The Temple of Venus and Rome and the Olivetan church and monastery complex served not only as a source of material, but also as a project inspiration as we have seen in the Palazzo Venezia.

At urban level, the *Passeggiata Archeologica* is remarkable in its continuity as a project over centuries, confirming the idea expressed by Alberti. Initiated in Roman times, revisited with the triumphal entry of Charles V, the tree boulevard of the seventeenth century, and the De Tournon and Baccelli's projects, to this day with the projects in the central archaeological area and the *Parco del Colosseo,* the strong design idea is that this area wants to be linear, scenographic and open, very different from the first, enclosed, Roman Forum described above.

In the Temple of Venus and Rome we can also test the permanence of the project. From the beginning, this was dual, not only because of its original design, but also because of how it has evolved. While its western part, towards the centre of the city, has been architecturally developed as part of an inhabited building, its east part, towards the Colosseum, has been consolidated in its condition of ruin in the picturesque landscape.

Marguerite Yourcenar (1992) tells us that time is the great sculptor, and certainly this important historic site is a good example. Many people acted on the building and lived in it, but the place, the entity and the scale of the building made time itself dictate 'laws', well intuited and interpreted by architects and clients. This resulted in the complex we see today, with an incredible diversity of styles and materials, but with a *concinnitas* created in some way by people, materials and time. Perhaps the excessive interest in trying to establish a position of each era with its past has distracted from the true understanding of the architectural transformations that have happened in time, in an intertwining of political, philosophical, economic and material reasons.

Despite the attempts to theorize about architectural conservation and establish parallels with the pictorial works, the differences are obvious: an architectural work has many times more than one author. It is created over longer periods of time with the collaboration of many other professions, and designed for a particular place. But the biggest difference is that buildings have a function and are occupied.

7.2 The Skilful Conservation of the Architectural Idea

The advances in archaeology over the last two centuries have helped immensely in our understanding and knowledge of the past, but it has also "scared" the architectural practice. Architects, most of the time not equipped well enough to understand old buildings and structures, have to be subject to the judgment of historians and archaeologists, on the other hand fairly: historical and cultural values are the easiest to cancel. These values are also the most difficult to transmit and integrate into our contemporary culture, and this work of the architect as a creative interpreter is also problematic.

Although Boni is best known in the field of archaeology, his studies and work in the field of architectural conservation are tremendously important, not only theoretically but also practically. When Boni completed a work, it was built, documented and written with exceptional value not only for the history of archaeology, architecture and conservation, but also as an example of project methodology. His relationship with Mussolini must be understood in its historical context and should not harm this great contribution. His rigour and meticulous intervention is not only an example for our generation, but it constitutes a value in itself and must be preserved and disseminated.

Crucial then is the classic question about what do we conserve today, to which we might conclude that what we conserve matters more than the creative idea (or ideas) for/from the work. It is the intangible aspect, the most delicate to convey: how the idea is preserved. We must promote the documentation of the ideas behind the buildings, which over time can be forgotten.

Without criticism and architectural interpretation, conservation cannot exist. Before 'touching' the building, we need to understand it, its value, meaning, significance and contribution in its urban and cultural context. The curators of paintings were initially painters and Argan and Brandi 'transported' conservation from the artistic-artisanal environment to the scientist. For Brandi, architecture, if it is not art, is pure tectonic, that is, the practical adaptation of a need, and if it is art, then it does not respond to a semantic structure. The curators of monuments are today architects; the 2013 reform of the Technical Building Code in Spain requires architects to have a thorough knowledge of the constructive-structural characteristics of the buildings. But this is not enough.

It is useful to look back at some of the practices of the seventeenth century, at a time when the figure of the architect-builder is consolidated with that of the architect-designer, with a continuous exchange of ideas with clients and the integration of other arts within their designs. It was also when the Italian architecture and architecture treatises began to be more widespread, just before the rediscovery of Pompeii and the development of archaeology as a science, as we have seen, with implications for architecture.

There are more and more opportunities (and necessity) for architects to design and work on existing architecture, but there are also more regulations and conservation charters. We have to give the new generations a better historical-critical and technical education that prepares them to face these new challenges in an intelligent way, understanding and interpreting the building before designing the intervention. As we have seen, the role and education of clients and architects was fundamental in determining the project.

On the other hand, Venturi and Scott Brown consider that there is too much doctrine and authoritarian personalities in architecture, and they attribute it to the system of teaching of projects with critical jurors, still following the French system of Beaux Arts. This is an interesting point to reflect on, think and discuss about how we could teach differently.

While a music critic is required to understand musical composition and structure, it is not uncommon to find a critic of architecture unable to understand structural and constructional aspects. Brandi was aware

170 *Conclusions*

of this complexity and discussed extensively the meaning of structure. However, spatial aspects did not seem to be important in the discussion.

7.3 The Conservation Project as Preservation and Transformation of Pre-existences

As we have seen, the conservation theories that were formalized, such as Brandi's, had been practised much earlier, as is the case with Boni. This gives us a clear indication that in architectural conservation, unlike in other sciences, conservation praxis always precedes and informs theory.

We are attending today a kind of rediscovery of the past, perhaps more for necessity and aesthetic reasons than for the romanticism of previous centuries. The powerful images of the new St Kolumba diocesan museum in Cologne that we discussed earlier, in which Peter Zumthor superimposes a large new building on the existing ruins have attracted much attention and interest. In the case of Scarpa's intervention in Castelvecchio and the related Venice Charter, they were informed in our view from previous works carried out after Boni and Cirilli's intervention at the cloister of S. Maria Nova.

Both Zumthor and Scarpa's projects convey the poetic sensibility of their authors and their ability to add structures through a masterful composition of old and new. Although Scarpa was not the first to transform an old building, he was perhaps the first to do so in a way that old and new are clearly visible, with their characteristic stratification. We could call it 'stratigraphic architectural design', the same one that Boni did for the first time in the cloister of the monastery of S. Maria Nova and that, as we have discussed, could have been transmitted through Cirilli, Boni's collaborator and Scarpa's teacher: in our view, this intervention was the paradigm shift in architectural conservation.

A similar operation, one hundred years later is the aforementioned Neues Museum in Berlin. The fact that the project was divided into two different competencies in terms of the new and the old arouses a controversy that, however, has not been reflected in the profession and in public opinion, which does nor seem to be too interested on the debate about architectural conservation. The general public seems more alert to the conservation of works of art. This is confirmed by the 2012 case in Borja (Spain) where someone in the local church, with the intention of conserving a *Ecce Homo* painting, repainted it with disastrous consequences and international exposure, something that does not happen with an equivalent architectural work, although there are many interventions of a similar nature.

Despite all the advances in communication, there are still 'parallel worlds' in regard to the theory and practice of architectural design and conservation, and even heritage science and architectural conservation. The historiography and criticism of architecture, present and past, have created a fictitious separation—from the point of view of architectural design—between the new architecture and the conservation of existing buildings, as in the mentioned case of the Neues Museum in Berlin. It seems that this separation has been dictated more by prejudices than by the rigorous analysis of the previous works, in which we can learn how pre-existences has influenced quality architecture.

As demonstrated in this site, intervening on an existing building is an architectural design act, but whose methodology is more complex than that of designing a new building, since it requires a series of additional studies, a historical-critical process of interpreting existing architecture and specialist technical skills. This methodology involves a detailed study not only of the building's fabric, but also of its physical, historical and cultural context.

This understanding of the characteristics and values of the building informs the project, in the sense that it is certainly not the same to intervene in the Pantheon than in a simple building devoid of architectural value. Knowing the building well and understanding why it should be preserved is the first step to know how its conservation should be designed. Although this statement seems obvious, we find every day 'standard' actions, such as the very popular 'façadism' or the addition of 'bland' volumes: parallelepipeds of wood or zinc on or next to historic buildings, denoting both a lack of understanding of the existing architecture and the design skills to deal with it. The consequence is a misunderstanding and lack of critical interpretation of the architecture of the existing building and a bad conservation practice, especially as regards the complete emptying of historic buildings, leaving only the façade.

The study of the monumental complex of the Temple of Venus and Rome and Santa Francesca Romana has allowed reflection on the subject in a time frame of more than two thousand years. Despite being a unique site in many respects, this extreme case of preservation and transformation has been the best example for studying the nature of the architectural project at different times, and the effect of patrons, clients, architects, politics and the environment, on architecture. This monumental complex is a rare survivor in the middle of the Roman Forum, surrounded by huge archaeological excavations and ruins with the particularity that the most recent larger intervention was carried out by Boni, also responsible for many of these excavations. Ultimately, the very reason why the building has arrived to our days with all its layers is because it has been always occupied.

In the best cases, the architecture books and even the architectural guides are full of vague references to previous phases of buildings, without explaining the importance of these in the project process and the final realizations. Most of the time there is no reference to these pre-existences, treating buildings as completely new or privileging one of its phases, limiting criticism to visual and formal aspects, forgetting those cultural and tectonic. Unfortunately, this occurs not only on a theoretical level but also on a practical level, and many monuments are returned to a fictional state of original or former 'glory'.

7.4 Conclusion

This is the first time that the historic site of the Temple of Venus and Rome and Santa Francesca Romana in the Roman Forum has been studied as a whole. This allowed for a new holistic identity of this important architectural site to emerge, which has been disintegrating for reasons rather related to ownership. An attempt was made to get to know in depth all the projects that have transformed the buildings and the place along their history, also set as a historical and cultural framework, and including urban developments.

The main hypothesis was the one guided by the intuition that despite the radical transformations, the monumental site has preserved the richness of its architecture and history in full. This history was very much developed in parallel with that of conservation, to the point that even the early nineteenth century intervention in the Arch of Titus, widely considered an emblematic case of conservation in the modern sense, is part of the monumental site. Nevertheless, as we have discussed, it should not be as emblematic as is considered at the moment. The project was of restoration and reconstruction rather than conservation: it is very much the result of the demolition of a significant part of the monastery, disassembly and reconstruction. Our conclusion and the argument put forward here is that the monumental site of the Temple of Venus and Rome and Santa Francesca Romana is undoubtedly a better example of architectural conservation, despite its radical transformations.

The survey, archival research, literature review, historical study and extensive in-situ observations and discussions with a large amount of people have produced a historical-critical analysis. This has allowed to identify the key architectural phases, their relation in space and time (the vestibule of Nero's *Domus Aurea*, the Temple of Venus and Rome, the church and abbey of S. Maria Nova/Santa Francesca Romana) and their various transformations.

The research revealed phases and aspects of the projects unknown till now. The coincidence of the levels of the nave of the current church and the building from Nero's era, as also seen in the presence of the still-visible rests of the *Via Sacra* underneath, seem to point to the existence of a Christian structure, much earlier than the visible one from the eighth century, commemorating the miracle of the fall of Simon Magus in this location. It was also possible to demonstrate that Hadrian reused the platform of the Nero's vestibule to a larger extent than what was originally believed, i.e. the major part of the platform of the temple that is seen nowadays was actually built by Nero for the vestibule of his

Domus Aurea, keeping even some of the adjacent spaces. Hadrian preserves these spaces by extending the platform towards the Colosseum, keeping them still in use in later periods, reaching our times relatively accessible, like for example the cryptoporticus at the north-east corner. This indicates an interest in reusing pre-existing fabric and a tolerance towards the coexistence of diverse architectures and users, a much different attitude compared to projects by other Roman emperors, Trajan in specific.

A further conclusion is that the Temple of Venus and Rome would have been fully vaulted from its origins, in contrast with the established view that these vaults dated from the later works by Maxentius. The cellae would communicate through a door at the apse and the absence of occupation of the cellae was due to their precarious structural state rather than religious reasons. In fact, the crypt of the church was built on the voids left by taking apart what would be an altar at the front of the Roman temple.

A more detailed study of ancient sources, to understand better how the Temple of Venus of Rome was used and the details about the rituals it hosted and new technologies to explore the platform contents in full, including the extensive water infrastructure within it and its functional and technical relationship with the Colosseum, could give a new light on the site. The difficulty in the study of this and many other complex buildings is the need for a multidisciplinary and interdisciplinary approach, time and funding. It is fundamental to research more about these complex buildings to inform policies, globally.

Over the centuries, an organic and stratified architecture has been created above the temple of Venus and Rome until the arrival of the Olivetan monks in 1352, Boni and the *Soprintendenza* in the twentieth century, who performed more global architectural design and conservation projects. We have to thank Boni for his foresight leaving many parts exposed for the benefit of future scholars, something in which he was also a pioneer. The study of the complex stratification of the north elevation of the abbey, the only one left without rendering, permitted the identification and interpretation of the distinct phases of the building, which sets a sound base for any conservation works. The fact that this fabric has been left exposed indicates cultural changes that recognize in the ancient walls values not only of structural and documentary nature but also aesthetic and even educational.

The most radical transformation occurred in early seventeenth century, when the architect Carlo Lambardi gave signs of virtuosity by 'engulfing' the fabric of the medieval church in a new architecture, hiding most of the original church. However he also preserved and exposed important elements, producing a very effective integration between the medieval and baroque architecture. Gianlorenzo Bernini would carry on this spirit in his *Confessione*, exploring design strategies (use of light and geometry) that he would later employ in his better-known projects such as the Cornaro Chapel and St. Peter's Square.

The site suffered extensive demolitions during the French occupation, in their aim to isolate the ancient monuments and impose an aesthetic unity, which will be followed with further damage during Italian Reunification. This was discussed in Valadier's intervention in the south elevation and the adjacent Arch of Titus, which is often mentioned as a paradigm of the modern approach to conservation, a view that, as we have explained, needs to be reconsidered.

The project by Giacomo Boni at the start of twentieth century is pioneering for the contemporary practice of conservation and influenced to a great extent conservation theory, which, as has been demonstrated, always followed to the practice and study of the building. His method, which we would call today 'interdisciplinary', the techniques he used and in particular his intervention are a clear paradigm shift concerning how to design in order to incorporate building fabric from diverse periods. As we have discussed, this approach will influence later on Scarpa's intervention in Castelvecchio and the Venice Charter.

The principal theoretical developments concerning architectural conservation have also been analysed with the objective to amplify the context, which made evident the influence Boni's work had internationally. In particular, his close relationship with the Society for the Protection of Ancient Buildings (SPAB) resulted in mutual influence in the development of their ideas. Indications have also been presented about the influence of Boni in Brandi's Theory of Conservation, and of Brandi in Robert Venturi's architectural criticism.

It became evident that while the *Domus Aurea* and later the Temple of Venus and Rome provided the place with the solidity of their platform, its monumental scale and symbolism, continuity and preservation of the Roman temple was achieved through the church and monastery of S. Maria Nova/Santa Francesca Romana, which further became a focus of urban activity in the area. It is evident that it was not only religious reasons that prohibited the use of the cellae of the temple by the Christian buildings, but issues relative to safety due to the continuous failure of parts of the vault. In fact, the medieval and Christian fabric used extensively the materials and spaces from the pagan buildings, and it is evident that pagan and Christian worship coexisted in peace in the place, which has accommodated at least two millennia of continuous worship, symbolism and even materiality. The cult of the goddess Rome, represented with the goddess Nike in her hand, as was seen in the case of "Roma Barberini", is succeeded with that of Santa Francesca Romana, very similarly accompanied by an angel. The colourful marbles that used to decorate the temple were fragmented and used at the pavements of the church, serving as inspiration and reference for materials and colours in new designs.

    The balance between archaeology and architecture needs to be established in a much clearer form. The striking examples of the façade of the church of Santa Francesca Romana and the Arch of Titus, which appear to float above the roman ruins, show how far architecture can be deformed if buildings are treated only as archaeological objects.

    The temple has been archaeologically excavated, the ruin has been consolidated and was made accessible again to the public until the ongoing construction of the new underground line started. Interventions in the church and monastery have been scarce since the intervention of Boni, partly due to the fragmentation of their property. In 1984–1989, the Ministry of Cultural Property (*Soprintendenza del Lazio*) financed dehumidification work in the crypt and the nave of the church, the maintenance of the roof and façades on the south side, as well as the conservation of the entrance. Since, there have also been conservation works in the façade of the church and monastery and there is scaffolding at the moment in the church to carry out conservation work in the wooden coffered ceiling of the church. The Olivetan monks continue to reside in part of the monastery and take care of the church, with the consequent needs to adapt the building to make it more accessible. These operations have included the insertion of a lift at the bottom of the medieval campanile carried out by the late D. Mauro Dell'Orto. Recently, the architect of the *Soprintendenza* Claudia Del Monti, who sadly left us too soon, intervened in the facade of the monastery towards the Colosseum and the cloister, and there was an opportunity to further inspect the building fabric. Del Monti completed also the conservation of the Imperial Ramp which goes from the Roman Forum to the Palatine (Fortini, 2015), previously also conserved by Boni. Both intervened in a similar line with regard to the 'stratigraphic architectural design', showing all the phases of the fabric, adding new simple forms with modern materials which help to read the monument, conserving in situ and facilitating future research.

    On the other hand, it is evident that tourism and merchandising have reached massive proportions in Rome, the Roman Forum and beyond, which seem to suffocate the monumental site. The recent events such as the interruption of Holy Mass and the damage on Bernini's balustrade as well as the current problems with the coffered ceiling of the church indicate the vulnerability of the site, not to mention the adjacent massive excavation works for the new line of the metro. The Forum had free entrance for a period, but now is once again ticketed and accessibility is considered limited and complex.

    This monumental site has a deep relationship with its surroundings and the city. The place and its buildings reflect the development of the entire city of Rome: the periods of intense construction activity, the ambition but also the abandonment of architecture. The word palimpsest is often encountered in reference to historic buildings that have undergone many transformations. While this can be very obvious in painting or writing, in architecture it occurs only on limited occasions. On the contrary, in architecture, most of the time, a clear intention can be seen to reveal and expose the previous phases, as it happens in this site. Using it as an example, we believe that, although Brandi's theory could be applied to individual elements, the effective conservation of the site requires a specific tool: an architectural design and conservation project.

The form in which existing architecture is conserved, preserved and transformed reflects the culture of its time, to the same degree that new architecture does. The dialectics and attitudes of its architects, builders and patrons are expressed in the relationship that is formed between the new and the existing fabric, and how this is expressed in the final project. Interventions until the eighteenth century had the aim to 'bring' the building to the present, including its function, and in line with the contemporary fashion. Since then, the importance of the aspects related to the material culture has become a priority and the historical and archaeological aspects prevail in the intervention.

The projects discussed were deliberate acts of design aiming to transform the building, promoting a new contemporaneity while preserving the original fabric, which is still easy to recognize. The role of the patron or client was fundamental in this process and the quality of the architecture produced, and whether it was a successful response to the expectations depended largely on the skills of the architects working on the monuments.

The most recent projects are punctual or emergency interventions, but the recent conservation of the elevation towards the Colosseum, the cloister and the ongoing conversion to Museum of part of the building, indicate that proper design projects may start once again, after being stalled for almost a century. We have seen how interventions in the site have reflected the history of the city; therefore the site needs to evolve in parallel, but ultimately ensuring that the the buildings are properly conserved, used and presented to the public.

Despite the existence of recommendations and generic criteria, there are not any specific and universally applied ones that dictate interventions: each monument, project and context are different. Historically, architects have done interventions in various manners, depending on the conditions of the place and the restrictions imposed by the client, who used to be engaged with the project in a much more substantial manner than architecture books suggest.

As we have seen, many patrons were directly responsible of the decision to preserve the existing buildings, at least for financial reasons, but also religious or for family legacy. It is ironic that preserving the existing fabric was then a saving exercise while today it is perceived many times as more expensive than considering demolition. This is due to a very different treatment of conservation of the historic fabric. This contemporary conception has to be challenged. The reason why some conservation projects are sometimes more expensive than new build is because the lack of conservation skills and capacity and thereafter they require expensive techniques or research that are not at the moment easily available, but it is hoped that they will become mainstream in the near future. Also good modern practice does not allow the historic structure to support the new one in any manner. It is however something to be considered case by case.

The interest in research to discover unpublished documents can paradoxically detach us from an careful observation of the material evidence. In the case of architecture, written documentation and even original drawings should never take a primary role, as its origin and reliability have always to be checked against the actual building fabric. An equilibrium must be struck between the study of documentary and material evidence: when these two aspects are in harmony, we are no doubt much closer to the understanding of the true significance of the architecture.

In order to finish with what can be called routine interventions in existing buildings, for example stone replacement or clear juxtapositions of new versus old, it is important to learn from the best tradition of architects in history, especially those who were capable of operating in a historic building, transforming it into contemporary architecture of quality. Obviously, this praxis should be updated, operating within the framework of our contemporary historic and conservation consciousness, in order to protect the value, significance and integrity of monuments. Away from classifying practices, this approach aims above all to observe each project in its own terms, using the monument also to improve the knowledge and skills that will be employed in the new project, and, above all, avoiding monuments becoming only museums of themselves, losing many of their architectural qualities. One of their fundamental qualities is their ability to be used and transformed: this is an intrinsic value in architecture that sets it apart from painting or sculpture.

In contrast to what happens in these arts, in architecture, materials and structure are reused. Architectural conservation goes far beyond the idea of an object and can only be created and analysed as an individual project, where the aspects of function and spatiality are crucial. It is a complex architectural project that is capable of integrating rigorous studies of existing buildings, sites and objects and their interpretation within their context (physical, historical, artistic and cultural but also economic and social). This has to include the education and necessary skills to conserve an existing building and to produce a new creative project.

Excellent patrons and professionals (Hadrian, the Olivetan Order, Lambardi, Valadier, Boni and the *Soprintendenza*) are certainly the responsible parties for the survival of this important monumental complex. All of them have in common the knowledge of history, design creativity and innovation. But the single most important aspect determining the effective conservation of the building is the fact that it has been continuously used by people who care for it: this is most powerful force in conservation. Together with the usual principles of conservation (minimum intervention, compatibility and distinguishibility), the appropriate use of the building and occupants who care for it must be added to the list. This monumental complex has been robust enough to cope during periods in which this was not the case; unfortunately, other buildings have not been able to survive similar processes.

However, it is important that the appropriate use of the building continues and that further investigations are carried out. Complex areas such as the apse of the church should be carefully studied before any intervention is proposed, as it contains extremely important remains from Nero's to Medieval times.

The Olivetan patronage in S. Francesca Romana has been very close to the work and very sensitive to the innovations and artistic trends of its time, taking care of the overall design of the whole complex. The transformations have occurred in such a way that they have retained the footprint of the previous building, operating in a respectful manner and compatible with existing fabrics. We could certainly say that these interventions follow the basic principles of the modern concept of conservation: minimal intervention, compatibility and, in some ways, reversibility. As well as the architecture, history and memories of the existing buildings and site and the surrounding environment, the functional needs are also very important when deciding how to intervene. This includes the need to sometimes tell clients that their building is not suitable for the function they intend to give it: we must always work in accordance with the building's 'vocation'. Architectural heritage should be a living and contemporary reference, without forgetting the ultimate need to conserve the architecture as well as the memories and traditions so important for people and civilization in its broader sense.

Abbreviations

ACS: *Archivio Centrale dello Stato* (Rome)
ASMN: *Archivio di S. Maria Nova*
ASR: Archivio di Stato di Roma
DG AA.BB.AA: *Direzione Generale Antichità e Belle Arti, Ministero della Pubblica Istruzione*
ICR: *Istituto Centrale del Restauro*
m.a.s.l.: metres above sea level
SCVA: *Sacra Congregazione della Visita Apostolica, Archivio Segreto Vaticano*
SPAB: Society for the Protection of Ancient Buildings

References

Alberti, L.B. 1450. *Descriptio urbis Romae*. Boriaud, J. and Furlan, F. (eds.). Firenze: Olschki, 2005.

Annoni, A. 1946. *Scienza ed arte del restauro architettonico. Idee ed esempi*. Milano: Edizioni Artistiche Framar, p. 14.

Argan, G.C. 1979. Prologue to Debenedetti, E. 1979. *Valadier, diario architettonico*. Rome: Bulzoni Editori.

ASMN. 1793. Archivio di S. Maria Nova. Capo Terzo 3. Indicazione. Con tutti i libri D.C. con li Canoni e Censi passivi che esistono nell'Archivio di S. Maria Nova, fatta l'anno 1793. D.C. Canoni e Censi Passivi E. n. 2.

Atti del Congresso internazionale di scienze storiche (Roma, 1–9 aprile 1903), pp. 137–138. Available at: http://archive.org/stream/attidelcongress05romgoog/attidelcongress05romgoog_djvu.txt [Accessed 25 December 2019].

Augenti, A. 1996. *Il Palatino nel Medioevo: archeologia e topografia (secoli VI-XIII)*. Roma: L'Erma di Bretschneider.

Augustus. *Monumentum Ancyranum*, IV, 1–7 y sigg.; X, 2 y sigg.

Baglione, G. 1642. *Le vite de' pittori, sculturi et architetti: dal pontificio di Gregorio XIII del 1572 in fino a' tempi di Papa Urbano Ottavo nel 1642*. Hess, J. and Röttgen, H. (eds.). Città del Vaticano: Biblioteca Apostolica Vaticana, 1995 (Include facsimile dell'edizione di Roma, nella stamperia d'Andrea Fei, 1642), vol. I, Vita di Pietro Paolo Olivieri, Scultore e Architetto, p. 76.

Baldini, U. 1978. *Teoria del restauro e unità di metodologia*. Firenze: Nardini.

Barosso, M. 1938. "Edificio Romano sotto il tempio di Venere e Roma", *Atti del III Convegno nazionale di storia dell'architettura*, Roma.

Barosso, M. 1940. "Le Costruzioni sottostanti la Basilica di Massenzio e la Velia", *Atti del V Congresso Nazionale di Studi Romani* II, pp. 58–62.

Barosso, M. 1952. "La Velia y S. Maria Nova", *Rivista Storica Bendittina*, p. 65.

Bartoli, A. 1996. *Cento Vedute di Roma Antica*. Firenze, 1911. Tav. IV, anche in A. Augenti, *Il Palatino nel Medioevo: archeologia e topografia (secoli VI-XIII)*, Roma: L'Erma di Bretschneider.

Bellanca, C. 2003. *Antonio Muñoz. La politica di tutela dei monumenti di Roma durante il governatorato. Bullettino della Commissione archeologica comunale di Roma*., Supplementi, 10 Roma: L'Erma di Bretschneider.

Bellanca, C. 2004. *Antonio Muñoz: 1884–1960. Una vita per i monumenti e per la città di Roma*. Roma: L'Erma di Bretschneider.

Bellini, A. 1997. "Dal restauro alla conservazione: dall'estetica all'etica", *Ananke: cultura, storia e tecniche della conservazione*, 19, p. 18.
Bellori, G.P. 1690. *Veteres arcus Augustorum triumphis insignes . . . cum imaginabus triumphalibus restituti*. Rome.
Benedetti, S. 1999. "La facciata maderniana: principali cadenze e caratteri", in *Basilica di S. Pietro, restauro e conservazione*. Fabbrica di S. Pietro in Vaticano, Mariano Comense (CO), Eni Comunicazione, p. 36.
Benzi, F. 1990. *Sisto IV renovator urbis: architettura a Roma 1471–1484*. Roma: Officina.
Bernard, J.F., Bernardi, P. and Esposito, D. (eds.). 2008. *Il reimpiego in architettura: recupero, trasformazione, uso*. Rome: Collection de l'École française de Rome, p. 418.
Bianchi, A. 1937. "Le vicende urbanistiche della Roma Napoleònica", in *L'Urbe,*, II, 3. Rome: Fratelli Palombi.
Bianchi Bandinelli, R. 1961. *Archeologia e Cultura*. Milano and Napoli: Riccardo Ricciardi Editore, p. 7.
Bilancia, F. 2006. "La chiesa di S. Maria Nova (S. Francesca Romana) di Carlo Lambardi con altri soffitti di chiese", *Palladio*, n.s., 19 (2006/2007), 37, pp. 73–104. Original documents in ASR, *Trenta notai capitolini*, Trenta notai capitolini, Uff. 33, t. 64, atti Michelangelo Cesio, c. 167, documento n. 6, 22 maggio 1614; cc. 211–212 v.e. 227, documento n. 2, 25 gennaio 1612; Uff. 33, t. 67, atti Michelangelo Cesio, c. 235–236, v238–239, v.e. 249, 246, documenti n. 3, 4. 27 gennaio 1612; Uff. 33, t. 71, atti Michelangelo Cesio, cc. 474–476 v.e. 488–489, documento n. 7, 26 giugno 1614.
Biondo, F. 1450. *Roma instaurata*. Available at: https://brbl-dl.library.yale.edu/vufind/Record/3587002 [Accessed 5 January 2020].
Blunt, A. 1982. *Guide to Baroque Rome*. London: Granada, p. 274.
Bonelli, R. 1945. "Teoria e metodo nella storia dell'architettura", *Bollettino dell'Istituto artistico orvietano*, 1, pp. 2–10, 93–94.
Bonelli, R. 1963. "Restauro Architettonico", in *Enciclopedia Universale dell'Arte*. Venezia-Roma: Instituto per la Collaborazione Culturale, vol. XI.
Boni, G. n.d.a. *Il suolo di Roma*. Boni-Tea Archive at the *Istituto Lombardo-Accademia di Scienze e Lettere*, XXII, 2–2bis.
Boni, G. n.d.b. Typewritten report. Boni-Tea Archive at the *Istituto Lombardo-Accademia di Scienze e Lettere*. Folder 12-B, 5–10.
Boni, G. n.d.c. *Il Foro Sacro*. Boni-Tea Archive at the *Istituto Lombardo-Accademia di Scienze e Lettere*. Cartella 12-A.
Boni, G. n.d.d. "Disegni in pulito (as esempi di maniera di disegnare)/Rilievi e appunti diretti dal vero (*come documenti del procedimento dell'indagine*)", Boni-Tea Archive at the *Istituto Lombardo- Accademia di Scienze e Lettere*. Folder 2, Cartella 28.
Boni, G. n.d.e. *Autenticitá dei monument*. Boni-Tea Archive at the *Istituto Lombardo- Accademia di Scienze e Lettere*. Folder 2, Cartella 7.
Boni, G. 1901. "Il metodo negli scavi archeologici", *Nuova Antologia*, Serie IV, XCIV, 16 julio, Rome, pp. 312–322.
Boni, G. 1913. "Il 'Metodo' nelle esplorazioni archeologiche", Congreso Arqueológico de Roma, 1911. In *Bollettino d'Arte*, 1–2.
Boni, G. 1924. Letter of G. Boni dated 4 decembre 1924, apologising for not being able to attend the opening of the academic year for health reasons,

Boni-Tea Archive at the *Istituto Lombardo- Accademia di Scienze e Lettere*. Cartella 2, 1ab.

Borromeo, C. 1577. *Instructionum Fabricae et Supellectilis Ecclesiasticae.* Monumenta studia instrumnta liturgica, 8). Città del Vaticano: Libreria Editrice Vaticana, 2000.

Borsi, F et al. (eds.). 1976. *Roma antica ei disegni di architettura agli Uffizi di Giovanni Antonio Dosio*. Rome: Officina, p. 133.

Boyer, F. 1943. "La conservation des monuments antiques à Rome sous Napoléon", *Comptes-rendus des séances de l'Académie des Inscriptions et Belles-Lettres*, 87e année, N. 1. pp. 101–108.

Bracciolini, P. 1723. *De Varietate Fortunae*. Available at: https://warburg.sas.ac.uk/pdf/nah3175b2638881.pdf [Accessed 5 January 2020]

Brandi, C. 1963. *Teoria del Restauro*. Roma: Edizioni di Storia e Letteratura. Torino: Einaudi, 1977.

Brandi, C. 1967. *Struttura e Architettura*. Torino: Giulio Einaudi Editore.

Brizzi, G. 1989. *Il coro intarsiato dell'abbazia di Monte Oliveto maggiore*. Monte Oliveto Maggiore: Silvana.

Bruschi, A. 2008. "Le vicende della chiesa di San Pietro in Montorio e qualche nota sui problema storiografici dell'architettura romana del quattrocento", *Quaderni dell'Istituto di storia dell'architettura*, 51, pp. 17–34.

Buls, C. 1903. "L'esthetique de Rome", *Revue del'Université de Bruxelles*, pp. 401–410.

Burns, H. and Beltramini, G. (eds.). 2008. *Palladio*. London: Royal Academy of Arts, p. 146.

Byron, Lord. 1817. *Childe Harold's Pilgrimage*, Act III, Scene IV, Song IV, LXXVIII. Available at: https://www.gutenberg.org/files/5131/5131-h/5131-h.htm [Accessed 2 November 2020]

Cagiano de Azevedo, M. 1954. "La Dea Barberini", *RIASA*, III, pp. 108–146.

Canina, L. 1863. *Supplemento all'opera sugli edifizi antichi di Roma dell'architetto A. Desgodetz. Parte I [-II.] ... Supplemènt à l'ouvrage sur les édifices antiques de Rome de l'architecte A. Desgodetz. Partie I.* Roma: dai tipi della Rev. Cam. Apostolica, v.1.

Capitel, A. 2008. "CaixaForum, caja sin sorpresas", *Arquitectura*, 352.

Capitel, A. 2009. *Metamorfosis de Monumentos y Teorías de la restauración*. Madrid: Alianza Forma. 2ª edicion.

Carbonara, G. 1990. Contribution to the '*Assessorato per gli Interventi sul Centro Storico di Roma*'. In "L'Area Archeologica Centrale", *Romacentro* 12/90. Roma: F.lli Palombi, stampa, p. 55.

Carbonara, G. 1995. Preface of Bonelli, R. *Scritti sul restauro e sulla critica architettonica*. Roma: Bonsignori.

Carbonara, G. 1996. "Teoria e metodi del restauro", in Carbonara, G. (ed.). *Trattato di Restauro Architettonico*. Torino: Utet, vol, 1, pp. 1–107.

Carbonara, G. 1997. *Avvicinamento al Restauro. Teoria, storia, monumenti*. Naples: Liguori Editore.

Carbonara, G. 2011. *Architettura d'Oggi e Restauro. Un confronto antico-nuovo*. Turín: Utet.

Carbonara, G. 2012. "An Italian Contribution to Architectural Restoration", *Frontiers of Architectural Research*, 1, p. 2–9.

Casiello, S., Pane, A. and Russo, V. (eds.) 2010. *Roberto Pane tra storia e restauro Architettura, città, paesaggio*. Venezia: Marsilio.

Cassanelli, C., David, M., De Albentiis, E. and Jacques, A. 1998. *Frammenti di Roma antica nei disegni degli architetti francesi vincitori del Prix de Rome (1786–1924)*. Novara: Istituto Geografico de Agostini, p. 99.
Cassius Dio, *Historia Romana*, LXIX, 4, 5; LXXII, 31, 1.
Castagnoli, F. 1946. "Il Tempio dei Penati e la Velia", *Rivista di Filologia e d'Istruzione Classica* 74:157–65. Torino: Bona.
Cavaceppi, B. 1768. *Raccolta di antiche statue busti bassirilievi ed altre sculture restaurate da Bartolomeo Cavaceppi scultore romano*. Roma, vol. I.
Cellini, P. 1950. "Una Madonna molto antica", *Proporzioni*, 3, pp. 1–8.
Ceschi, C. 1970. *Teoria e Storia del Restauro*. Roma: M. Bulzoni, p. 115.
Ciampi, I. 1887. "Vita di G. Valadier", *Opuscoli Vari, storici e critici di Ignazio Ciampi*.
Ciampini, G.G. 1690–1699. *Vetera monumenta, in quibus praecipuè musiva opera sacarum profanarumque aedium structura, ac nonnulli antiqui ritus, dissertationibus, iconibusque illustrantur*. Roma: Ex typographia Joannis Jacobi Komarek, Bohemi, apud S. Angelum custodem, vol. 2.
Cicero, *De Re Publica* II, 53; *De Haruspicum Responso* 16.
Cirilli, G. and Boni, G. 1909. Report dated 15th June 1909. ACS, Ministero della Pubblica Istruzione, Direzione Generale Antichità e Belle Arti, Divisione I (1908–1924), busta 869.
Cirulli, B. 2009. "Documenti sulla fondazione e dedicazione della cappella delle Oblate di Santa Francesca Romana in Santa Maria Nova e una ipotesi sulla sua più antica decorazione (1442-1448)", in Bartolomei Romagnoli, A. (ed.). *Francesca Romana. La Santa, il monastero e la città*. Appendice documentaria 6. Sismel—Edizioni del Galluzzo.
Cirulli, B. 2013. "La cappella delle oblate in Santa Francesca Romana nella prima metà del seicento. Continuità e discontinuità", in Bartolomei Romagnoli, A. (ed.). *La canonizzazione di S. Francesca Romana. Santità, Cultura e Istituzioni a Roma tra Medioevo ed Età Moderna*. Firenze: SISMEL- Edizioni Del Galluzzo.
Clark, K. 1964. *Ruskin Today*. London: John Murray.
Clinton, K. 2016. "The Eleusinian Anaktoron of Demeter and Kore", *Journal of Ancient History*, 4(1), pp. 40–56.
Coarelli, F. 1983. Il Foro Romano. Roma : Quasar.
Coarelli, F. 1989. *Guida Archeologica di Roma*. Milano: Mondadori.
Colini, A.M. 1933. "Scoperte tra il Foro della Pace e il anfiteatro", *Bullettino Communale*, LXI, pp. 79–87.
Colini, A.M. 1983. "Considerazioni su la Velia da Nerone in poi", *Città e architettura nella Roma imperiale*, atti del seminario del 27 ottobre 1981 nel 250 anniversario dell'Accademia di Danimarca. Odense: Odense University Press, pp. 129–145.
Conforti, C. 2018. "Soffitti figurati nelle chiese di Roma", *Opus Incertum*, 3, pp. 68–79. https://doi.org/10.13128/opus-23051.
Connoly, R.H. (ed.). 1929. *Didascalia Apostolorum*. Oxford: Clarendon Press, cap. XII II.57–58.
Consolato, S. 2006. "Giacomo Boni, l'archeologo-vate della terza Roma", in De Turris, G. (ed.). *Esoterismo e fascismo: storia, interpretazione, documenti*. Rome: Edizioni Mediterranee.

Cornell, T.J. 1995. *The beginnings of Rome. Italy and Rome from the Bronze Age to the Punic Wars (c. 1000–264 BC)*, Routledge History of the Ancient World. London: Routledge.
Coulton, J.J. 1977. *Greek Architects at Work*. London: Granada.
Creti, L. 2010. *In Marmoris Arte Periti. La bottega cosmatesca di Lorenzo tra il XII e il XIII secolo*. Sapienza- Universitá di Roma. Dipartimento di Storia dell'Architettura, Restauro e Conservazione dei Beni Architettonici. Edizioni Quasar, pp. 58–59.
Cristallini, E. 2006. "Carlo Ludovico Ragghianti, Bruno Zevi e il dibattito sulla tutela del patrimonio artístico negli anni della ricostruzione (1945-1960)", in Andaloro, M. (ed.). *La teoria del restauro nel Novecento da Riegl a Brandi*. Firenze: Nardini, pp. 122–123.
Cristinelli, G. 2008. "Nuovi edifici nei centri storici?" *Italia Nostra*, 437, pp. 30–31.
Croce, B. 1920. *Nuovi saggi di estetica*. Bari: Laterza, 1969.
Dal Co, F. 2007. "L'infondatezza del vecchio- l'aleatorietá del nuovo", *Casabella*, LXXI(4), p. 754.
Dante, *La Divina Comedia*, Il Purgatorio, Canto VI, 114.
Davey, P. 2007. "Diocesan Dialoguue", *The Architectural Review*, November.
De Angelis D'Ossat, G. 1935. "Il Sottosuolo dei Fori Romani e l'Elephas antiquus della Via dell'Impero", *Bullettino della commissione archeologica comunale di Roma*, 63.
De Angelis D'Ossat, G. 1961. "Restauro: Architettura sulle preesistenze diversamente valutate nel tempo", *Palladio*, 1978, III, XXV(2).
De Rossi, F. 1727. "Descrizione di Roma moderna formata nuovamente con le auttorità, del Card. Cesare Baronio, Alfonso Ciaconio, Antonio Bosio, e Ottavio Paniroli", in De Rossi, F. (ed.). *Descrizione di Roma antica: formata nuovamente con le auttorita' di Bartolomeo Marliani, Onofrio Panvinio, Alessandro Donati e Famiano Nardini, e d'altri celebri scrittori antichi, & antiquarii moderni . . . .* Roma: Fratelli dè Rossi, vol. II, Descrizione di Roma Moderna.
De Rossi, G.G. (ed.). 1684. *Insignium Romae Templorum: prospectus exteriores interioresque*, Madrid, Instituto Juan de Herrera, 2004 (reprodución facsímil de la ed. Roma 1684).
De Tournon, Count. 1831. *Etudes statistiques sur Rome*. Paris. Articles I, II.
Debenedetti, E. 1985. *Valadier, Segno e Architettura*, Catalogue of the Exhibition 5 Nov. 1985–15 Genn. 1986), Rome, 1547 [80].
Del Monti, C. (ed.). 2010. *Il Tempio di Venere e Roma nella Storia*. Milano: Soprintendenza archeologica di Roma.
Desgodets, A.B. 1682. *Les édifices antiques de Rome: dessinés et mesurés très exactement*. Paris: Jean Baptiste Coignard.
Dezzi Bardeschi, M. 1991. *Restauro: punto e dacapo. Frammenti per una (impossibile) teoria*. Locatelli, V. (ed.). Milano: Franco Angelli.
DG AA.BB.AA. 1891–1897. ACS Ministero della Pubblica Istruzione, Direzione Generale Antichità e Belle Arti, II Versamento, II Serie, busta 403, fasc. 4493.
DG AA.BB.AA. 1907. ACS Ministero della Pubblica Istruzione, Direzione Generale Antichità e Belle Arti, Letters of the *Ufficio Tecnico di Conservazione dei Monumenti* dated 15 and 31 October 1907 and 19 December1907. ACS. DG AA.BB.AA. busta 869.
DG AA.BB.AA. 1908–1924. ACS, Ministero della Pubblica Istruzione, Direzione Generale Antichità e Belle Arti, Divisione I, busta 869.

Di Stefano, R. 1969. *John Ruskin, interpret dell'architettura e del restauro*. Napoli: Edizioni Scientifiche Italiane.
Donato, M.P. 1992. "Dell'antico Culture and Culture of the Lumi to Rome in the Settecento: The politicizzazione dello scambio culturale during the pontificato di Pio VI", *Mélanges de l'Ecole française de Rome, Italie et Méditerranée T*, 104(2), pp. 503–548, 513, 521, 526, 548.
Du Pérac, 1577. *Vestigi dell'Antichitá di Roma*.
Ducati, P. 1938. *L'arte in Roma dalle origini al sec. VIII*. Bologna: Istituto di Studi Romani.
Duchesne, L. (ed.). 1955–1957. *Le Liber Pontificalis*. Paris: E. de Boccard, Paul I, Nicholas I, Leo IV, Alexander III, Gregory XI.
Dumser, E.A. 2005. "The Architecture of Maxentius: A Study in Architectural Design and Urban Planning in Early Fourth-Century Rome", PhD Thesis, University of Pennsylvania.
Dumser, E.A. 2018. "Visual Literacy and Reuse in the Architecture of Late Imperial Rome", in Ng, D.Y. (ed.). *Reuse and Renovation in Roman Material Culture: Functions, Aesthetics, Interpretations*. Cambridge: Cambridge University Press.
Dyonysius, I, 68; V, 19.
Eco, U. 1968. *La struttura assente*. Milano: Bompiani, pp. 279–280.
Eco, U. (ed.). 2004. *Storia della belleza*. Milano: Bompianti, pp. 249–251.
Erder, C. 1986. "Our Architectural Heritage: Form Consciousness to Conservation", *Museums and Monuments*, XX, Unesco, pp. 44–45.
Fabiani, U. and Fraioli, F. 2010. "Note sull'allineamento del Tempio di Venere e Roma", *FOLD&R FastiOnLine documents & research*, 193, pp. 1–10.
Facciotti, G. 1616, *Le nuove et antiche meraviglie dell'alma città di Roma*. Roma: Appresso Guglielmo Facciotti, pp. 45–46.
Fea, C. and Valadier, G. 1822. *Gli edifizi antichi di Roma misurati disegnati esattissimamente sui luoghi dal fu M. Desgodetz architetto del Re* traduzione with note and il testo originale a lato, Rome. 76, n4.
Fedele, P. 1900. "Tabularium S. Mariae Novae", *Archivio della Societá romana di Storia Patria*, XXIII, p. 174.
Fedele, P. 1900–1903. "Tabularium S. Mariae Novae", *Archivio della Societá romana di Storia Patria*, XXIII (1900), pp. 171–237, XXIV (1901), pp. 159–196, XXV (1902), pp. 169–209, XXVI (1903), pp. 21–141.
Felini, P.M. 1969. *Trattato nuovo delle cose maravigliose dell'alma Città di Roma*. Berlin: B. Hessling, pp. 159–160.
Ferrajoli, R. 2016. "Il Tempio di Venere e Roma—Ipotesi di ricostruzione", PhD thesis in Scienze storiche, archeologiche e storico-artistiche. Università degli Studi di Napoli Federico II.
Festus, 154, 348.
Forcella, V. 1873. *Iscrizioni delle chiese e d'altri edificii di Roma dal secolo XI fino ai giorni nostri*. Roma: Tipografia delle scienze matematiche e fisiche, v. II, parte 1, 11.
Forssman, E. 1989. *Dorico, ionico, corinzio nell'architettura del Rinascimento*. Bari: Laterza.
Fortini, P. and Taviani, M. (eds.). 2014. *In Sacra Via. Giacomo Boni al Foro Romano. Gli scavi*. Milano: Electa.

186 References

Fortini, P (ed) 2015. *La Rampa Imperiale. Scavi e restauri tra Foro romano e Palatino*. Electa Milano

Fréart de Chambray, F. 1650. *Parallèle de l'architecture antique et de la moderne*. . . Paris: E. Martin.

Freeman, E.A. 1846. *Principles of Church Restoration*. London.

Freud, S. 1930. *Civilization and its Discontents*. New York: W. W. Norton, 1989.

García-Gutiérrez Mosteiro, J. 2014. "La 'replica sapiente' Algunas consideraciones sobre el legado teórico de Paolo Marconi (Roma 1933–2013)", Cuadernos de Proyectos Arquitectónicos. N. 5. Available at http://polired.upm.es/index.php/proyectos_arquitectonicos/article/view/2084/3155. [Accessed 5 January 2020].

Garnham, T. 2013. *Architecture Re-Assembled. The use (and abuse) of history*. New York: Routledge.

Giovannoni, G. 1927. "Il Prefetto de Tournon e la sistemazione edilizia di Roma", *Nuova Antologia*, Vol. II, 16 abril (446).

Giovannoni, G. 1929. *Questioni di architettura, nella storia e nella vita*. Roma: Biblioteca d'arte Editrice, pp. 133–175.

Giovannoni, G. 1931. *Vecchie città ed edilizia nuova*. Torino: UET.

Giovannoni, G. 1932. "The International Conference of Athena for the Restoration of Monument", *Bolletino d'Arte*, 9, pp. 408–409, 411, 415–417.

Giovannoni, G. 1936. "Restauro dei monumenti", in *Enciclopedia Italiana di Scienze, Lettere e Arti*. Roma: Istituto della enciclopedia italiana, vol. XXIX.

Glass, D.F. 1980. *Studies on Cosmatesque pavements*, "British Archaeological Reports", International Series 82.

Gjerstad, E. 1953. *Early Rome*. Lund: C.W.K. Gleerup, 1953–73. vol. IV–2.

González-Longo, C. 2006. "Giacomo Boni at the Antiquarium Forense: Construction History as a Source for Architectural Innovation", in Dunkeld, A. et al. (eds.). *Proc. 2nd International Congress on Construction History*. Exeter and Cambridge: Short Run Press, vol. 2, pp. 1341–1361.

González-Longo, C. 2008. "Conserving, Reinstating and Converting Queensberry House", Sinha, B. and Tanacan, L. (eds.). *ISSM08, Proceedings of the 8th International Seminar on Structural Masonry*. Istanbul: Cizgi Basim Yayn Ltd.

González-Longo, C. 2013. "Da S. Maria Nova a S. Francesca Romana: Architettura e committenza Olivetana nella transformazione della chiesa dal Trecento al Seicento", in Bartolomei Romagnoli, A. (ed.). *La canonizzazione di S. Francesca Romana. Santità, Cultura e Istituzioni a Roma tra Medioevo ed Età Moderna*. Firenze: SISMEL- Edizioni Del Galluzzo.

González-Longo, C. 2014. "Can Architectural Conservation be Mainstream?" ICOMOS Scientific Symposium, Florence.

González Longo, C. 2015. "Conservación y transformación: el complejo monumental del templo de Venus y Roma—Santa Francesca Romana en el Foro Romano", Thesis (Doctoral). Escuela Técnica Superior de Arquitectura de Madrid (ETSAM), Universidad Politécnica de Madrid. Available at: http://oa.upm.es/43718/. [Accessed 5 January 2020].

González-Longo, C. and Theodossopoulos, D. 2005. "The Vaulting Structure of the Temple of Venus and Rome at the Roman Forum", in Modena, G. et al. (eds.). *Structural Analysis of Historical Constructions*. London: Taylor & Francis.

González-Longo, C. and Theodossopoulos, D. 2008. "The Architecture and Technology of Stratification in the Masonry of the Abbey of Santa Maria Nova at the Roman Forum", in Sinha, B. and Tanacan, L. (eds.), *ISSM08, Proceedings of 8th International Seminor Structural Masonry*. Istanbul: Cizgi Basim Yayn Ltd pp. 549–556.

González-Longo, C. and Theodossopoulos, D. 2009. "The Platform of the Temple of Venus and Rome", in Kurrer, K. E. et al. (eds.). *Proceedings of the 3rd International Conference on Construction History*. Cottbus, Berlin: NEUNPLUS1

González-Longo, C. and Theodossopoulos, D. 2013. "The stratification of S. Maria Nova at the Roman Forum: Construction, Materials and Conservation", in *Construction & Building Materials*. Elsevier, vol. 41, April 2013, Pages 926–941.

Gregorovius, F. 1988. *Storia di Roma nel Medioevo*. Calvani, V. y Micchia, P. (eds.). Roma: Newton Compton editori.

Greville, Charles C.F. 1874. *The Greville Memoirs, A Journal of the Reigns of King George IV and King William IV, Volume 1 (of 3)*. London: Longmans, Green, and Co, Henry Reeve.

Guarducci, M. 1989. *La più antica icone di Maria: un prodigioso vincolo fra oriente e occidente*. Roma: Istituto Poligrafico e Zecca dello Stato.

Guidobaldi, F. 1992. *San Clemente. Gli edifici romani, la basilica paleocristiana e le fasi altomedievali*. Romae: Apud S. Clementem.

Guidobaldi, F. 2008. "Le carte del archivio Boni-Tea all'Istituto Lomabardo di Milano. Cenni sul ritrovamento, sulla consistenza e sullo stato della pubblicazione" in Fortini, P. *Giacomo Boni e le istituzioni straniere apporti alla formazione delle discipline storicoarcheologiche*, Atti del Convegno Internazionale, giugno 2004, Roma, SSBAR.

Guidolbaldi, F. 2016. "Note dall'Archivio Boni-Tea. La progettata e mai realizzata pubblicazione di Giacomo Boni sugli scavi del Foro e del Palatino", in Favaretto, I, and Pilutti Namer, M. (eds.) *Tra Roma e Venezia, la cultura dell'antico nell'Italia dell'Unità. Giacomo Boni e i suoi contesti*. Conference Proceedings, vol. 66/76. Venice: Istituto Veneto di Scienze, Lettere ed Arti

Hart, V. and Hicks, P. 1996. *Sebastiano Serlio on architecture*. New Haven: Yale University Press, vol. 1, p. 196.

Haskell, F. and Penny, N. 1984. *L'antico nella storia del gusto*. Torino: Enaudi.

Hibbard, H. 1967. "Giacomo della Porta on Roman Architects, 1593", *The Burlington Magazine*, 109(777), p. 713. The original document is at the Archivio della Pia Casa degli Orfani di Santa Maria in Aquiro (Orfanelli), Roma, t. 69, f. 154 (93).

Hill, M. 2001."The Patronage of a Disenfranchised Nephew: Cardinal Scipione Borghese and the Restoration of San Crisogono in Rome, 1618–1628", *The Journal of the Society of Architectural Historians*, 60(4) (December), p. 448, n. 69. It refers to L. Pastor, *History of the Popes*, 26: 381 n. 1.

Hillard, George Stillman. 1853. *Six Months in Italy*. London.

Holloway, R.R. 1994. *The Archaeology of Early Rome and Latium*. London, New York: Routledge, pp. 142–149.

Huemer, C. 2008. "Giacomo Boni e i borsisti americani a Roma", in P. Fortini (ed.). Giacomo Boni e le istituzioni straniere apporti alla formazione delle discipline storico-archeologiche, Atti del Convegno Internazionale, junio 2004, Roma, SSBAR, 2008, pp. 57–69.

Insolera, I. 1976. *Roma moderna, un secolo di storia urbanistica 1870–1970*. Torino: Giulio Einaudi Editore.

Krautheimer, R. 1937–1977. *Corpus Basilicarum Christianarum Romae. The Early Christian basilicas of Rome (IV-IX cent.)*. Città del Vaticano: Pontificio istituto di archeologia cristiana.

Krautheimer, R. 1959. *Corpus Basilicarum Christianarum Romae*. Città del Vaticano: Pontificio Istituto di Archeologia Cristiana, 1 edition, vol. I, 1937.

Krautheimer, R. 1983. *Rome, Profile of a City, 312–1308*. Roma: Princeton, 1980.

Krautheimer, R. 1985. *The Rome of Alexander VII*. Princeton: Princeton University Press.

La Padula, A. 1969. *Roma e la Regione nell'epoca napoleonica. Contributo Alla Storia Urbanistica Della Città E Del Territorio*. Roma: Istituto Editoriale Pubblicazioni Internazionali

Lancellotti, S. 1623. *Historiae Olivetanae. Venetiis, ex Typographia Gueriliana*.

Lanciani, R. 1893. "Il panorama di Roma scolpito da P.P. Olivieri nel 1585", in *Bullettino della Commisssione Arcjeologica Comunale*. Roma, vol. XXI, pp. 272–277.

Landi, F. 1771. *Istoria di S. Francesca Romana e della sua Nobile, e Venerabile Congregazione delle Signore Oblate di Torre di Specchi*. Lucca.

Lauro, G. 1699. *Romanae magnitudeinis increases quae urbem illam orbis dominam velut redivivam . . . restituta et aucta*. Rome, pl. 71.

Lavin, I. 1980. *Bernini and the Unity of the Visual Arts*, New York : Pierpont Morgan Library by Oxford University Press,

Linstrum, D. 1982. "Giuseppe Valadier et l'arc de Titus", *Monumentum*, 25, pp. 50, 52.

Livy (II, 7).

Lorenzatti, S. 1990. "Vicende del tempio di Venere e Roma nel Medioevo e nel Rinascimento", *Rivista Istituto Nazionale di Archeologia e Storia dell'Arte*, XIII, pp. 119–138.

Lugano, P. 1900. *S. Maria «olim antiqua nunc nova». S. Maria Anti-qua e le origini di S. Maria Nova de Urbe al Foro Romano rivendicate su documenti fino-ra inediti. Saggio storico topografico*

Lugano, P. 1922, "La Basilica di Santa Maria Nova al Foro Romano (Santa Francesca Romana). Memorie e Opere d'Arte", in *Rivista Storica Benedettina*.

Lugano, P. 1924, "San Benedetto sul Palatino e nel Foro Romano", *Rivista Storica Benedettina*, 15.

Lugano, P. 1933. "Santa Francesca Romana in Tor de' Specchi", in AA.VV. *La nobil casa delle Oblate di Santa Francesca Romana in Tor de' Specchi*. Città del Vaticano: Tipografia Poliglotta Vaticana

Lugli, G. 1935. "Il restauro del Tempio di Venere e Roma", in *Pan*, 5, 7, pp. 364–375. Milano, Firenze, Roma: Rizzoli

Manieri Elia, M. 1992."Note sul significato del Tempio di Venere e Roma", En *Saggi in onore di Renato Bonelli*, Quaderni dell'Istituto di Storia dell'Architettura, 1990–1992, 15–20: 47–54. Roma: Multigrafica.

Marconi, P. 1993. *Il restauro e l'architetto*. Venezia: Marsilio.

Marta, R. 1995. *L'Architettura del Rinascimento a Roma (1417–1503). Tecniche e tipologie*. Roma: Edizioni Kappa, p. 222.

Matero, F. 2007. "Loss, 'Compensation and Authenticity: The Contribution of Cesare Brandi to Architectural Conservation in America'", *Future Anterior*, IV(1) (Summer), pp. 45–58.

Matthiae, G. 1967. *Mosaici medioevali delle chiese di Roma*. Roma: Libreria dello stato, p. 315.
Mazzarino, S. 1966. *Il pensiero storico classico*. Bari: Laterza, vol. 1, p. 193.
Miarelli Mariani, G. 1989. "Il 'cristianesimo primitivo' nella riforma cattolica e alcune incidenze sui monumenti del passato", in Spagnesi, G. (ed.). *L'Architettura a Roma e in Italia (1580–1621)*. Roma: Centro di Studi per la Storia dell'Architettura, vol. 1, pp. 152–153.
Miarelli Mariani, G. 1999. " 'Durata', 'intervallo' . . . restauro; singolarità in architettura", in *Architettura: processualità e trasformazione, Proceedings of the International Conference*. Roma: Bonsignori, 2002.
Milizia, F. 1768a. *Le vite de più celebri architetti d'ogni nazione e d'ogni tempo*. Roma: Arnaldo Forni, 1978, pp. 144, 145.
Mola, G.B. 1663. *Breve racconto delle migliori opere d'Architettura, Scultura et Pittura fatte in Roma et alcuni fuor di Roma descritto da Giov. Battista Mola l'anno 1663*. Berlin: B. Hessling, 1966.
Momigliano, A. 1989. *Roma Arcaica*. Firenze: Sansoni.
Montenovesi, O. 1926. "Roma agli inizi del secolo XV e il monastero di S. Maria Nova al Foro", *Rivista storica benedettina*, XXVII.
Morganti, G. 2006. "Un possibile laboratorio per la Teoria: il restauro di Santa Maria Antiqua ad opera di Giacomo Boni", in Andaloro, M. (ed.). *La teoria del restauro nel Novecento da Riegl a Brandi*. Proceedings of the international meeting, Viterbo, 12–15 Novembre 2003. Firenze: Nardini.
Moroni, G. 1840–1861. *Dizionario di erudizione storico-ecclesiastica*. Venezia: Tipografia Emiliana, vol. XLI, p. 225.
Morricone, M.L. 1987. "Edificio sotto il tempio di Venere e Roma", *Studi per Laura Breglia*, 3, p. 69, *Bollettino di numismatica. Supplemento*, 6, pp. 69–82.
Muffel, N. 1999. *Descrizione della città di Roma nel 1452: Delle indulgenze e dei luoghi sacri di Roma (Der ablas und die heiligen stet zu Rom)*. G. Wiedmann (ed.). Bologna: Pàtron.
Muñoz, A. 1935a. "Il tempio di Venere e Roma", in *Capitolium*.Roma
Muñoz, A. 1935b. *La sistemazione del tempio di Venere e Roma*. Roma: Governatorato di Roma, vol. XII, p. 85.
Nash, E. 1961. *Pictorial Dictionary of Ancient Rome*. London: Deutsches Archäologisches Institut, A. Zwemmer, Fig. 419, p. 347.
Nibby, A. 1839. *Roma nell' anno 1838*. Tipografia delle Belle Arti.
Ojetti, U. 1960. *Cose Viste*. Firenze: Sansoni, pp. 650–656.
Orbaan, J.A.F. 1920. "Documenti sul Barocco in Roma", *Miscellanea della R. Società Romana di Storia Patria*, 114, p. 231.
Osborne, J. and Claridge, J.A. 1996. *Early Christian and Medieval Antiquities*. London: Mosaics and Wallpaintings in Roman Churches, Harvey Miller, vol. 1.
Overbeke, B. van. 1763. *Reliquiae antiquae urbis Romae, quarum singulas Innocentio XI. Alexandro VIII. & Innocentio XII. . . . diligentissime perscrutatus est, ad vivum delineavit, dimensus est, descripsit, atque in aes incidit Bonaventura ab Overbeke. Opus postumum Michael ab Overbeke suis sumptibus edi curavit. MDCCIX. Tomus I*. Hagae-Comitum 1763.
Palladio, A. 1554. *Descritione de le chiese de Roma*. Murray, P. (ed). 1972. Rome: Five Early Guides to Rome and Florence. Farnborough, Gregg.
Palladio, A. 1570. *I Quattro Libri dell'Architettura*. Venezia, vol. IV.

Pane, G. 2009. "Tafuri e Roberto Pane: colloquio inedito sul destino del lavoro storiografico", in Di Marino, O (ed.). *Manfredo Tafuri: oltre la storia*. Napoli: CLEAN.

Pane, R. 1965. "Gli architetti moderni e l'incontro tra antico e nuovo", Convegno di Venezia 23–25 aprile. In Pane, R. *Attualità dell'ambiente antico*. Firenze

Panella, S. 1985. "Scavo nella platea del Tempio di Venere e Roma", in *Archeologia nel centro, I: L'area archeologica centrale*. Roma, 106–112.

Panella, S. and Cassatella, A. 1990. "Restituzione dell'impianto adrianeo del Tempio di Venere e Roma", In *Archeologia Laziale*. Roma, vol. X, pp. 52–54.

Panella, S. and Del Monti, C. 1992. "Il Tempio di Venere e Roma", *AA.VV. Architettura di Roma Antica*. Milano: Federico Motta, vol. I, pp. 48–60.

Paribene, A. 2008. "Personalitá e Istituzioni stratniere dalle carte dell'Archivio Boni-Tea", in Fortini, P. (ed.). *Giacomo Boni e le istituzioni straniere apporti alla formazione delle discipline storico-archeologiche*, Atti del Convegno Internazionale, June 2004. Roma: SSBAR.

Parker, J.H. 1876. *The Roman Forum*. Oxford and London.

Parker, J.H. 1879. *The Archeology of Rome, 1874–76 and A Catalog of 3.391 historical photographs of Antiquities in Rome and Italy*.

Parlato, E. 2004. "Carlo Lambardi", in *Dizionario Biografico degli Italiani*. Roma: Treccani, vol. LXIII.

Parlato, E. 2006. "Dal rudero all'anastilosi: il restauro nella scrittura militante di Cesare Brandi", in Andaloro, M. (ed.). *La teoria del restauro nel novecento da Riegl a Brandi*, Atti del Convegno Internazionale, Viterbo 2003, Firenze: Nardini, p. 404.

Patrizi, M. and Giovannoni, G. 1927. "Il Prefetto de Tournon e la sistemazione edilizia di Roma", *Nuova Antologia*, II (16 April), p. 446.

Pelissier, L. 1893. "Le Spese d'una canonizazione a Roma", *Archivio della Societá Romana di Storia Patria*, 16, p. 239.

Petrelli, M. 2008. "L'influsso della cultura inglese su giacomo Boni: John Ruskin e Philip Webb", in Fortini, P. (ed.). *Giacomo Boni e le istituzioni straniere apporti alla formazione delle discipline storico-archeologiche*, Atti del Convegno Internazionale, June 2004. Roma: SSBAR, pp. 57–69.

Piacentini, M. 1925–1926. "La Grande Roma". In *Capitolium*, 1: 413–42

Pietrangeli, C. 1979. *Rione X- Campitelli*. Guide Rionali di Roma. Parte III, seconda edizione. Roma: Fratelli Palombi.

Pisani Sartorio, 1983. "Una domus sotto il giardino del Pio Istituto Rivaldi sulla Velia", Accademia di Danimarca. Città e architettura nella Roma imperiale: atti del seminario del 27 ottobre 1981 nel 250 anniversario dell'Accademia di Danimarca. Odense University Press.

Platner, S.B. and Ashby, T. 1929. *A Topographical Dictionary of Ancient Rome*. London: Oxford University Press.

Plinio the Elder: *Naturalis Historia* (III.69; XXXV, 171; XXXVI, 45).

Plutarch, *Vita Pompeo*, 42, 3.

Pollak, L. 1838. "Note sulle statue di culto del grande tempio di Roma e Venere costruito dall'imperatore Adriano a Roma", Atti del Congresso di Studi Romani, vol. II, pp. 209–10.

Prandi, A. 1937. "Vicende edilizie della Basilica di S. Maria Nova", *Atti della Pontificia Accademia Romana di Archeologia*, s. III, *Rendiconti*, 13, II–IV, pp. 197–228.

Priester, A. 1993. "Bell Towers and Building Workshops in Medieval Rome", *The Journal of the Society of Architectural Historians*, 52(2), pp. 199–220.

Procopius, *Bellum Gothicum*, IV, 2.
Quatrèmere de Quincy, A. 1832. *Dictionnaire d'architecture*. Paris.
Quilici, L. 1979. *Roma primitiva e le origini della civilta laziale*. Roma: Newton Compton, p. 68 y ss.
Racheli, A. 1995. *Restauro a Roma 1870–1990: Architettura e citta*. Venecia: Marsilio.
Racheli, A. 2007. "Restauro e Architettura. Teoria e critica del restauro architettonico e urbano dal XVIII al XXI secolo", Roma: Gangemi Editore, p. 19, n. 8, 56, 57; p. 85. cif. F. Borsi, L'Architettura dell'Unitá d'Italia, Le Monnier, 1969, p. 195.
Rebert, H.F. 1925. "The Velia: A Study in Historical Topography", *Transactions and Proceedings of the American Philological Association*, 56, pp. 54–69.
Riegl, A. 1903. *Der Moderne Denkmalkultus. Sein Wesen und seine Entstehung*, Wien und Leipzig 1903. Trad. Italian: Scarrocchia, S. *Il culto moderno dei monumenti. Il suo carattere e i suoi inizi*. Bologna 1990. Trad. English: KW Forster and D. Ghirardo, "The Modern Cult of Monuments: Its Character and Origin," *Oppositions* 25 (1982), pp. 20–51.
Riegl, A. 1927. *Spätrömische Kunstindustrie*. Österr. Staatsdruckerei.
Rivera Blanco, J. 1999. "El Patrimonio y la Restauración Arquitectónica. Nuevos Conceptos y Fronteras", paper presented at the Universidad Internacional Menéndez y Pelayo, 1999, published in Rivera Blanco, 2008. *J. De varia restauratione*, Madrid: Abada Editores, pp. 20–21.
Rosatelli, B.M. 1911. "Memoria del Monastero di S. Maria Nova di Roma ricavate dai registri d'archivio e da altri documenti manoscritti", Manuscript at the Archivio dell'Abbazia di Monte Oliveto Maggiore, including the *Inventario della Chiesa di S. Maria Nuova en Campo Vaccino*, 1726. Archivio Segreto Vaticano. Sacra Congreagazione della Visita Apostolica, 125, vol. 17.
Rossi Pinelli, O. 1996. "The Surgery of Memory: Ancient Sculpture and Historical Restorations", in Price, S., Kirby Talley, N.M. y Melucco Vaccaro, A. (eds.). *Historical and Philosophical Issues in the Conservation of Cultural Heritage*. Los Angeles: Getty Conservation Institute.
Ruskin, J. 1849. *The Seven Lamps of Architecture*. London: Elder Smith.
Ruskin, J. 1853. "Lectures on Architecture and Painting", Delivered at Edinburgh in November 1853 (Lecture III., Sect 101).
Russo, L. 2006. "Cesare Brandi e l'estetica del restauro", in Andaloro, M. (ed.). *La teoria del restauro nel novecento da Riegl a Brandi*, Atti del Convegno Internazionale, Viterbo 2003. Firenze: Nardini, p. 314.
Ryberg, I.S. 1940. *An Archaeological Record of Rome from the Seventh to the Second Century* BC. London: Christophers; Philadelphia: University of Pennsylvania Press.
Santangeli Valenzani, R. 2011. *Edilizia Residenziale in Italia nell'Alto Medioevo*. Carocci.
Scappin, L. 1997. *Il restauro di Palazzo Ducale*. Venezia: Tesi di laurea, AA 1996–97, IUAV.
Scarpa, C. 1976. "Conferencia en la Academia de Bellas Artes de Viena", 16 de noviembre de 1976, in Dal Co, F. and Mazzariol, G. (eds). 1985. *Carlo Scarpa: the complete works*. New York: Electa/Rizzoli.
Scarpa, C. 1978. "Lecture given in Madrid (1978)", in Dal Co, F. and Mazzariol, G. (eds.). 1985. *Carlo Scarpa: The Complete Works*. New York: Electa/Rizzoli.

Scarpini, M. 1952. *I Monaci Benedettini di Monte Oliveto*. Alessandria: Edizione "L'ulivo".

Scherer, M.R. 1955. *Marvels of Ancient Rome*. London: Phaidon Press, pp. 15, 34.

SCVA (Sacra Congregazione della Visita Apostolica). 1726. *Inventario della chiesa di S. Maria Nova in Campo Vaccino*. Archivio Segreto Vaticano, 125, vol. 17.

Servius (Maurus Servius Honoratus). *In Aeneiden*, I, v.422.

Símboli, R. 1906. "El Foro Romano", *Hojas Selectas*, abril 1906, pp. 291–98. (Copy in the Boni-Tea Archive at the *Istituto Lombardo-Accademia di Scienze e Lettere*).

Slessor, C. 2007. "Funky Fouquet", *The Architectural Review*, November.

SPAB. 1877. *Manifesto*. Available at: www.spab.org.uk/what-is-spab-/the-manifesto/ [Accessed 25 December 2019].

SPAB. 1885. Report, June.

Spartianus *Hadrian* xix.

Stendhal. 1826. *Journal d'Italie*. Rome: Naples and Florence.

Stendhal. 1828, Voyages en Italie. Paris 1973.

Stendhal. 1829. *Promenades dans Rome*. Available at https://gallica.bnf.fr/ark:/12148/btv1b8618414q/f28.item [Accessed 25 December 2019].

Suetonious. *Augustus* 28, 3, 29.

Suetonius. Nero. 31, 1.

Susmel, E. 1956. *Opera Omnia di Benito Mussolini*. Firenze: La Fenice, vol. XXI.

Tacito. *Annales*. XV, 39, 42.

Tafuri, M. 1986. "There Is No Criticism, Only History", in *Design Book Review*. Spring issue. Berkeley: Calif.

Taylor, G. and Cresy, E. 1821. *The Architectural Antiquities of Rome*. London: James Moyes.

Tea, E. 1921. "La Rocca dei Frangipane alla Velia", in *Archivio della Societá Romana di Storia Patria*. Roma.

Tea, E. 1932. *Giacomo Boni nella vita del suo tempo*. Milano: Ceschina.

Tea, E. 1940. "Introduzione alla corrispondenza fra Philip Webb e Giacomo Boni", in Annales Institutorum, XIII (1940-1941), pp. 127-145. Roma. The letters are at the Courtauld Institute in London.

Tea, E. 1952–1955. "L'opera di Giacomo Boni al Foro e al Palatino", Archivi (manuscript at the Boni-Tea Archive at the Istituto Lombardo- Accademia di Scienze e Lettere).

Thumser, M. n.d. *Cencio Frangipane*. Dizionario Biografico degli Italiani, Roma: Treccani.

Titi, F. 1674. *Studio di pittura, scultura, et architettura*, I.

Torsello, B.P. 2005. *Che cos'é il restauro? Nove studiosi a confronto*. Venezia: Marsilio Editori.

Totti, P. 1638. *Ritratto di Roma moderna*. Roma: Mascardi, p. 433.

Valadier, G. 1822. "Narrazione Artistica dell'operato finel nel ristauro dell'Arco di Tito", read at the *Academia Romana di Archeologia* on 20 Decembre. Available at: https://archive.org/details/narrazioneartist00vala/page/n21/mode/2up [Accessed 25 December 2019].

Van Deman, E.B. 1923. "The Neronian Sacra Via", *American Journal of Archaeology*, 27(4), pp. 383–424.

Van Deman, E.B. and Clay, A.G. 1925. "The Sacra VIa of Nero". Rome: *Memoirs of the American Academy in Rome*, vol. 5 pp. 115–126.

Van Heemskerk, Marteen. 1535. *Vedute di Roma dal colle Capitolini*. Belino: Foto Anders, Published in *Storia dell'Arte Italiana*, parte seconda, v. 1, *Dal Medioevo al Quattrocento*. Torino: Giulio Einaudi editore, 1983, Fig. 280.

Varagnoli, C. 2004. "Antichi edifici, nuovi progetti. Realizzazioni e posizioni teoriche dagli anni Novanta ad oggi", in Ferlenga, A., Vassallo, E. and Schellino, F. (eds.). *Antico e Nuovo. Architetture e architettura*, atti del convegno internazionale (Venezia 31 marzo-3 aprile 2004). Padova, IL: Poligrafo, pp. 841–860.

Varagnoli, C. 2015. "Fare architettura restaurando", in Pallottino, E. and Pinelli, A. (eds.). *Paolo Marconi architetto-restauratore. Filologia della ricostruzione e cultura del patrimonio*. Ricerche di storia dell'arte, nn. 116–117, pp. 99–101. Roma: Carocci.

Varagnoli, C. 2016. "Monumenti e diplomazia: i progetti di Jacques Carlu (1957–1958) e i restauri di Jean-Claude Rochette e Paolo Marconi (1970–1990) nella Trinità dei Monti", in Di Matteo, C. and Roberto, S. (eds.). *La chiesa e il convento della Trinità dei Monti. Ricerche, nuove letture, restauri*. Roma: De Luca Editori d'Arte, pp. 249–258.

Venturi, A. 1939. *Storia dell'Arte Italiana, XI, 2*. Milano: Casa Editrice Libraria Ulrico Hoepli, pp. 936–944.

Venturi, R. 1966. *Complexity and Contradiction in Architecture*. New York: The Museum of Modern Art.

Viollet-le-Duc, E.-E. 1869. *Dictionnaire raisonné de l'architecture*. Paris, viii, 14ff.

Vitruvius Pollio, De Architectura, II, 3, 5, 6; IV, 7, I; V, 9, I; VII, I, 2, 4.

Vivio, B. 2010. *Franco Minissi: musei e restauri. La trasparenza come valore*. Roma: Gangemi.

Vlad Borrelli, L. 2006. "L'archeologia Italiana prima e dopo la Teoria del Restauro", in Andaloro, M. (ed.). *La teoria del Restauro nel Novecento da Riegl a Brandi. Atti del convegno internazionale di studi*, Viterbo 12–15 Novembre 2003. Firenze: Nardini Editore., pp. 215–224.

Walbank, F.W. (ed.). 1989. "The rise of Rome to 220 B.C", *Cambridge Ancient History*, 7(2), pp. 63–81.

Ward-Perkins, J.B. 1954. "Constantine and the Origins of the Christian Basilica". *Papers of the British School at Rome*, vol. 22, p. 85. Rome.

Watkin, D. 2011. *The Roman Forum*. London: Profile Books.

White, L.M. 1990a. *Building God's House in the Roman World: Architectural Adaptation Among Pagans, Jews and Christians*. Baltimore: Published for the American Schools of Oriental Research by Johns Hopkins University Press.

White, L.M. 1990b. "Texts and Monuments for the Christian Domus Ecclesiae in Its Environment", Social Origins of Christian Architecture, nos. 32–35. Harvard Theological Studies.

Winckelmann, J.J. 1755–67. *Il bello nell'arte. Scritti sull'arte antica*. Torino: G. Einaudi, 1942.

Wollheim, R. 1973. "Giovanni Morelli and the Origins of Scientific Connoisseurship", *Art and the Mind: Essays and Lectures*. London. Available at: www.gutenberg.org/files/25700/25700-h/25700-h.htm [Accessed 2 January 2020].

Yourcenar, M. 1992. *That Mighty Sculptor, Time*. New York: Farrar Straus & Giroux.

Zorzi, A. P. 1877. *Osservazioni intorno ai restauri interni e esterni della basilica di San Marco in 1877*. Venezia: Ongania. Cited in Clegg, J. 1981. *Ruskin and Venice*, London: Junction Books, pp. 184–187.

Index

Page numbers in *italic* indicate a figure on the corresponding page.

Academy: American in Rome 155; Brera (Accademia di Brera) 121; French 118; French in Rome 104, 107, 119; of Architecture in Paris 104; Platonic 27
Acropolis 1, 28, 141
aedicule 41, 98–100
Aeneas 13
Agrippa, Marcus Vipsanius 15, 27, 35
Alaric 48
Albano, Mount 3, 5
Alcántara Bridge 26
Alexander III (Pope) xxxi–xxxii, 41, 59–60, 65–66
Alexander VI (Borgia) (Pope) 79
Alexander VII (Pope) 96
Anacletus II (antipope) 58
anastylosis 145–146, 149, 162
Ancus Marcius 6
Annoni, Ambrigio xvii, 148
Antiquarium Forense xxvii, 11, 137–138, *137*
Anti-Restoration Movement 120
Antonines 39
Antoninus Pius 28, 38, 39
Antoninus and Faustina, Temple of 4
Apollodorus of Damascus 26–27, 35
Archaeological Conservation 150
Archaeological Park 107, 113, 125
Archaeological Park of the Colosseum *see Parco Archeologico del Colosseo*
archaeological strata 130
archaeology xviii, xxvii, 106, 117, 120, 125–126, 129–132, 143, 157, 159, 166, 168–169, 175; Christian 81

architects xxii, xxvii–xxxi, 11, 19, 22, 80, 84, 92, 94, 104–106, 108–110, 112–116, 121, 131–133, 141, 145, 155, 158–164, 167–169, 171, 176–177; *see also* Celer
architectural conservation: active 105; creative xvii; critical xvii; debate about 170; example of 172; in Italy xxix; modern 141; optical 127; and pictorial works 168; pioneer of 139; principles of 163, 177; research in xxii; tactical 127; unifying systems 161; urban 141; *see also* Architectural Conservation Project; stratigraphic architectural conservation design
Architectural Conservation Project 167–178; as preservation and transformation of pre-existences 170–172
architectural design xx, xxii, xxvii–xxx, xxxii, 136, 170–171, 173, 176
architectural heritage 164, 178
Architectural Idea: skilful conservation of 168–170
architectural preservation 70–103
architecture: Byzantine 155; Caesarian 14; Christian 43, 46, 89; classical 104; Conservation Theory and 150; contemporary 27, 81, 91; courses in 130; criticism of 169–170; domestic 9; Etruscan 10; existing 161, 169, 171, 176; experimental 132; Flavian 23–25; French 104; Gothic 155; Greco-Roman 118; Greek 14; history of xv; improvement of xx; iron 122; Italian 169;

Index 195

materiality of 133–134; medieval 140; modernization of 72, 155; monumental 46, 158; new 161, 163–164, 171, 173, 176; principles of 152; representation of 131; research in xxx; Roman 14, 26, 104, 155; Romanesque 155 ; theory of 158, 162
Arch of Constantine 46, 144
Arch of Pius 118
Arch of Septimius Severus 96
Arch of Titus xvi, 5, 15, 24–25, 57–58, 67, 74, 83, 96, 102, 111–113, 115–120, 124, 138, 172, 174–175
Arco dei Pantani 18
Argan, Giulio Carlo 114, 148, 169
Asia Minor 16, 38
Assumption procession 95
astanza 155
Athenaeum 27, 129
Athens 1, 11, 13, 26, 28, 29, 30, 35, 141, 145, 167
Athens Charter 141, 145
atrium 9, 18, 46, 53, 94
Augustus 14–15, 17–18, 25; Mausoleum of 17; temple and library of 18; theatre of xvii
aula ecclesiae 43–45, 47
Aurelian wall 125
Austria 122
Aventine (hill) 125
Avignon 69

Bacco, temple of 38
Baldini, Umberto 150
balustrade 61, 81, 97–99, 101, 103, 175
Baroque age xv
Baroque art 126
basalt 9, 50, 53, 67, 71
basilical configuration 84
Basilica Nova 39
Basilica of the Nativity in Bethlehem 46
basilicas 7, 43, 47; Constantinian 45–47
Baths of Trajan 125
Bellini, Amedeo xvii, 161, 164–165
Bembo, Marco (Cardinal) 18
Benedict III (Pope) 88
Benedict VIII (Pope) 55
Benedict XIV (Pope) 103

Berlin 163, 170–171
Bernini, Gianlorenzo xv, xxxi–xxxii, 97–101, 104, 107, 112, 151, 173, 175; *see also Confessione*
bifora windows 74–75, 79
Boario Forum 14, 109, 125
Boito, Camillo xviii, 121–122, 124, 130, 132, 141, 148
Bonelli, Renato xvii, 156–157
Boni, Giacomo xvi–xviii, xxi, xxix, xxxi–xxxii, 2, 4, 14, 53, 66, 103, 111, 125, 128–166, 168, 170–171, 173–175, 177
Boniface IV 48
Borgia, Cesare 79
Borromeo 81–82, 84, 90, 93–94
Bramante, Donato 85
Brandi, Cesare xvi–xvii, xxxii, 133, 140, 148–153, 155–156, 161–162, 164, 169–170, 174–176
brick 5, 13–14, 16–18, 21, 37, 39–40, 46, 49, 55, 60, 65–66, 77, 111, 116–117, 119, 139, 147
Britain 106, 108, 120; *see also* Great Britain
Bussa de' Leoni family 99
Byron, Lord 119
Byzantine Rome 48–49

Calcarium 49, 55
Caligula 18
Callistus II (Pope) 57, 65
Campidoglio *see* Capitoline Hill
Camporese, Giuseppe xvi, xxxi–xxxii, 104, 108–110, 112–115, 117
Canaletto, Antonio 102, 105–106
Canons Regular of the Congregation of San Frediano in Lucca 65
Capitoline Hill xxv, 1, 8, 9, 11, 13, 28, 30, 35, 93, 96, 109, 112, 136, 143, 147
Capitoline Jupiter, temple of 23
Capitolium 10
Capua 25
Carbonara, Giovanni 156, 159–165
Carinae 1, 12, 15
Caröe, William Douglas 133
Castelvecchio (Verona) xvii, 153, 155, 166, 170, 174
catacombs 42–43
Cavaceppi, Bartolomeo 106, 117
Celer (architect) 19
Celestine I (Pope) 48

196 Index

Celestine II (Pope) 58
Celio 3, 125
cella(e) 10–11, 13, 17–18, 28, 31, 34–36, 38–40, 47, 50, 55, 64, 86, 102, 113, 124, 138, 145, 147
Central Institute of Conservation xvii; *see also Istituto Centrale di Restauro*
Cesare Ottaviano 15
Charlemagne 49
Charles V (Emperor) 79–80, 167
Christian worship 41, 43, 46, 48, 60, 174
chromatic abstraction 150
Cibeles 25
Cicero 12, 120
Cipriano 44
Circus Massimus 125, 129, 144
Cirilli, Guido xvi–xvii, xxxii, 135–140, 153–154, 170
civitas 60, 64–69
classicist restoration 106
Claudius 18
Clement III (antipope) 57
Clement VI (Pope) 70
Clement VIII (Pope) 91
Clement XII (Pope) 102
Clemente 42
Cloaca Massima 10, 15, 106–107
Cock, Hieronymus 67, 74–75, 82
Colbert, Jean-Baptiste 104
Cologne 163, 170
Colosseum xv–xvi, xx, 1, 9, 22, 23–24, 28–30, 34, 38–39, 53, 62, 66, 69, 72, 78, 102, 109, 111–113, 116, 125, 144–145, *154*, 160, 168, 173, 175
Colossus of Nero xv, 19, 23, 27, 28, 62, 144
Column of Trajan 59
'*com'era, dov'era*' 135–140
Commodus 39
Confessione 97–101, 112
Congregation of Saint Benedict of Monte Oliveto 70; *see also* Olivetans
conservation (*restauro*) xv–xviii, xx–xxiii, xxvii, xxix–xxxiii, x, 27, 48, 66, 84, 88, 102, 104–111, 113, 115–118, 120–122, 124–141, 144–178 and Architectural Project 128–166; of cultural heritage xviii; definition 148; vs. restoration 120–122; Roman School of 155–157; critical conservation xvii, 128, 140, 155–157, 161 theory of xv, 140, 148–153, 155, 170; urban 141, 157–161; *see also* Archaeological Conservation; architectural conservation; conservation charters; Critical Conservation; preventive conservation; scientific conservation
Conservation Charters xvii–xxi, xxx, 166, 169; Athens Charter (1931) 141,145; Italian Charters (1883) 121; (1932) 145–147; (1972) xvi, 152; Venice (1964) 118, 153, 163, 166, 170, 174
Constantine 39, 45–47
Constantinian Basilicas 45–47
Constantinople 49
Constanzo II 47
Constitutio Antoniana 43
Continuous Architecture 167–168
Corinthian columns 13, 34–35, 38–39, 60, 74, 93
Corinthian order 84, 94
Corinthian pilasters 91, 93
Cosmati pavements 59, 61–62, *61*
Council of Trent 81
Critical Conservation (*Restauro Critico*) xvii, 128, 140, 155–157, 161
Croce, Benedetto xxxi, 156
cruciform windows 67, 78
Crusades 60–61
cultural heritage xviii–xxix, 159
Curia 3, 129

Dante 69, 148
Dea Roma 25
de Beaufort, Pietro Roger 70; *see also* Gregory XI (Pope)
Della Porta 91, 93
Demeter 26; Temple of 26, 28
Desgodetz, Antoine 104–105
De Tournon, Count Camille 107–113, 142, 167–168
Dezzi Bardeschi, Marco xvii, 161, 164
diaconicum 47, 53, 55–56, 64–65, 67, 72
Didascalia Apostolorum (Syrian order of 270) 44
Diocletian 14, 44, 47

Dionysius 12
diradamento 141–142
Divus Hadrianus temple of 39
Domitian 17, 23–27
Domus Aurea xv, 19, 20, 23, 28, 30, 66, 109, 172–174; *see also* vestibule
domus ecclesiae 43–44, 47
Domus Transitoria 19
Doric colonnade 13, 47
Du Pérac, Étienne 79, 82
Doyle, Arthur Conan 121
Dyonysius 12

earthquakes 23, 49, 53, 55, 63–64, 69, 70–71
Edict of Milan 46
Edinburgh 158, 164
Eleusinian Mysteries 25–26, 31
Eleusis (Lepsina) 26
Elio bridge 27
England xviii, 105, 120, 129, 132–134; *see also* Britain; United Kingdom
Epictetus, Hierapolis 27
Eros 36, 150
Esquiline 2, 4, 19, 124
Etruscans 8–11
Eugene IV (Pope) 78, 80
Europe xviii, xxviii, 61, 63, 96, 105, 107, 121–122, 141, 164, 167
Eusebius 44

Fagutal 4
Fascist Era xvi, 141–143
Felix IV (Pope) 50
fires: of 83 BC 10, 13; of AD 64 15, 19, 24; of AD 80 23, 27; of AD 283 xxxii, 14, 38–40; of AD 191 23, 39; at the church of Santa Maria Nova 53, 62, 66; destruction from 63; protection strategy 21, 35
First Renaissance 77–83
Flavian architecture 23–24
Flavian dynasty 23–24
Flavian Palace 19, 23
Flavius Odoacer 48
Florence 149
Foro della Pace 2, 23
Foro Italico (*Piazza Venezia*) 143–144, 159
Fortuna Virile 14, 109
Forum of Trajan 115

France xviii, 60, 104, 122, 124, 143
Francis of Assisi, St. 57
Franco, Giacomo 130, 154
Frangipane, Cardinal Latino Orsini Malabranca 62, 65, 67, 78
Frangipane, Cencio 56–58
Frangipane family xxxi–xxxii, 57–58, 65
Frangipane period 56
Frangipane *Rocca* 56–58
Franks 49
French Academy 118
French Academy in Rome 104, 107, 119
Freud, Sigmund 121, 157

Gallic invasion 9
Gelasius II (Pope) 56–57
Ghibellines 56
giant order 93–94
Giardino del Campidoglio 112
Giovannoni, Gustavo 121, 140–143, 156–158, 162
Giulia basilica 14
Giuliano the Apostate 47
Giulio Claudia Dynasty 15–19
Goethe, Johann Wolfgang von 107, 119
Golden House of Nero, 19; *see also* *Domus Aurea*
Gothic 63, 77, 121, 155, 163
Goths 48
Grand Tour 106, 119–120
granite 28, 49
Gratian 49
Greco-Roman foot 11
Greece 5, 16, 25, 128
Greek cross 60, 85
Greeks 5, 8, 48
Gregory of Tours, Saint 41
Gregory the Great I (Pope) 48
Gregory V (Pope) 55, 81
Gregory VII (Pope) 56
Gregory XI (Pope) 70, 72, 75, 81, 88, 89, 98, 113
Gregory XIII (Pope) 80
Gregory XVI (Pope) 122
guardian angels 89–90
Guelphs 56
Guiscard, Robert 56

Hadrian xv–xvi, xxix, xxxi–xxxii, 15, 17, 19, 25–28, 30, 34–35, 37–40, 46, 50, 55–56, 64, 119, 139, 167, 172–173, 177

198 Index

Heemskerk, Maerten van 74, 79
Hell 10
Hellenism 13–14, 17, 25;
 phylo- 25–26
Henry IV (Emperor) 56
Henry V 56
Heraclius 49
Herculaneum 106
Historical Restoration 133, 136
Honorius (emperor) 47
Honorius I (Pope) 37, 49–50
Honorius II (Pope) 57–58
Honorius III (Pope) 62–64, 66
Horatius Pulvillus (Marcus) 10
Horrea Piperataria 21
hypogeum 18

Imperial Forums 26, 125, 147, 149
Imperial Rome 11–15, 48, 142
Innocent II (Pope) 58, 60
Innocent X (Pope) 99–100
International Style 59–62
Ionic columns 75, 89
Iron Age 3
Isis, Temple of 102, 104–105
Istituto Centrale del Restauro (ICR) 148, 152, 155
Italian Charter of Conservation (1932) 145–147, 157
Italian Conservation Charters xvi, 144–148
Italy xviii, xxix, 47–48, 55, 58, 60, 107, 112, 121–124, 130, 140, 162–164, 166
Itinerary of Einsiedeln 49, 59

jasper 98–99
Jerusalem 24, 46, 116
Judea 28
Julius II (Pope) 80
Julius III (Pope) 81
Juno 10
Jupiter 4, 10, 13; temple of Capitoline Jupiter 11, 13, 23, 30, 35; temple of Jupiter Optimus Maximus 6, 10–11
Jupiter Stator, temple of 7, 12
Justinian 48

Knights of Rhodes 18
Kunstwollen 125–127
lacune xvii, 118, 149–150, 152–153, 163

Lambardi (Lombardi), Carlo (Lambardo da Arezzo) xv–xvi, xxix, xxxi–xxxii, 76, 83, 85, 88–99, 114, 173, 177
Lapis Niger 128
Lares, temple of the 4, 6–7, 17
Lateran 47, 57–58, 72
Lateran Basilica (church of San Giovanni in Laterano) xvii, 46, 80, 105
Lateran Canons 65
Lateran Council, third 60
Laterano xvii, 46, 80, 105, 123
Latin (language) 13, 48
Latin-cross plan 84
Leo III 49
Leo IV (Pope) xxxi, 53, 64
Leo X (Pope) 80, 111
Leo XIII (Pope) 124
Liszt, Franz 123
Livy 12
loggia 18, 102
Louis XIV (King of France) 104
"L'universale ristabilimento" 101–103
Lupercale 129

Madonna dei Monti 91
Madonna Glycophilousa 53
marble 14, 49; Cipollino 13, 105; golden 100; Pentelic 117; polychrome 37, 98–100; Proconnesian 37, 49
Marcus Aurelius 39
Marcus Porcius Cato 13
Marcus Salvius Otho 21
Marcus Vipsanius Agrippa 15
Mars 6–7; temple of 18
martyrs 55–56, 81
Maxentius xv, xxxii, 34, 38–40, 45, 50, 173
Maxentius, Basilica of 1, 11–12, 21, 39, 69, 71, 94, 119
Mediterranean 8, 17
Meta Sudans 24, 144
Michelangelo 80, 85, 93
Middle Ages xv, 80, 120, 167
Milan 103, 105, 121–122, 132, 148; Edict of 46
Minerva 10
Mithraism 25–26
Mithra 25
modernity xvi, 140–143

Index 199

Mole Adriana 27
Mondrian, Piet 153
Monte Cassino 70
Monte Oliveto Maggiore 72, 75, 77, 82, 107
monumental complex xxi, xxvii, xxix, xxxiii, 66, 102, 122–125, 144, 158, 167–168, 171, 177
Morelli, Giovanni 121, 126
Morelli Method 121
Morris, William xvii, 120, 129, 133–134
mosaics xvi, 53, 59–60, 62, 71, 82, 88–90, 99
musealization 153
Mussolini xxix, 2, 22, 95, 103, 110, 129, 137, 140–144, 158, 168–169

Napoleon III 124
Napoleonic Empire 108, 111
Napoleonic era xxxii, 122, 143
Napoleonic invasion of Rome 100, 107, 112, 141
Napoleonic Rome 107–112
Napoleonic Wars 119
neoclassicism 114, 121
Neri, San Filippo 81
Nero xv, xxxi, 15, 17, 19, 23–28, 30, 35, 41, 50, 52, 56, 62, 66, 144, 159, 172; Urban Project 19–22; *see also* Colossus of Nero; Golden House of Nero, vestibule of
Nero's vestibule *see* Golden House of Nero, vestibule of
Neues Museum 163, 170–171
New Conservation Ideology 104–127
New Testament 42
Nicholas I (Pope) 53, 64
Nicholas III (Pope) 62
Nicholas V (Pope) 78
Normans 56–57
Numa Pompilius 4

Oblates of Tor de' Specchi, Order of 74
Olivetans xv, xxv, 70–72, 77, 82–83, 90–92, 96–98, 100, 123; Benedictine monks xv, 70–103
Olympeion of Athens (Temple of Olympian Zeus in Athens) 11, 26, 30, 35, 167; *see also* Temple of Olympian Zeus in Athens
Oppio hill 19
Orsini Frangipane, Cardinal Latino Malabranca 62, 65, 67, 78
optical 19, 126–127
Orsini family 78
Ostrogoths 48
Otricoli, basilica of 39
Ottone (Saint) 56

Paul V (Pope) 85
pagan worship 47, 49, 174
painting(s) xvii, 53, 63, 74, 89, 100, 102, 105, 108, 112–113, 119–120, 139, 148–150, 152–153, 169–170, 175, 177
Palace of Diocletian (Spoleto) 47
Palace of Diomitian 37
Palatine 2–5, 7, 9, 13–15, 18–19, 23, 37, 48, 53, 57, 96, 110, 116, 123–125, 129, 132, 140
Palazzo dei Conservatori 93
Palazzo Venezia 78, 167
Paleo-Christian art 125–126
Palladio, Andrea 78, 81, 84, 93–94, 104–105, 115, 159
Pamphili Edict 108
Pantheon (of Agrippa) 27, 34–35, 48, 99, 110, 118, 151, 167, 171
Papal States 107–108
Parco Archeologico del Colosseo (*Parco del Colosseo*) xxi–xxii, xxv, 3, 138, 168
Paris 60, 104, 107, 109–110, 116, 118–119, 124, 157, 163
Passeggiata Archeologica 125, 167
patina xvii, 150–152, 160
patronage 43, 46, 70–103, 108, 178
patrons xxviii, xxxi, 81, 92, 171, 176–177
Paul I 50
Paul II (Pope) 77–78
Paul III (Pope) 79
Paul V (Borghese) (Pope) 83, 90, 97
Pax Augusta 17
Pax Romana 17
Penates, temple of the 6–7, 11, 17–18
peperino 5, 11, 30, 49, 78, 105
Pericles 162
Philippi porticus 17
Philological Conservation 121
phylo-Hellenism 25

200 Index

Piacentini, Marcello 142–143
Piazza Colonna 91, 109
Piazza Venezia 143–144, 159
Pisa 132
Pius VII (Pope) 108, 111
Pius IX (Pope) 123
plague 69, 97, 123
Platonic Academy 26
Pliny the Elder 3, 16
Plotinus 43
Plutarch 14, 162
Pompeii 14, 106, 169
Pompeo 13–14
pontifex maximus 3, 6
porphyry 36–37, 49, 60, 62
Porta Maggiore 18
portico xvi–xvii, 10, 14, 21, 23, 39, 46, 71, 75, 84, 88–89, 91, 93–95, 109, 138; crypto- 139
portico order 93
presbytery 53, 61, 75, 81, 88–89, 98–100
preservation (*conservazione*) xxi, xxiii, xxvii, 12–13, 40, 70–103, 117, 128, 147, 151–152, 156–157, 161–166, 170–172
Preventive Conservation (*Restauro Conservativo*) 150, 152
Principality 6
prothesis 47, 53
Psyche 36
Publius Valerius (Publicola) 12

Rabirius (architect) 23, 26
Raphael 80, 85, 111
Ravenna 47–49, 148
red jasper 98
Regia 6–7
Regular Canons of the Congregation of S. Frediano di Lucca 56
Remus 37, 129
Renaissance xxviii, xxxii, 77, 80, 126, 153
Republic, the xv, 5–6, 11–12, 14–15, 21, 107–108, 112
Republican era 5, 12, 15
Republican Rome 11; *see also* Republic, the; Republican era
Restauro Critico 140, 156; *see also* critical conservation
restoration (*ripristino*) xvii–xviii, xx, xxii, xxxii–xxxiii, 18, 27, 44, 60, 78, 106, 108, 118, 129, 121, 125, 130, 134, 135, 139, 145, 150, 153, 161, 163–166, 172 vs. conservation 120–122
Reunification of Italy 110, 123–124, 136, 142
Riegl, Aloïs 125–127, 128
rigatino 150
Risorgimento movement 121
'Roma Barberini' fresco 36, 39, 174
Roma Capitale 122–125
Roman art 105, 108, 125–126
Roman Composite Order 115
Roman foot 9; *see also* Greco-Roman foot
Roman Forum xv–xvi, xx–xxi, xxvii–xxviii, xxxiii, 1–7, 9, 15, 18, 26, 28, 38–39, 45, 53, 72–74, 79–80, 89, 95–96, 102, 106–110, 112–113, 116, 119–120, 125, 128–129, 131–132, 135, 137, 143, 148, 168, 171–172
Roman School of Conservation 155–157
Roman Settecento 105–107
Romana, Francesca (Saint) xxv, 71, 72, 79, 83, 95, 97, 99–100, 107, 112; canonization of xxv, 72, 83, 89
Romanità 129, 140–143, 147
Rome: architecture of 12, 157; churches in 42, 45, 75; city of xv, 48, 120, 124, 175; cultural restoration of 119; founding of 5, 13; history of 5; invasions of 100, 111, 141; kings of 1, 129; people of xx, 13, 23, 41, 57, 78; political restoration of 119; territory of 8; *see also* Aeneas; Byzantine Rome; Imperial Rome; Napoleonic Rome; Remus; Republican Rome; Romulus; square Rome (*Roma Quadrata*); Temple of Venus and Rome
Rome and Augustus: cult of 25; temple of (Ankara) 17
Romulus 3–4, 7, 37, 129
Romulus (son of Maxentius), Temple of 50
Rosini, (Abbot) Pietro Maria 55, 107
Rule of St. Benedict 82
Ruskin, John xvii, 119–121, 128, 132–135, 138, 152, 158, 164

sacristy 53, 63, 81, 97, 102
Saint Bernard (Bernardo Tolomei) 70

Index 201

San Clemente, Basilica of 42–43, 47
San Crisogono 45, 47
San Giovanni in Laterano, church of xvii, 46, 80, 105
San Marco, Basilica of (Venice) 134–136
San Martino ai Monti, church of 43
San Salvador de Spoleto, church of 47
Sansovino, Jacopo 94
Santa Francesca Romana (church) 72–77; charitable work at 113; church of xx, 15, 20, 41, 42, 53, 72, 73, 76, 106, 175; conservation in 153; construction of 83; façade of 16, 92–96, 175; Isis, Temple of 102, 105; monastery of 105, 110, 112, 116, 122–124, 131; and S. Maria Nova 73
Santa Maria in Cosmedin, church of 136
Santa Maria Maggiore, church of 105
Santa Maria Nova 73; church of 41, 53, 59, 70, 72, 78, 81; cloister of 135–140, 152; demolition and reintegration of 112–115; history of 53–56; monastery of 59, 92, 112–115, 135–140; Olivetans in 70–72; Tridentine Reforms in 77–83; *see also* Romana, Francesca (Saint)
Saracens 53
Saturn, Temple of 7
Scarpa, Carlo xvii, 153–154, 170, 174
Schism of 1054 56
scholasticism 60
Scientific Conservation 121, 136, 140, 151
sculpture 89, 98, 100–101, 107, 148, 152, 177
Second World War *see* World War II
Segovia Aqueduct 26
Semper, Gottfried 126, 128
Senate 39, 59
Senate Palace of the Capitol 13
Septizonium 57–58
Sergius II (Pope) 53
Servius Tullius 8
Severus, Settimius 19, 23
Severus (architect) 19
S. Francesco della Vigna, church of 94
S. Giorgio Maggiore, church of 93–94
Siena 49, 59, 72, 97
Sulla, Lucius Cornelius 12–13, 23

Simon Magus 41, 90, 172
Sixtus III 48
Sixtus IV (Pope) 79
Sixtus V (Pope) 108, 141
S. Maria ad Martyres, church of 48
S. Maria Antiqua, church of 53, 55–56, 65, 152
S. Maria in Trastevere, church of 60, 99
S. Maria sopra Minerva, church of 63
Society for the Protection of Ancient Buildings *see* SPAB
Soprintendenza Archeologica di Roma see Parco Archeologico del Colosseo
SPAB (Society for the Protection of Ancient Buildings) xvii–xvii, 120, 132–135, 174
Spain xviii, xxii, 26, 148, 162–163, 169–170
spolia 167
S. Prisca, church of 86, 93
square Rome (*Roma Quadrata*) 7
Ss. Cosma and Damiano, church of 17, 50
Ss. John and Paul, basilica of 45, 47
Ss. Peter and Paul, Church of 41, 50–53, 52, 71, 82, 90
Stendhal (Marie-Henri Beyle) 118–119
Stern, Raffaele 108–109, 116–117, 138
St. John Lateran, baptistery of 36
St Kolumba church/museum 163, 170
Stoics 27
St. Peter's, basilica of 47, 49, 59, 80, 85, 90
St. Peter's Square 99, 174
Stradone di Campo Vaccino 79
stratigraphic architectural conservation design 135–140, 170, 175
stratigraphic excavation 130–131
stratigraphy xviii, 137, 154
St. Sebastian in catacomb, church of 59
Stylistic Restoration 121, 133
sventramenti xvi, 142
Sylvester (Pope Saint) 41
Syria 38, 44, 48

Tabernacle 89, 98–99
Tabularium 13, 55
Tacitus 120
tactile 126–127

202 Index

Tafuri, Manfredo 158–159
Tarquinius Superbus Lucius 10, 12
Tarquinius Priscus, Lucius 5, 7, 10, 12
Telesterion (Eleusina) 26, 28, 35
Temple of Hadrian 19, 55–56, 64
Temple of Peace 23, 111, 119
Temple of Solomon (Jerusalem) 46
Temple of Venus and Rome xv, xx, xxvii, xxxii–xxxiii, 1–2, *2*, 7, 8, 10–11, 14–15, 18, 22, 23–40, *24*, *32*, *36*, *37*, 41, 45, 52–53, *52*, 57, 64, 72, 77–78, 83, 88, 93–94, 105, 107, 113–114, *114*, 117, 119, 122, 125, 138–140, 158, 167–168, 171–174; construction of 25; Expolio of 49–50; platform of *30*, *31*; restoration of 144–148
Templum Sacrae Urbis 28, 50
Terme di Caracalla 125
Theodoric 48
Theodosius 26
Theory of Substitutes 157
Third Rome 123
Tiberian domus 18
Tiber Island 14, 67
Tiberius 18
Tiber River 1, 5
tituli 42–43
Titus 19, 23, 112, 115, 116; *see also* Arch of Titus
Toesca, Pietro xvii, 148, 153
Totila 48
Tower House 67–68, 78
Trajan 17, 26–28, 116, 173; *see also* Baths of Trajan; Column of Trajan; Forum of Trajan
travertine 14, 18, 30, 49, 78, 84, 91, 93–95, 105, 115–117
tuff 9–10, 12, 14, 24, 49, 67, 79, 139
Tullus Hostilius 6, 12
Turin Exhibition 124
Turner, Joseph Mallord William 112, 119

UNESCO 164
United Kingdom xxii, 162
United States 162
Urban II (Pope) 56–57
Urban VIII (Barberini) (Pope) 97, 99–100
urban conservation 141, 157–158
Urbs 1, 8, 25–26, 40
use-marks 126

Valadier, Giuseppe xvi, xxxi–xxxii, 24, 64, 104–105, 108–110, 112–118, *114*, 124, 139, 174, 177
Vandals 48
Vatican, the 53, 64, 72, 80, 108, 142
Vatican Museum 24, 108
Velia: destruction of xvi, 143–144; hill xv, xxxii, 1–4, 6–7, 11–12, 19, 21, *32*, 103, 115, 144, 159; rebuilding of 157, 159–160
Venere Felix and *Roma Aeterna*, temple of 28
Venice 93, 94, 108, 121, 122, 128–129, 132–134, 136, 140, 153, 156, 161; *see also* Venezia; Venice Charter
Venice Charter (1964) 118, 153, 163, 166, 170, 174
Venturi, Adolfo 91, 121, 128, 141
Venturi, Robert xvii, 155, 158, 169, 174
Venus 28, 31, 35–36, 102, 145; *see also* Temple of Venus and Rome
Verdi, Giuseppe 122
Verona xvii, 80, 130, 153
Vespasian 23, 115 vestibule of the Domus Aurea (Goldern House)
Vespasian temple 115
Vesta, temple of 6–7
Vestales 6; House of the 6, 19, 39
Via Appia 4, 9, 125
Via Crucis 38
Via dei Fori Imperiali 9, 142; *see also* Via dell'Impero
Via dei Trionfi (*Via di San Gregorio*) 142, 144
Via dell'Impero 2–3, 9, 14, 21–22, 142–144; *see also Via dei Fori Imperiali*
Via del Mare 143
Via del Monte 143; *see also* Via dell'Impero
Via Sacra 2, 5–7, 9, 13, 15, *16*, 17, 19, 21–22, 25–26, 28, 41, 50, 52, 72, 95, 116, 172
Vienna School 125–127
Villa Adriana 27
Viollet-le-Duc, Eugene Emmanuel xviii, 118, 120–122, 133, 151, 161, 164
Virgin Mary 53, 60
Vitellio 23
vitruvianism, age of 91

Vitruvius Pollio, Marcus 10, 11, 14–16, 35
Vittorio Emanuele (monument) 143, 154

Webb, Philip xvii, 128, 132–135
Wickhoff, Franz 125–126
Winckelmann, Johann Joachim 106, 108, 119, 126

World War I 129
World War II 153, 158, 163

zenithal light 98, 100
Zenodoros 19
Zeus 13, 18, 26, 28, 29, 35
Zevi, Bruno 155, 159
Zola, Émile 120
Zumthor, Peter 163, 170

Taylor & Francis eBooks

www.taylorfrancis.com

A single destination for eBooks from Taylor & Francis with increased functionality and an improved user experience to meet the needs of our customers.

90,000+ eBooks of award-winning academic content in Humanities, Social Science, Science, Technology, Engineering, and Medical written by a global network of editors and authors.

TAYLOR & FRANCIS EBOOKS OFFERS:

- A streamlined experience for our library customers
- A single point of discovery for all of our eBook content
- Improved search and discovery of content at both book and chapter level

REQUEST A FREE TRIAL
support@taylorfrancis.com

Printed in the United States
By Bookmasters